Created and Directed by Hans Höfer

INSIGHT GUIDES

Korea

Edited by Leonard Lueras and Nedra Chung
Photography by Leonard Lueras, Greg Davis,
Lyle Lawson and others
Updated by Bruce Cheesman and Mike Breen

Editorial Director: Geoffrey Eu

APA PUBLICATIONS

Korea

Sixth Edition
© 1992 APA PUBLICATIONS (HK) LTD
All Rights Reserved
Printed in Singapore by Höfer Press Pte. Ltd

ABOUT THIS BOOK

Land of the Morning Calm. The Kingdom of White-Clad People. Choson. Korea. The Republic of Korea is one of the last countries in Asia to open its doors to the outside world, and – in both ancient and contemporary journals – one of the world's most misunderstood countries.

Insight Guide: Korea, like all APA's *Insight Guides*, was a long time in the making but worth the wait. Indeed, this book by a team of creative people represents more than a century of first-hand human experience in that country.

When freelance editors **Leonard Lueras** and **Nedra Chung** first visited Korea in January 1976, they were aware of the sobriquets and stereotypes associated with Korea, and they hoped the place would surprise them, but they had no notion that it would entrance them the way it did.

Lueras has worked for many years as a reporter for *The Honolulu Advertiser*, has written and edited several books on Asia-Pacific subjects, and has contributed to numerous publications in the United States and Asia.

Editor Chung, meanwhile, has worked on APA's *Insight Guides* to Hawaii and the Philippines, and has written on Korea-related subjects for prominent Korean literary publications. Chung co-wrote with Lueras most of the travel section of this book, and compiled and wrote most of the Travel Tips supplement.

This new edition of *Insight Guide: Korea* was prepared by **Michael Breen** and **Bruce Cheesman**, two British journalists based in Seoul. Breen arrived in Korea in 1982 and writes for *The Washington Times* and *The Guardian*. Cheesman has been in Korea since 1987 and is the correspondent for *The Daily Telegraph* and *The South China Morning Post*. They also added to this edition their articles on Korean business culture and the box insert on matchmaking.

Probably the first person to join Lueras and Chung in the creation of the book was Tokyo-based photographer **Greg Davis**. Davis and Lueras have worked together on various Asia-related projects over the years, and Davis, who has been regularly visiting and photographing Korea during the past decade, was a logical contributor to this book. The reader will find numerous sensitive photos by Davis throughout *Korea*.

(The late) **James Wade**, columnist-composer-author, contributed the first section essay on Korean life cycles. He also wrote and edited several anthologies of Korea-related books, including titles such as *One Man's Korea* and *West Meets East*.

Barbara Mintz, who takes the reader on a proper and serendipitous stroll through old and new Seoul, was born in Honolulu but has lived since 1962 in Korea. Leaving her teaching position at Ohio State university, she came to Korea as a Fulbright lecturer in English.

Norman Thorpe, an expert on "toasting spirits," has been in Korea since 1968 – first with the U.S. Army, then as a student and freelance writer, and as Seoul staff correspondent for *The Asian Wall Street Journal* till 1982. Thorpe has a masters degree in Korean studies from the University of Washington at Seattle.

Jon Carter Covell takes the reader by the hand on a cultural tour of this artistically exciting country. Covell has authored sev-

Lueras

Chung

Davis

Mintz

Covell

eral books on Korean and Japanese art. She has lived much of her life in the Far East, where she specializes in Buddhism and its artistic expressions.

Gary Clay Rector came to Korea in 1967 as a Peace Corps volunteer. After studying Korean music for several years under Kim Byung Sup, Korea's eminent solchanggo (hourglass folk drum) player, Rector has become one of the foreign community's most-respected authorities on the subject. Rector wrote the story on Korean music and dance.

Laurel Kendall is our resident expert on Korean shamans and housewives. After conducting extensive field work in the shamanist spheres of a Korean village, she received a doctors degree in anthropology from Columbia University in 1980.

Norman Sibley is a native of New Hampshire who first came to Korea at age four with his Christian missionary parents. He grew up in Korea – at Taegu, Koje-do and Seoul – and later, after graduating from the College of the Atlantic, co-edited *Korea Quarterly* with his wife Greta and their friends. Norman, a multi-talented author-architect-graphic designer and photographer, penned the essay on Korea's south crescent, contributed numerous photographs, an architectural rendering of Kyongju's Pulguk Temple, and gave much appreciated guidance to *Insight Guide Korea*'s editors.

Gertrude Ferrar, who orients the reader to Korea's creation, geology, geography and flora and fauna in a sympathetic opening essay, is a native New Yorker who first came to Korea in 1963 "where I've resided ever since." In her own words, "I run a language school, write (both over my own name and as a ghost-writer), study Korean flora and fauna,

and take people on long walks about which some complain mightily."

Insight Guide: Korea's historian is **Michael E. Macmillan** from Honolulu. He has variously worked as a radio broadcaster, newspaper reporter (for *The State* of Columbia, South Carolina, and for *The Honolulu Advertiser*). Macmillan was also publications editor at the University of Hawaii's Center for Korean Studies.

Korea's diverse religious spectrum was reviewed by **Tom Coyner**, a former Korean Peace Corps program developer and Seoul-based bank executive.

Another longtime Koreaphile who contributed to the delicate "cultural balance" of this book is **Ken Kaliher**, a journalist who has lived in Korea on and off since 1969. He edited the English copy of and wrote for *Orient Press*, then one of Korea's two general news agencies, and reported for ABC Radio in the United States.

Yeoman graphics support came from several fine sources. Prominent among individual photographers were the contributions of **Emil Alfter**, who was stationed in Korea for several years as a deputy attaché with the German Embassy in Seoul; **Mi Seitelman**, a former chief command photographer with the U.S. 8th Army's headquarters staff; and **Lee Nam Soo**, one of Korea's finest native photographers.

Other key shots were clicked by Barbara Mintz, Tom Coyner, **Stanford Zalburg**, **Alain Evrard**, **Dallas & John Heaton**, **Manfred Gottschalk**, **Jean Kugler**, **Robin Nichols** and **Paul Barker**. Thanks are due to the **Korea National Tourism Corporation** office in Singapore for its kind assistance.

– APA PUBLICATIONS

N. Sibley   *Rector*   *Kendall*   *Ferrar*   *Macmillan*

CONTENTS

Culture and Heritage

Places

Maps

TRAVEL TIPS

*For detailed information
See Page 265*

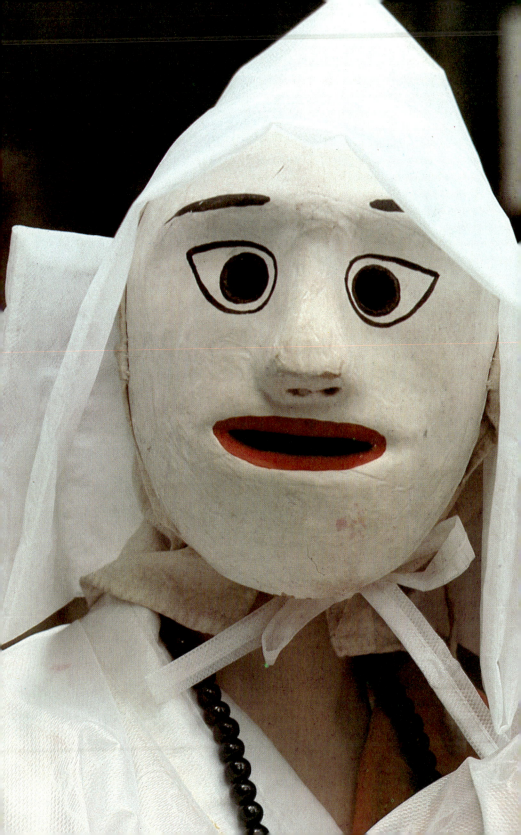

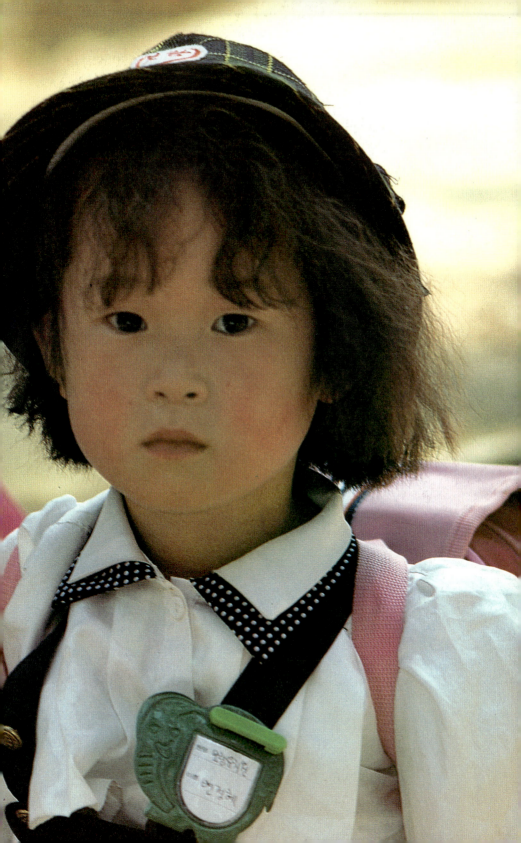

SHINING WITH NEW LIGHT

Part of the beauty of Korea is provided by its colorful history. Squeezed as it is between its bigger neighbors – Japan, China and the Soviet Union – Korea has survived invasions, wars and colonial rule, remaining fiercely distinct.

In modern times, the peninsula was first known as the "Hermit Kingdom" due to its official 19th-century policy of shielding itself from foreign influence. For 36 years, it became the "inferior" part of colonial Japan. More recently the Korean War images of poverty and destruction, sustained long after they ceased to be relevant by the American TV comedy *MASH*, provided the pre-dominant impression. Then in the 1980s came the exaggerated images of student protests.

It was not until the 1988 Summer Olympics in Seoul that the Koreans burst into the international scene. In two short weeks, millions of viewers around the world saw Korea as it is – a modern and vibrant nation, with a long and rich cultural heritage, coming of age as an economic and political power in its own right.

Today, part of Korea's attraction is its pulsating modernity. In Seoul, the country's capital for 600 years, skyscrapers reach toward the heavens and traffic jams stall the human race below. Neons light the city at night and workers pile into vehicles early in the morning. Business suits are as common here as in New York city and the pace of life is quickly approaching that of the frantic Western bustle.

Yet in the neighborhoods of Seoul and throughout the country-side, women still hang peppers to announce the birth of a baby boy, children bow to their grandparents, fortune-tellers warn of future trouble and offer portents of luck, Buddhist monks wander the streets for alms, and families take to the mountains to worship the natural beauty of their land.

The country is dotted with Buddhist temples and contains some great Buddhist treasures. It also has a rich Confucian legacy from its Yi Dynasty period when it was said that the Koreans were more Confucian than the Chinese. In this century, Korea has become one of the great success stories of Christian evangelizing and now boasts six of the world's 10 largest congregations.

But Korea's greatest pull is its people. Described by Westerners as the Irish of the East, the Koreans are their country's greatest resource. Raised on the strictures of Confucianism and the tolerance of Buddhism, and fashioned by a land of bitter winters and roasting summers, the Koreans have emerged a proud, fierce and strong race. With their mixture of bravado and insecurity, their passion and cool good sense, their austere traditions and lively characters, the Koreans are an ancient people shining with new light in the world.

Preceding pages: soaking in the sights at Hwachae-bong Peak and Flying Dragon Waterfall, Sorak-san; traditional mask dancers; schoolmates; early morning walk; solitary pathfinder. **Left**, entrance of Sunamsa (temple), Chollanam-do.

Alone, cup in hand,
I view the distant peaks.
Even if my love came to me,
Would I be any happier?
The peaks neither speak nor smile;
But what happiness, O what joy!
                    – New Song in the Mountain
                    by Yun Son-do (1587-1671)

Wherever one walks, drives or flies in Korea, one sees the hills, the mountains, "... the distant peaks." Whether in the joyous lyricism of the great *sijo* poet Yun, or in the many paintings of Korea's amazing Diamond Mountains, those peaks rise figuratively and literally in any reference to this country.

From Manchuria south to Cheju Island in the East China Sea, the entire country is ribbed by low-rising, sharp and often bare mountain ridges. Because those "mountains" never rise more than 9,200 feet (2,800 meters) in elevation, armchair geologists were quick to jump to the conclusion that Korea is a young land. To the contrary, Korea is in fact one of the world's oldest known land areas, dating back to the pre-Cambrian period (1,600 to 2,700 million years ago) in the earth's evolution.

Korea's basic foundation of granite and limestone is old and tough, like her people. And were it not for strenuous reforestation programs conducted during the past two decades, she might look even older.

The Korean peninsula is relatively small – about the size of Rumania or New Zealand – but it becomes even smaller when you consider that only about 20 percent of its total land area is flatland. The peninsula's overall size (including north and south) is about 620 miles (1,000 kilometers) long and 134 miles (216 kilometers) wide at its narrowest points. Seoul, Korea's major city, is, as the crow flies, about 680 miles (1,100 kilometers) from Beijing and about 870 miles (1,400 kilometers) from Tokyo.

As you cruise up and down this peninsula, take note that you are traveling on an ancient land-bridge that is tilted toward the west and into the Yellow Sea. This tipping, caused by volcanic pressure on the peninsula in ancient geologic times, has left the offshore area of Korea's west coast dotted with hundreds of islands. Also, in concert with the Yellow Sea's tremendously wide tide changes, this west side sinking produced far-reaching, shallow inlets which look like huge, placid, sky blue lakes at high tide.

The east coast fronting the Japan Sea features mountains marching right down to a coastline marked by tiny coves. These eastern waters produce great tasty coldwater catches of cuttlefish and salmon, while the west coast supplies clams, oysters, large and small shrimp, sea snails and abalone.

Migratory Pit Stop: Where the water is shallow enough, there are great expanses of sedge to play host to a variety of water birds. The most glorious of them is the Manchurian crane. This bird was presumed to be nearly extinct but in 1977, Dr. George Archibald, head of the International Crane Foundation, found a large colony in Korea's demilitarized zone.

The shallow waters and inlets of the western side of the country are home to the white-naped crane and many different kinds of ducks, geese and swans. Korea also acts as part-time home for birds which follow migration routes cutting through the country.

The total bird population has been rising in recent years in concert with government regulations prohibiting the shooting of feathered friends. Where only a few years ago, the pheasant seemed on its way to extermination, it is now common. The sparrow population has increased so enormously as a result of this bird-killing ban that sparrow netting is now permitted for a limited period every autumn.

There are several seriously endangered bird species in Korea. The aforementioned Manchurian crane has been greatly reduced in numbers and the Tristram's woodpecker population is way down, but its numbers are increasing. Birdwatchers report that more than 20 birds are now living in the protected area of the Kwangnung Forestry Research Institute Branch.

Left, pine covered ridges of mountain between Yanggu and Inje.

Bears and Wildcats: Wild mammals have not fared so well as birds. The Korean tiger is still celebrated in art, but he is extinct. So is the local leopard, though some speculate that leopards may still be roaming forests in the remote north of Korea.

One of life's great ironies is that the demilitarized zone (DMZ) between North and South Korea has provided a place of peace and quiet where wildlife can proliferate.

One creature carrying on in this DMZ refuge is a small wildcat which has all but completely disappeared in mountains south of the 38th parallel. There are also some of the small native Korean bears. These bears are now protected, but they almost disap-

peared for good because the eating of bear meat has long been considered to be very good for one's health. An entire community of otters – about 100 of them – was found along the Naktong River at about the same time bears were found on Mt. Chiri.

Snake Consommé: Korea has a large snake population, but none of these serpents are aggressive and only one is truly deadly. Quick treatment for any snake bite, however, can prevent tragedy. If you see a snake, stand still and give it time to go away.

Cheju Island off Korea's south coast is famous for its horses. Because of this island's sub-tropical climate, there is forage for horses all year round and Cheju horses are permitted to run free.

Korea also has a unique breed of dog, Chindo, which is a medium-sized, short-haired canine with a moderately pointed snout, heavy shoulders, and a coloring that varies from light cream beige to almost brown. The breed seemed in danger of extinction a few years ago, but the government now forbids, as a preservation measure, the taking of Chindo dogs from their native island.

"Too Many Azaleas": Korea's forest flora is closely related to that of neighboring China and Japan. The nation's indigenous plants are most likely to be preserved in temple gardens where, for centuries, Buddhist monks have tended Korea's living things with loving care. It is here that the finest specimens of gingko trees, a variety of maple, and herbaceous plants thrive.

Korea has such a large population of azaleas that it is often impossible to walk across a forest clearing without trampling on them. Indeed, wild weigelia, spirea, viburnums, hydrangeas, boxwood, holly, daphne, and a host of other plants are all considered "weeds." However, it is now against the law to dig up such plants in the wild or cut down a tree without government permission, however, ever. The woody plants have become common in Korea as a result of successful reforestation programs.

Korean roadsides in the autumn are iced with a floral froth of lavender, pink, white and deep red cosmos. City streets are often edged with gingkos, aialanthus, London plane trees, sumac and pawlonia, and just about every village has an ancient zelkova or persimmon tree.

Oddly enough, the azalea which covers almost every mountainside and fills every untilled field is not the national flower. That official honor was bestowed on the rose of Sharon. During the Japanese occupation, Japanese officials in some areas tried to stamp it out, but that only served to make the Korean population even more determined to cultivate it.

Above left, a pair of dancing Manchurian cranes in the demilitarized zone north of Seoul. **Right**, wild cosmos blossoms.

猛
見
書
龜
迷
縱
生
東
海

Centuries of existence in the shadow of stronger neighbors has given Korea a history filled with turbulence that belies the familiar nickname, "Land of the Morning Calm." Located at a strategic crossroads of northeast Asia, the Korean peninsula has been trampled on by armies of Chinese and Japanese, Mongols and Manchus, Russians and Americans. Despite these onslaughts, Koreans have maintained a distinct political and cultural identity.

Koreans, of course, have borrowed many attributes of Chinese civilization and in turn, transmitted elements of that civilization to Japan. Still, Korea is neither China in miniature nor an offshoot of Japan, and the ability of Koreans to preserve their identity while enduring the depredations of intruders is one of the most striking themes in modern history. The Koreans have not merely endured, but have produced artistic, scientific and literary achievements of great distinction.

Tan'gun, the Bear-Woman's Son: The retelling of Korean history begins with the mythical founder of the nation, Tan'gun. According to myth, Hwanung, the son of the Divine Creator, descended to earth and proclaimed himself king on hearing the prayers of a bear and tiger who wished to become human beings. He gave each of them 20 pieces of garlic and a piece of artemisia and told them they would be transformed if they eat the plants and withdraw from sunlight for 100 days. The animals ate the offering and retired to their caves, but the tiger's restlessness drove him out. The bear remained for 100 days and emerged as a woman.

The first wish of the bear-woman was to have a son. So she prayed beneath a sandalwood tree, became pregnant and bore a son, Tan'gun, whose reign is said to have begun in 2333 BC. He ruled, the story goes, until 1122 BC when Kija, supposedly a descendant of the Shang royal line of China, arrived in Korea and established himself as ruler.

Preceding pages, an old Chinese-Korean map identifies China as the "Middle Kingdom" and other countries as peripheral states. **Left**, the now extinct Korean tiger, once worshiped as a messenger of mountain spirits.

Thereafter, Tan'gun resumed his spirit form and disappeared.

Although little credence may be given to the myth, archaeological studies demonstrate that human life on the peninsula is very old. Paleolithic sites were discovered in the 1960s, and yielded stone tools estimated to be about 30,000 years old. The oldest evidence of a Neolithic society has been assigned a date of 4270 BC.

After the collapse of the Later Han dynasty, one of the Korean tribal states, Kogu-

ryo, had begun to emerge as a tribal alliance of nomadic people in southeastern Manchuria in the 1st century AD. By the 4th century, Koguryo had grown into a kingdom with a centralized government built around a hereditary military aristocracy. Frequently at war with the Chinese, the Koguryo people came by the 5th century to dominate the northern half of the Korean peninsula, and all of Manchuria to the regions of the Amur, Sungari and Liao rivers.

The Three Kingdoms Period: The southern part of the peninsula was peopled by a number of distinctive but related tribes that had, by the 3rd century AD, formed three weak tribal confederations: Mahan, Chin-han, and Pyonhan. It was in this area – during the 3rd and 4th centuries – that the Paekche and Silla tribes arose, who, with Koguryo, dominated the so-called Three Kingdoms period in Korea.

Paekche emerged among the Mahan tribes of the southwest. Led by a royal clan, Paekche occupied the area south of the Han River and initially placed its capital in the vicinity of modern Kwangju. In subsequent years Paekche expanded its territory, organized a bureaucratic government along Chinese lines, and established relations with the Eastern Chin state of south China.

Last to develop as a major kingdom was

Silla, whose origins consisted of a loose federation of tribes in the southeastern corner of Korea. Silla's transition from tribal league to kingdom took place in the late 4th and early 5th centuries.

Another tribal federation, the Kaya league, occupied the southern coast of the peninsula in the lower reaches of the Nakton River. Until its annexation by Silla in 562, the Kaya territory was an important point of contact between the Korean states and the inhabitants of Japan.

The centuries during which these three kingdoms were emerging were full of strife. Between 396 and 404, Koguryo King

Kwanggaet'o forced Paekche to withdraw from the Han River valley and move its capital farther south. In 433 Silla joined forces with Paekche to fight Koguryo; a few years later Silla turned and attacked Paekche. China, then under the Sui dynasty, launched unsuccessful attacks against Koguryo in 598 and 612. These military failures contributed to the collapse of Sui in 618 and the rise of the T'ang dynasty. T'ang China also sent unsuccessful expeditions against Koguryo in 645 and 647, failing which it allied with Silla and attacked Paekche as a preliminary to striking Koguryo from the south. By 660, T'ang had destroyed Paekche, and the two allies turned on Koguryo, which fell in 668.

After the defeat of Paekche and Koguryo, the Chinese tried to establish an administration to govern the peninsula, including Silla. Silla's response was to help the Koguryo resistance movement in the north, and also move against the T'ang troops in the south. By 671, Silla had taken the old Paekche capital and by 676 Silla had expanded to the Taedong River. The Chinese had to withdraw into Manchuria. Finally, in 735, China was forced to recognize Silla's dominion over all the areas south of the Taedong.

The Sillan conquest of the peninsula is often taken as the beginning of a unified Korean state that continued to exist until the division of north and south Korea took place in 1945. However, Silla's unification was, at best, tenuous.

Luxurious Buddhism: Chinese civilization had flowed into Korea throughout the Three Kingdoms period. Buddhism and Confucianism, art and architecture, the written language of China, and bureaucratic organizational principles were all introduced.

Of all the importations from China, none flourished more luxuriantly under unified Silla than Buddhism. Believing that Buddhism would protect the state and bring good fortune, Silla's rulers lavished state funds on temples and Buddhist images, and dispatched monks to China and India to study the religion. The epitome of the Buddhistic art of the period may still be seen in the Sokkuram stone grotto near the Sillan capital of Kyongju. It and Korea's most famous temple, Pulguk-sa, were begun in 751 when Silla was at its height of glory.

The early influence of Chinese civilization was profound, but it did not supplant native culture. In fact, Silla's success in unifying the peninsula stemmed in part from the strength of such native institutions as the *hwarang* and *kolp'um* systems. The *hwarang,* or "bone-rank," was a paramilitary youth organization for the training and education of the sons of Silla elite. Some of Silla's most able leaders were shaped by the *hwarang* precepts. The *kolp'um* system was a highly stratified hierarchy of rank based on birth, with royalty and aristocracy monopolizing the high offices.

The T'ang administrative system became the model for the state structure and unified Silla, but Chinese forms were altered to meet Korean needs. Nowhere is the difference between the Chinese model and the Sillan adaptation clearer than in the recruitment of officials for government. In T'ang China, officials were selected on the basis of examinations. In Silla, positions were filled according to birth, not talent. While the T'ang dynasty did not impose direct rule on Korea, it did dominate Silla and later Korean kingdoms through the tributary system. As long as the ceremonial obligations of the tributary system were met, the Koreans were free to conduct their affairs as they saw fit.

Koreans in Japan: The Three Kingdoms and united Silla periods constituted centuries of profound Korean influence on Japan. There were frequent migrations of Koreans to Japan from the 4th through the 7th centuries, especially during times of turmoil in the Korean kingdoms. With the emigrants went Korean and Chinese technological, intellectual and cultural influences. Monks from Paekche and Koguryo staffed the first Buddhist monastery in Japan, built in the 6th century. Architects and builders from Paekche were largely responsible for the great burst of temple construction that occurred during that century.

Men from the peninsula became the tutors of Japan's famed Prince Shotoku; others brought with them expertise in calendrics and Chinese embroidery has been attributed to women from Koguryo who became prominent at the Japanese court. Nearly one

third of the nobles in the register of families compiled in 815 were of Korean descent.

Silla reached its zenith in the middle of the 8th century, then entered upon a century and a half of civil strife and disintegration. The growth of the royal clan led to intense internal rivalries over the crown. Moreover, the heart of the social and political order, the *kolp'um* system, came under attack from lower echelons who felt excluded from power. Another discontented element was the merchants who were amassing great wealth. At the same time, the greed of large provincial landowners contributed to the weakening of government. By the late 9th century many farmers were abandoning their fields to survive by banditry.

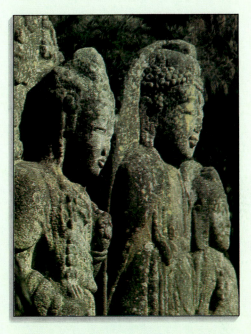

The 9th and early 10th centuries were years of upheaval. As early as 768, major revolts broke out among the aristocracy and in 780, King Hyegong was assassinated. Uprisings also raged in the countryside.

Out of this chaos arose rebel chieftains who struggled for centuries until the appearance of Wang Kon. Supported by the landlord and merchant class from which he sprang, Wang Kon grew in power over the next two decades. In 935, King Kyongsun handed over the government to Wang Kon who reunited the peninsula, named his new state Koryo, and began a dynasty that lasted more than 450 years.

Left, an early portrait of the 8th-century Sokkuram Buddha at Kyongju. **Above right**, serene Buddhas of Silla.

The founding of Koryo represented more than a mere change of dynastic names. Wang Kon's power was based on a non-aristocratic elite. He was also helped by some Silla aristocrats whose power derived from their landholdings and by some discontented Sillan intellectuals.

Although the *kolp'um* system had been destroyed, Koryo was still a society founded on status consciousness and sharp class distinctions. Ancestry continued to be of great importance in determining one's position in the

social hierarchy. Whereas the old ruling class had consisted of warrior-aristocrats, the elite of Koryo came to be the literati who occupied the civil offices in the government.

For the first time in Korea, Wang Kon invoked the Chinese notion of the "mandate of Heaven" as his rationale for assuming the throne. He justified his rule by claiming moral superiority. In the 10th and 11th centuries, Wang Kon and his successors built a centralized government, but subordinated it to the wishes of an oligarchy. A competitive civil examination system was created in 958 to fill the highest offices with those members of the ruling class most highly schooled in Chinese

literature and Confucian Classics. Advancement depended greatly on social status.

Although the government apparatus outwardly resembled the Confucianized government of China, the influence of Confucianism as a way of life was limited in Koryo times. Buddhism remained the most pervasive spiritual force throughout the dynasty. Wang Kon himself was a Buddhist and patronized the religion, and monasteries wielded considerable secular power and influence by accumulating land and wealth through money-lending and commercial activities.

An abrupt change came about in August 1170. A military escort conveying the king and royal party on an outing revolted and killed every man in the party, except the king himself. The latter was banished to Koje Island, where he was murdered.

Historians have interpreted the coup as a military revolt against discrimination suffered at the hands of civilian officials and against the debauchery of the royal court under King Uijong (1146-1170). It introduced a period in which most important positions in government went to military men. More reliance was placed on native political and economic institutions and a period of general breakdown ensued. The dominant figure to emerge from a series of uprisings was Ch'oe Chung-hon, who built an independent base of power while suppressing the provincial uprisings. He then turned against rival military leaders, whom he eliminated by 1196.

The military rulers found that they lacked the administrative expertise to run the country so they began luring civilian scholar-officials into service. An unprecedented fusion of the two groups through intermarriage followed. In time the civil aristocracy revived, building strength toward an eventual challenge of the military supremacy. In the mid-13th century, the Mongol invasions took place.

The Mongols Take Over: The Mongols were the most formidable of a number of peoples with whom the Koreans clashed during the Koryo period. As early as 916, in the wake of the collapse of the T'ang dynasty in China, the Khitan had begun to dominate Manchuria and Mongolia and sought formal relations with Koryo. As with the Jurchen and the Mongols, the Koreans regarded the Khitan as culturally inferior and resisted their approaches.

By the 980s, the Khitan had established a Chinese-style state called Liao, overran Parhae and begun attacking the Jurchen tribes along the middle reaches of the Yalu River. A new bid for diplomatic relations with Koryo was repulsed; in 993 the Khitan invaded. The peace settlement suspended contacts with China's Sung government.

In 1010, the Khitan invaded again; then again in 1018 when the Koreans rejected Khitan demands that Koryo cede strategic

against the Liao state, which they eliminated. Then they proclaimed the Chin dynasty in 1115 and took all of north China from the Sung dynasty. Koryo was compelled to declare fealty to Chin and cut its ties with the southern Sung court.

A century after the Chin conquest, there were more clashes as the Mongols swept into China and Manchuria from central Asia, pressing the Khitan down into the peninsula. The Koryo government agreed to ally with the Mongols to end the Khitan threat, but they had no taste for a lasting alliance with the invaders.

border areas and become a vassal of Liao. this incursion led to stalemate, but the wary Koreans began building a stone wall reminiscent of the Great Wall of China. Completed in 1044, it stretched from the mouth of the Yalu on the west coast to Kwangp'o on the east.

More trouble came as the 12th century opened. The Jurchen invaded northern Koryo in 1104 and remained until a large army was sent against them in 1107. Repeated engagements were indecisive; the Jurchen turned

Left, Confucius is *Kongja* to Koreans. <u>Above</u>, Unjn Miruk (Buddha of the Future) at Kwanchok Temple, near Nonsan.

The Mongol armies were not easily appeased, however, and Koryo reluctantly began meeting demands for large tribute payments in return for the help the Mongols had given. These payments began in 1219 and continued until 1224, when relations were broken off after the murder of a Mongol envoy to Korea. Only the Mongols' preoccupation with other campaigns and their own internal politics spared Koryo from immediate retaliation.

The reckoning came in 1231. The Mongols quickly overran most of northern Korea, laid siege to Kaesong, the capital, and forced the government to surrender. But when the Mongols relaxed their grip the following year, the

Koryo government fled from Kaesong with most of the city's population, and took refuge on Kanghwa Island at the mouth of the Han River on the west coast.

Thereupon the Mongols invaded Korea in force, but could not cross the narrow channel separating Kanghwa from the mainland. Thus the government remained inviolate, though isolated and helpless, during further Mongol incursions. In the next 25 years, all the major cities were sacked and widespread destruction was inflicted on the countryside.

The question was: Should they continue resistance or capitulate? In 1258, Ch'oe Ui was overthrown by another military official, Kim Chun.

Wonjong himself went to the Mongol court and offered complete submission in return for aid against the military clique. He even agreed to marry his crown prince to a Mongol princess in order to seal the bargain. Yet when he returned to Korea with a Mongol army at his disposal, a large part of the military faction still refused to give in. Open rebellion broke out.

Some military units held out on the offshore islands as late as 1273. But the rebellion signalled the end of the military dictatorship and the restoration of civilian bureaucracy. By 1279 the Mongols, who were firmly lodged in north China, adopted the dynastic name Yuan and proceeded to take over the rest of China.

The Mongols allowed the Koryo govern-

In 1259, a truce was struck with the Mongols and a decade of comparative peace began. However, the military officials who dominated the government refused to capitulate and the government remained on Kanghwa rather than return to Kaesong.

In 1269, Kim Chun fell victim to an internal power struggle and was ousted by another military figure, Im Yon, who had obtained King Wonjong's support. Im deposed Wonjong in favor of a younger brother of the king, but Wonjong's crown prince, who had been sent to Beijing under the terms of the truce with the Mongols, returned with a large force and restored his father to the throne.

ment in Korea to remain in control, except in far northern areas and on the island of Cheju, but always subject to directions of the Yuan court. Koryo crown princes were sent to Beijing as children, compelled to marry Mongol princesses, and kept there until the death of the reigning king. In this way, the Koryo court was thoroughly Mongolized and neutralized.

Extracting Female Quotas: The Yuan overlordship placed a severe strain on Korea. The Mongols extracted large annual tribute – gold, silver, horse, ginseng, hawks for hunting, artisans, eunuchs, and women. An office was set up to select girls and young widows to fill the annual quotas. In addition, Korea had to build hundreds of ships and furnish soldiers for ill-fated invasions of Japan in 1274 and 1281.

The period of Mongol domination, however, had important cultural effects. There was, for example, the transmission of ideas and techniques for others under the dominion of the Mongols. Koreans gained knowledge of astrology, medicine, artistic skills, calendrics, and cotton cultivation.

In the 14th century, rebellions in China, which upset the Mongol regime, culminated in the founding of the Ming dynasty in 1368. There was a revival of Korean independence during these years, especially after the enthronement of King Kongmin in 1352.

Kongmin rejuvenated the government, reorganized the army, reasserted control over the northwest territories, and reorganized and enforced the civil examination system. He began in the mid-1360s to restore illegally appropriated slaves to their rightful owners.

The landholders proved so powerful, however, that Kongmin was forced to compromise. Eventually, he had to give up the reform program entirely. That did not satisfy his opponents at court. They had him assassinated and installed his 10-year-old son on the throne.

This was the prelude to the rise of a major new leader who swept the Koryo dynasty aside, Yi Song-gye. Descended from a family of military leaders in Hangyong, Yi distinguished himself by suppressing local rebellions and combating Japanese pirates called *wako*. He also carried out a reform program to break the power of the old landlords, reduce the influence of the Buddhist establishment, and increase the strength of the government.

The Rebirth of Choson: In 1392, Yi ousted the king and took the throne to become the founder of his own dynasty. Surviving for more than 500 years, it was Korea's last ruling house, and a watershed in the history of Korea. The new kingdom promptly resumed tributary relations with Ming China and took the ancient Chinese name for Korea, Choson.

The reformers around Yi Song-gye were men who had embraced the ideas of the Chinese Confucian thinker Chu Hsi. These Neo-Confucianism doctrines gave the traditional ethico-political cult metaphysical underpinnings. It made of it a virtual religion and imbued its followers with a zealous spirit of reform. Once the new dynasty was pro-

claimed, the reformers i
to impose Confucian no

The changes wrought (
ing of the very fabric of
ples: In burying the dead
practiced rituals that we
customary and Buddhist tr
ingrained customs, includi
thrust aside in favor of Confucian ancestor worship and its related rituals. Until the end of Koryo times, marriage customs had admitted endogamy, polygamy and remarriage of widows. Yi-period reforms, however, broadened the circle of kin with whom marriage was prohibited, forbade the practice of giving equal social status to multiple wives and discouraged remarriage.

The rise of Confucianism spelled the decline of Buddhism. By confiscating land and forcing the closing of many temples, the new regime reduced Buddhism to a subservient position. It was never able to recover its former status in Korean society.

The founder of the dynasty was content to be more a figurehead than dictator. Not so the third king of the dynasty, T'aejong, who came to power in 1401 after killing his youngest brother, then the heir-apparent, in 1398. Under his rule, the government was reorganized to strengthen the throne.

T'aejong's successor was Sejong (1418-1450), a man considered by many to have been the greatest of Korean kings. Intelligent and scholarly, he presided over the conception of the remarkable Korean alphabet, *han'gul*, and, indeed, over the flourishing of cultural activity. As an administrator, he was meticulous and indefatigable, but he was succeeded by men of lesser capacity, Munjong (1450-1452) and the ill-fated boy-king Tanjong (1452-1455). This unfortunate boy was forced to abdicate by his uncle, imprisoned, and finally strangled. His murderous uncle took the throne as King Sejo (1456-1468).

Sejo assumed direct control, intimidated his critics with purges and executions, instituted banishments, and seized property. When his reign was over, the power of the Korean monarchs again diminished and the Yi dynasty began a long decline.

The decline of the Yi dynasty may be attributed in part to the threat of foreign invasion, which recurred in the 1590s. This time it came from Japan, newly reunified under Toyotomi Hideyoshi who, in April 1592, invaded Korea.

Left, statue of Admiral Yi Sun-sin.

s": The Koreans had little military presence on land, but at sea the story [was] different. Korea's naval hero, Admiral Yi [Sun]-sin, commanded a naval force of 80 ships, [ba]sed at Yosu. Among his fleet were several "turtle ships," which he used to break the back of the Japanese invasion by choking off the flow of supplies and troop reinforcements.

The "turtle ships" averaged 100 feet in length, were propelled by oars, and were faster and more maneuverable than the Japanese ships. An armored canopy studded with pointed objects made them invulnerable to enemy projectiles and raiders who come aboard. The vessels were heavily gunned, and the bow of each ship was decorated with a large turtle's head that could emit sulphur fumes masking the movements of the fleet.

From May to July 1592, Yi's fleet met smaller Pusan-bound Japanese ships carrying troops and supplies. In eight major engagements he sank more than 250 of them. In the naval campaign of 1592, Yi took his fleet into the Japanese base at Pusan and is said to have destroyed more than half the 500 ships there.

Yi's victories, plus the growing Korean guerrilla campaign and the intervention of Chinese troops, forced the Japanese to start pulling back. Negotiations resulted in the withdrawal of the bulk of the Japanese troops and the dispatch of Korean and Chinese envoys to Japan to conclude a settlement.

In January 1597 the Japanese renewed the war. They sent 100,000 men to punish Korea. This time, they met stiffer resistance from the Koreans and from the Chinese garrison. The invasion was confined to the southern provinces, but it was waged with great ferocity.

At sea, the Koreans did not fare as well as before. Yi Sun-sin had fallen victim to court intrigues and was given only a dozen ships. Once again Yi defeated the Japanese in a series of engagements, but in November 1598, standing at the bow of this flagship, he was struck by a bullet and killed. The death of Hideyoshi in September 1598 prompted the Japanese to bring the war to a close.

Some of the Korean losses in the war were distinct assets for Japan. A number of skilled makers of ceramics were taken to Japan as captives and thousands of books were looted by the Japanese. It was also through a Korean prisoner that the tenets of Neo-Confucianism began to take hold in Japan.

Within a few decades, Choson was under assault from the north. In the Manchurian highlands, the Jurchen tribes had united under Nurhachi. Sporadic attacks began along the northeastern border as early as 1583, and by the 1590s the Ming outposts in Manchuria were under pressure.

Choson sided with the Chinese against the rising Manchu state but in 1627, Nurhachi captured P'yongyang and then took the Yi capital at Seoul. The court fled to Kanghwa Island. Under the terms of a peace treaty, the Korean ruler committed his country to a Confucian-style, elder-younger brother relationship with the Manchus, and pledged aid against the Ming dynasty. The Koreans, however, did not take their pledges seriously. In 1632 the Manchus demanded annual tribute and the Koreans issued a declaration of war.

The Manchu cavalry blocked the escape route of Injo and his ministers, who capitulated on learning that the Manchus had captured Kanghwa and 200 hostages, including the queen.

The Manchus extracted a heavy price: a tributary relationship, severance of ties with the Ming court and submission of two Yi princes as hostages. The Manchus went on to conquer and rule China as the Ch'ing dynasty (1644-1912).

The Sirhak: In the 18th century, the Yi dynasty recovered some of its earlier vitality. Financial problems had been resolved and the reigns of Yongjo (1724-1776) and Chongjo (1776-1800) brought great progress.

Two important intellectual currents stimulated Korean thinkers of the late Yi period. One was the body of Western ideas flowing into Korea from China. The other was the Ch'ing School of Empirical Studies which emphasized critical reasoning. The most interesting products of these influences appeared in the works of the scholars of the *sirhak*, or "practical learning" school. *Sirhak* embraced a number of thinkers whose concerns varied widely. They had in common a focus on finding pragmatic solutions to Korea's economic and social problems. They stressed inductive reasoning in their studies and had little patience with the speculative metaphysics of the orthodox Neo-Confucian tradition.

The early 18th century saw scholars and statesmen such as Yi Chae (<u>right</u>) as avid *Kongja* disciples.

The 19th century was a century of crisis for Korea. Despite its longevity and occasional brilliance, the Yi dynasty did not give Korea an efficient administration. Decades of social unrest and popular agitation in the early 19th century, including major rebellions in 1811 and 1862, made the conservative ruling class reactionary and inward-looking. And that was a time when Korea, along with the rest of Asia, faced the challenge of an expansive and technologically superior West.

Korea's contacts with her main neighbors, with the enthronement of King Sunjo (1800-1834). In 1839, a new wave of persecution brought the deaths of 130 Christians. Apart from clandestine missionaries, direct contacts with the West continued to be limited until the 1860s. Korean officials, however, were badly shaken by the news that British and French troops had occupied Beijing in 1860. This strengthened their determination to exclude foreigners from the peninsula. This policy was confirmed upon the accession of a new monarch, Kojong(1864-1907).

China and Japan, had been closely regulated and direct exposure to Westerners had been limited. Over the next two centuries, however, a good deal of information on Western learning passed into Korea which was declared subversive to Confucian beliefs and social order by the Chinese and Koreans.

Despite the official persecutions in 1791, a number of Koreans embraced Catholicism. In 1794 a Chinese Catholic priest, Father Chou Wen-mo slipped into the country and began missionary work. During the next six years, the Korean Catholic community grew from 3,000 to 10,000.

Repression of Western learning deepened He began his reign as a 12-year-old youth with the dowager queen as the nominal regent. Actual power was in the hands of his father, better remembered by his title, Taewon'gun ("Great Prince of the Court"). The Taewon'gun, in pursuing an exclusionist foreign policy, won widespread support.

The year of Kojong's crowning also brought the intensification of Western pressures on Korea. The Russians began to demand trade and diplomatic relations but were turned down in 1866. That same year nine French Catholic priests and some 8,000 Korean converts were executed. In August 1866, the American-owned *General Sher-*

man, sailed up the Taedong River and ran aground. The ship was burned and her crew killed. In October, the French occupied Kanghwa Island but withdrew shortly.

In 1871, the American minister to China, Frederick Low, accompanied five warships to Korea to try to open the country to trade. A clash occurred. The Americans occupied Kanghwa Island where 350 Koreans and three Americans were killed before the mission was abandoned by the Americans.

Under the Tae-won'gun, the seclusion policy was applied even to the Japanese who, in 1875, were determined to press the issue. After a clash between Korean shore batteries and a Japanese ship, Japan pressed upon the Chinese to redouble efforts to preserve their traditional influence. This led to a series of confrontations. In 1882 Korean army soldiers killed their Japanese instructors, burned the Japanese legation, and attacked residences of the dominant family in the government, the Min clan of Yohung, the family of Kojong's queen. When rebellious soldiers went so far as to seize King Kojong, the Min clan sought help from the Chinese, who were happy to restore Min control. Japan won indemnity and permission to station a legation guard in Korea, but her political influence was eclipsed by the Chinese.

The Tonghak Uprising: After a Korean revolt, China and Japan agreed to withdraw

Korean government a treaty of friendship and commerce. It provided for the opening of three ports to trade with Japan and permanent Japanese diplomatic offices in Korea. Kojong and his advisors saw the treaty merely as the normalization of relations with a country Korea always had ties with.

Korea now became an international battleground for contending powers. The rise of Japanese influence after 1876 spurred the

their troops from Korea and not to intervene again but both countries continued to try to penetrate Korea through commercial trade. Western involvement in Korea, especially the growth of Protestant missions, also grew, sparking the Tonghak uprising in 1894 and, in its wake, the Sino-Japanese War.

The Tonghak ("Eastern learning") movement began as a religious society founded in 1860 under a philosophy that combined monotheism with the principles of Confucianism and other concepts from Buddhism, Taoism, Shamanism, and other sources. By the 1890s Tonghak was a religious and social movement of national significance, sup-

Preceding pages, Westerners at the Korean Court. Early Korean lithographs: *Korean Chief and Attendants* (left); *Islanders of Sir James Hall group* (above), sketched in 1817.

ported by many peasants and discontented elements from the upper classes.

The troubles in the spring of 1894 grew out of a peasant rebellion which reflected the serious economic problems caused in part by foreign merchants. The government attitude provided a large-scale armed revolt. When the Tonghak-led rebels defeated the troops of the central government in two major battles, an appeal went out to China for military assistance. China responded and duly notified the Japanese. Uninvited, the Japanese sent 7,000 men and warships.

The Chinese and Korean forces put down

the rebellion and Japan began processing the Korean government for a program of reform and modernization. In late July, the Japanese seized the government, occupied Kyongbok Palace, ousted the administration, and installed a progressive, pro-Japanese cabinet. The old Taewon'gun was declared the nominal head of state as regent for the king.

Soon Chinese and Japanese armies clashed and the Sino-Japanese War was on. It pitted the fading Ch'ing empire against the rising imperial power of Meiji Japan. The Japanese dealt China a startling defeat. China then formally acknowledged Korea's liberation from the old suzerain-vassal relationship.

The Murder of Queen Min: With the Chinese eliminated, the Koreans opposed to Japanese dominance found a new counterforce in the Russians. In 1895 Russia helped to weaken the Japanese position by compelling Japan to restore to China the Liaotung peninsula, seized during the Sino-Japanese War. On the heels of this *fait accompli,* a pro-Russian faction associated with Queen Min obtained the dismissal of the pro-Japanese minister to Korea and a professional soldier, Miura Goro, engineered the murder of Queen Min, said to be the real power behind the throne.

Then, with the connivance of the pro-Russian group, King Kojong slipped out of his palace and took refuge in the Russian legation whereupon he dismissed the cabinet and replaced it with a pro-Russian one.

For a year, Kojong reigned from the legation, returning to the palace only in February 1897 when he was convinced he could do so without fear of Japanese threats. Under Russian protection, he sought to reassert Korea's independence. In October 1897, he adopted the title of "emperor" in order to claim equality with the rulers of China and Japan. At the same time, the name of the country was changed from Choson to Taehan Cheguk, "Empire of the Great Han."

A novel group, The Independence Club, attempted to urge reform on the government. They founded a newspaper, *The Independent*, published exclusively in the Korean script, *han'gul*, which became an important means of popularizing reformist proposals.

The Russians soon became a primary target of the Independence Club. As the club grew, its criticism of foreign encroachment and of government policies became bolder. In November 1898 the government dissolved the club and jailed some of its leaders.

The Russo-Japanese War: As the end of the century neared, Japan and Russia maintained an uneasy truce in Korea but events beyond Korea's borders such as the 1902 alliance between Japan and Great Britain, began to turn the situation in Japan's favor.

The showdown came in February 1904 when Japan launched a surprise attack on the Russian fleet at Port Arthur. That set off the Russo-Japanese War. Korea had declared its neutrality, but as soon as the war broke out Japan moved into the peninsula in force. The Korean government had no choice but to authorize Japanese military occupation.

By the end of 1905, Japan's control of Korea was recognized, ending the war. In Western opinion, Japan's role in Korea was seen as one of uplifting and enlightening a backward people who had repeatedly proved their incapacity to eliminate corruption and build a modern society and government.

The next step was to get Korea's formal acceptance of Japan as her protector. To this end, Ito Hirobumi arrived in Seoul on 5 November 1905, to persuade the Korean ruler to approve a treaty transferring partial sovereignty to Japan.

Both Kojong and his cabinet resisted, but before two weeks had passed Ito had convinced a majority of the cabinet to accept the

tions. The emperor's aide, Min Yong-hwan, and a former prime minister, Cho Pyong-se, both committed suicide.

The regulations of the Residency-General went beyond the wording of the protectorate treaty. They claimed for the resident-general the right to maintain law and order; the right to intervene in Korea's internal administration; the authority to supervise Japanese officials in Korea, including those employed by the Korean government; and the power to issue ordinances.

In June 1907, Kojong sent a secret envoy to the Hague peace conference to generate international pressure for Japan's withdrawal from the peninsula. The mission

treaty. It was signed on 18 November and gave Japan control of Korea's foreign relations and the right to station in Korea a resident-general to manage external affairs.

When the treaty was made public, there was an outburst of protest and demands for the punishment of the "Five Traitors" who had approved it. Japanese gendarmes had to be called out to suppress public demonstra-

failed and in July, Kojong's cabinet, apparently to forestall Japanese retaliation, forced the emperor to abdicate in favor of his feeble-minded son (Sunjong, 1907-1910).

At the same time, the Japanese decided to disband the Korean army, and the two events sparked riots which were suppressed by 1912. In December 1907, the treaty between Korea and Japan was revised to give the resident-general a veto over all important administrative acts, internal reforms, and appointments and dismissals of high officials. By mid-1909, the administration of justice was in Japanese hands. A year later the Japanese had complete police power.

Left, Korean Prince Yi Eun was commissioned as "Captain Prince Ri" by conquering the Japanese. **Above**, bronze mural at Seoul's Pagoda Park to commemorate March 1 Movement.

Korean resistance was unflagging. Ito was assassinated by a Korean patriot in October 1909. But on 22 August, 1910, another treaty annexed Korea to Japan and extinguished Korea's existence as a separate nation.

The March 1 Movement: With annexation, the Residency-General became known as the Government-General and "Choson" was rendered "Chosen" by the Japanese. General Terauchi Masatake, the first governor-general, began a period of iron-fisted rule during which Korean opinion and political participation were thoroughly suppressed. Meanwhile, the Japanese were building an all-

powerful, centralized government designed to exploit their new colony.

Organized resistance was completely broken by the Japanese army and policy under Terauchi and his successor, but the Koreans still endured. This became evident with the March 1 Independence Movement of 1919, one of the most celebrated incidents in Korean history. To take advantage of the call for the self-determination of subjected peoples being heard at the Versailles Conference, a group of religious leaders planned a non-violent protest and appeal for independence. A declaration of independence was drafted, and on the afternoon of 1 March, signatories of the declaration dispatched a copy to the police and circulated others.

The Japanese were taken completely by surprise. When printed copies surfaced on 1 March, the authorities did not know what to do and when large crowds began to appear in the streets, the police panicked. The peaceful demonstration turned into a bloody riot. For seven weeks, public demonstrations for independence spread to every corner of Korea. As many as 7,000 were killed in the clashes or as the result of beatings and torture, and 50,000 injured.

The Japanese adopted a softer line after the 1919 uprisings. Officials and school teachers stopped wearing swords; the number of military police was reduced, but the total number of policemen continued to grow; and Korean-language newspapers, which had been suppressed, were revived but tempered by vigorous censorship.

In 1937 colonial policy turned toward the complete "Japanization" of Korea. Use of the Japanese language was made mandatory in schools and in public places, and Korean history was dropped from the curriculum. Koreans were compelled to adopt Japanese names and required to participate in Shinto rituals. As the war in China intensified and World War II approached, Koreans were mobilized into patriotic associations and exhorted to support Japanese expansionism. Between 1939 and the end of World War II, hundreds of thousands of Korean laborers were conscripted to fill the positions of workers in the Japanese army.

Japanese rule brought material improvements to Korea, but, as with most colonial societies, few of the improvements were undertaken with the Koreans in mind. The Japanese built highways, railroads, ports, and modern communications facilities related to strategic and defense concerns. Agricultural and industrial development took place along lines dictated by the needs of Japan's domestic economy. Where industries were built, the earnings went to the Japanese, not Koreans.

The Japanese shook Korean society out of its lethargy but the benefits of the colonial period hardly offset the costs of exploitation and suppression.

Above, a Korean courtesan of the 1880s. **Right,** Yi Kojong in a 1898 portrait by Hubert Vos.

Koreans were jubilant when Japan surrendered to the Allied powers in August 1945, but their celebrations were short-lived. Most Koreans had taken it for granted that Japan's defeat meant immediate liberation and restoration of an independent nation. Instead, Korea was once again caught in the turbulence of international politics.

In Cairo on 1 December 1943, the United States advanced the idea of a four-power trusteeship over the peninsula on the theory that Koreans would be unable to maintain a strong, stable government if left to their own devices. The British and the Russians were unenthusiastic about the plan, but did not reject it out of hand.

Americans to the south. Under pressure to reach a decision the planners chose the 38th parallel as the demarcation line.

The 38th parallel was not conceived of as a permanent division of the country. However, as soon as the two occupation armies were in place on opposite sides of the line it became a barrier that no amount of negotiation was able to dissolve.

The Allied foreign ministers met in Moscow in December 1945 and agreed to go ahead with an international trusteeship, which

strong, stable government if left to their own devices. The British and the Russians were unenthusiastic about the plan, but did not reject it out of hand.

As the war ground to a conclusion in 1945, the Grand Alliance was already split by the tensions that soon gave rise to the Cold War. Thus when the Russians entered the Pacific war on 9 August, American leaders were concerned that the Red army might deny the United States any voice in Korea's future. To counter this possibility, Washington officials proposed that a demarcation line be drawn across the peninsula. The Russians were to accept the surrender north of that line and the

was to direct Korean affairs through a provisional government, staffed by Koreans, for at least five years. Two protracted attempts were made in 1946 and 1947 to implement this agreement, which was bitterly opposed by most Koreans. Both attempts failed and the United States turned to the United Nations in September 1947.

In the meantime, the two occupation armies were creating the beginnings of two separate Korean states. In the north, the Russians moved ahead to establish a Communist regime that would be friendly to the Soviet Union. They recognized and worked through people's committees that sprang up immediately after the Japanese capitulation. Both Communists and non-Communists worked together in the early days of the occupation. By February 1946, however, the Communists had begun to dominate politics under the leadership of the man the Russians had chosen, Kim Il-song. In another two years, all pretense of coalition had ended, and the Communists under Kim were in full control.

In the south, the American army refused to recognize a rudimentary administration known as the People's Republic, which had organized hastily after the surrender. Instead, the Americans tried to retain some Japanese officials and established a military government with American personnel as executives and Koreans in subordinate positions. The military government was barely able to cope with the chaotic conditions resulting from the collapse of the Government-General, the separation of the south from the resources of the more-industrialized north, and the influx of refugees from the Russian zone and returnees from Japan.

The American policy was to hold important political and economic decisions in abeyance until a Korean government could be formed. This, of course, required the cooperation of the Russians, which was not forthcoming. As a result there were months of drifting when action was needed and the political arena quickly became a free-for-all. There was very little middle ground. Parties and individual leaders divided along sharp left-versus-right lines, and their constant strife further complicated the work of the military government.

The Republic of Korea: The United Nations General Assembly called for the creation of a unified and independent government for all of Korea and appointed a temporary commission to oversee elections. The commission was denied entry into the Russian zone, but decided to go ahead with elections in the south. On 10 May 1948, half of Korea chose a constituent assembly to draft a constitution and elect a chief executive.

The assembly picked as chairman, and later as first president, Syngman Rhee (Yi Sung-man), a 73-year-old conservative anti-Communist. He had returned to Korea in October 1945 after 36 years abroad agitating

Left, Korean refugees fleeing to the south from advancing armies.

for Korean independence, mostly in the United States. As a young man, he had had a minor role in the Independence Club and had been jailed for seven years as a result of his activities. He had earned a Ph.D. degree at Princeton University and in 1919, had been chosen premier of the Korean Provisional Government of expatriates in Shanghai.

Rhee was an authoritarian with scant regard for liberal democracy. Neither installed nor favored by the U.S. government, Rhee knew well how to manipulate Americans. He plied that skill repeatedly after being sworn in as first president of the Republic of Korea on 15 August 1948.

The creation of a separate government in the south had been reduced to an advisory group. The Russians supplied arms and assistance necessary to create a formidable north Korean army, but the United States refused to provide the south with armament beyond those sufficient for self-defense.

The Korean War: The stage was set for civil war. North Korean troops poured across the 38th parallel in strength early Sunday morning, 25 June 1950. The American response was to assume that unless the United States acted swiftly and decisively, the forces of global communism, directed from Moscow, would soon be on the march.

In Washington, President Truman promptly ordered U.S. forces into battle and asked the United Nations to sanction his intervention. At the time, the Soviet delegate was boycotting the United Nations in protest of the seating of Nationalist China and did not return to block Truman's request. Hence, a resolution was quickly passed, placing the American action under the flag of the United Nations and calling on other member nations to render aid. Sixteen other nations eventually contributed, but half the combat troops were supplied by the United States and most of the others were Koreans. An American general, beginning with Douglas MacArthur, was always in command.

By the beginning of September, South Korean and American forces had been pushed into a perimeter around Pusan. In mid-September, however, a counteroffensive was launched and by the end of the month the front had been pushed back to the 38th parallel.

With Rhee threatening to go ahead alone if necessary, MacArthur obtained U.N. authorization to push north and unite the peninsula. By the end of October, American and South Korean troops were nearing the Manchurian border. The Chinese government, however, had strongly warned the United States against going into North Korea. Tens of thousands of Chinese troops crossed the Yalu River, attacked the spreadout U. N. forces, and drove them back. They pushed south, crossed the 38th parallel, and retook Seoul.

For the next six months, the battlefront raged back and forth and finally stabilized in an area just north of the 38th parallel. The stalemate prompted the beginning of truce negotiations in July 1951 which dragged on for two years. As agreement appeared near in at P'anmunjom to discuss the armistice and exchange recriminations.

Korea Artificially Divided: At the end of the war, Korea lay in ruins. Several cities had been reduced to rubble and millions were rendered homeless. The United Nations Command lost nearly 37,000, of whom 33,629 were Americans. Another 117,000 were wounded. Civilian casualties were also heavy with 47,000 killed, 183,000 wounded and 70,000 missing in the south. On the northern side, total casualties, military and civilian, were estimated to have been 1½-2 million.

The war dealt a fatal blow to any hopes of reunification. The creation of the demilita-

the summer of 1953, Rhee, who opposed a negotiated settlement, almost sabotaged the accord by releasing 25,000 prisoners who had refused repatriation to the north. South Korea did not sign the agreement finally put into effect on 27 July 1953.

The armistice agreement created a demilitarized zone stretching from coast to coast along the line of battle. It set up a Military Armistice Commission consisting of officers from the opposing armies to administer the agreement and a Neutral Nations Supervisory Commission to monitor the truce. For four decades, the Military Armistice Commission has continued to meet periodically rized zone made the border between the two Korean states one of the most effective artificial barriers in the world, and the fighting hardened the hostility on both sides.

In the north, since the war, Kim Il-song has sought to construct a self-reliant socialist state based on Communist doctrines. He has skillfully steered North Korea away from total dependence on either China or the Soviet Union. Kim's political ideology is a kind of patriotic socialism revolving round a personality cult in which he is revered as the supreme leader. Kim was able to rebuild the shattered economy after the war with Soviet aid. However, years of central planning and heavy defense expenditures took their toll and by the 1980s the economy had stagnated. Today, in the 1990s, North Korea is still having difficulty feeding its people.

In the south, the period following the Korean War was one of stagnation and slow recovery, despite massive amounts of American aid. Throughout the 1950s there was little industrial growth, and the economy was plagued by shortages and inflation.

Favoritism and corruption were widespread in the government and in the upper ranks of the military. Rhee fell in danger of being ousted in the National Assembly balloting for president in 1952 and engineered a constitutional amendment to provide for popular

out in Seoul and other cities. On 19 April, police fired on a demonstration in Seoul, killing 115 persons. Rhee attempted to pacify the discontent by promising reforms, but the demonstrations continued until he resigned from office and took exile in Hawaii on 27 April.

Failure of the Second Republic: The collapse of Rhee's government was followed by a brief interim administration and in July, the constitution was changed to provide a government with a cabinet responsible to the legislature. Yun Po-Son won election to the figurehead position of president and took office on 15 August 1960, marking the beginning of the Second Republic. He chose

election, which he won. Before the 1956 elections came around, he coerced the National Assembly to drop the two-term limit for presidents and was subsequently returned to office for a third term. By 1960, however, it was apparent that Rhee's Liberal Party had become very unpopular.

The 1960 election was marred by fraud so blatant it could not be ignored. In March and April, massive student demonstrations broke

Left, U.S. General Douglas MacArthur makes an inspection tour of frontlines. **Above,** a North Korean general arrives for the 1953 peace talks at P'anmunjom on the DMZ.

Chang Myon to lead the new government as prime minister. Both were members of the former opposition, the Democratic Party.

The Chang government, committed to liberal democratic rule, proved incapable of maintaining itself in power. It fell on 16 May 1961, when a military junta, seized control. The junta immediately announced pledges to oppose Communism, to respect the United Nations charter and seek closer relations with the free world, to stamp out corruption, to build a self-supporting economy, and to work for reunification. When these revolutionary tasks were accomplished, the government would be returned to civilian hands.

The coup leaders imposed an absolute military dictatorship known as the Supreme Council for National Reconstruction and in July, Major General Park Chung-hee emerged as its chairman.

Park was a 43-year-old career officer of rural origin. He had been trained in Japanese military academies and had served as a lieutenant in the Kwantung Army in Manchuria during World War II. After the war, he had entered the Korean army for several years, had then become a civilian intelligence offi-

years later, he secured a constitutional amendment to open the way for a third term, to which he was elected in 1971, narrowly defeating Kim Dae-jung.

In an attempt to ensure his unchallenged command of Korean affairs, Park declared martial law on 17 October 1972, and called for a program of Yushin (revitalizing) reforms. The constitution was redrawn, establishing a National Conference on Unification, whose membership he controlled, which functioned as an electoral college. Under the

cer, but had returned to active duty when the Korean War began. By 1960, he had risen to become deputy commander of the Second Army but had always remained apart from the main political factions within the army.

Under Park's leadership, the military government continued to rule until 1963, when it could no longer resist pressures for a return to civilian government. With presidential elections scheduled for mid-October, Park retired from the army and ran as the candidate of the Democratic Republican Party, defeating Yun Po-son. He was inaugurated and the Third Republic was launched.

In 1967, Park won a reelection and two

terms of the new constitution, the Conference elected Park to a new six-year term as president with no limit on future terms.

Park's rule came to an end on 26 October 1979 when he was killed by his own intelligence chief, Kim Chae-kyu, who claimed he had assassinated Park in order to restore democracy. Kim was convicted, along with six accomplices, and was executed.

The long-term legacy of Park's 18 years in office comprised two trends: Park's idea of Korean-style democracy placed a strong emphasis on administrative efficiency, and he presided over a series of development programs that made Korea one of the most remarkable economic successes of the 1960s and 1970s. The immediate period of transition after his sudden death, however, was a period of uncertainty and contention.

Under the 1972 constitution, the prime minister Ch'oe Kyu-ha, became acting president. On 6 December the National Conference for Unification, Korea's electoral college, named him to serve out Park's term. Between Ch'oe's election and his inauguration on 21 December, an abrupt change occurred within the military establishment when Major General Chun Doo-hwan, head of the Defense Security Command, the agency responsible for investigating Park's murder, arrested the Army Chief of Staff, General Chong Sung-hwa, who was accused of complicity in the assassination of Park. A number of other senior officers were also arrested.

The arrests of military opponents marked the first step in a phased assumption of power by Chun. Suppression of civilian opponents in May 1980 led to a popular revolt in the city of Kwangju after special forces sent to control student demonstrations overreacted and brutalized protesters. At least 200 students and citizens and several soldiers were killed. Paratroopers retook the city after 10 days. With the opposition quelled, Chun was named President in August by the process of indirect election set out in Park's Yushin constitution.

In January Chun became the first head-of-state to be received by newly-elected American President Ronald Reagan. The haste with which Washington appeared to endorse Chun's takeover led Korean dissidents and students to conclude that America, which had 40,000 troops in Korea, had backed the new military coup from the outset. This perception was the basis for the anti-Americanism which characterized anti-government protests during Chun's rule and which remains in the 1990s.

It is one of the ironies of Korea's recent political history that Washington had in fact agreed to the Chun meeting in exchange for a secret agreement by Chun that he would step down at the end of his seven-year term as the constitution demanded and that he would commute a death sentence on opposition leader Kim Dae-jung. By the time Chun's rule neared its close, the opposition

was weakened by factional strife and the campus protest movement was alienating students and the public with its leftist slogans and violent protest tactics. However, when Chun anointed fellow coup-maker Roh Tae-woo as his successor, religious dissidents called for protests and hundreds of thousands of ordinary Koreans joined student activists in taking to the streets to demand direct popular elections. For three weeks Chun resisted but on 29 June 1987, Roh himself accepted all the protesters' demands. In December, Roh won the election, thanks to opposition rivals Kim Dae-jung and Kim Young-sam who failed to agree on a single candidate, thus splitting the opposition ticket.

Roh took power in February 1988 in what was the first peaceful transfer of power in Korean history. The pent-up frustrations of a rapidly developing society, held down by years of dictatorial rule, appeared to explode at once. For three years in succession widespread labor disputes rocked the nation. Wages rose so fast that Korea found itself no longer able to sell many of its products overseas competitively. Yet the country still managed to achieve growth rates which are the envy of the developing nations.

In the autumn of 1988, Korea staged the most successful summer Olympics to date. In two weeks, Korea shed its wartime rubble-and-ashes image and was seen by the world for the developed, fast-paced, modern nation that it is. In the wake of the Games, Seoul developed full diplomatic ties with East European nations and the Soviet Union.

While Korea advanced economically and diplomatically, politics appeared to drag. Even the surprise merger of Kim Young-sam and Kim Jong-pil's opposition parties with Roh's ruling party failed to further democratic reforms. Where North Korea was concerned, old habits which characterized earlier authoritarian rulers prevailed. Starry-eyed dissidents who traveled illegally to North Korea to encourage unification – after Roh had declared the North to be a "brother" and no longer the "enemy" – received heavy jail terms. Korea's critics, however, acknowledge that the country is moving in the right direction. On the economic front, Korea has become a major industrial powerhouse. In 1963, GNP was $100. By 1990, it had passed the $5,500 mark and the goal is to reach $10,000 by the end of the century.

To understand today's Koreans and their intriguing, paradoxical country; to survive potentially terminal cultural shock, and learn to get along smoothly with these fascinating people, it's necessary to give some consideration to the questions of who they are, how they become that way, and why they act the way they do.

The qualities that have enabled Koreans to survive, and which have become their most strongly ingrained attributes, are primarily three: patience, flexibility, and stubbornness.

side influences, it seems, and were there to be developed and orchestrated by the happenstance of proximity and event.

The Descent of Tan'gun: So far as it is now known, the Korean peninsula was first settled by wandering tribes from Central and Northern Asia some 30,000 years ago. These hardy nomadic people had their own language, a variant Ural-Altaic speech related to Turkish, Hungarian and Finnish. This uniquely Korean tongue, despite a later overlay of Chinese ideographic writing and vocabulary plus some

To these may be added a robust, satiric, and sometimes uncouth sense of humor.

Korean patience does not mean passivity, nor does flexibility imply lack of strong individuality. The third trait, stubbornness – sometimes dignified by calling it perseverance – explains and modifies the other two.

It would be easy but misleading to make a neat generalization here and say that these three basic Korean qualities are derived from the three major outside influences, and to speak of Chinese patience, Japanese adaptability, and American stick-to-it-iveness. But it goes deeper than that: these counterpointed national themes appeared earlier than the out-

elements shared with Japanese syntax, has remained an important factor contributing to national unity. This was especially so after the belated invention of an efficient phonetic alphabet, called *han'gul*, in the 15th century.

The early Koreans devised a national foundation myth in which a son of heaven descended to the peninsula and mated with a bear-woman, who represented the sturdy, independent totem-animal of the tribe, producing as progeny the semi-divine ancestor named Tan'gun.

As population increased during the Bronze and Iron ages, and the people settled into sedentary occupations such as farming and fishing, their social organization developed from tribal to clan level. Patriarchal chiefs of allied clans met in council over important issues such as war, a practice that led eventually to selection of a king who was merely "first among equals." The outspokenness and self-reliance of Koreans had taken firm root by the 1st century BC.

It was during this period too that the major influx of informative influence from China began. In addition to agricultural and manufacturing skills, there came the writing system which brought with it classical Chinese literature. The most important borrowings from the mainland, though, consisted of religio-philosophic creeds and the social system these implied or dictated.

Here we may be on somewhat firmer ground in seeking sources for our three characteristic Korean traits. For certainly Buddhism encouraged the cultivation of patience. Likewise, the Confucian system became in practice a pragmatic philosophy, presupposing adaptability in pursuit of advantage. And Taoism suggests a stubbornness embodied in its metaphor of water as the strongest of all elements, since it gradually wears away even the hardest stones.

With the establishment in Korea of these three interdependent systems of thought – none of which ever achieved full dominance over the others – the stage was set for the unfolding of the drama of Korean history.

Buddhism and the Golden Horde: The Silla kingdom, which first unified the peninsula under one government in AD 668, is generally regarded as a predominantly Buddhist monarchy but it was actually guided by firm Confucian tenets of ritual and conduct, as was the succeeding Koryo dynasty, which assumed power in 936.

During Koryo times, the Buddhist clergy did indeed attain powerful influence in government. It was during this period too that the Mongol armies of the Great Khan swept over the country in 1213. Suffering and destruction were unprecedented, and when the Korean king sued for peace he was forced to take a Mongol princess as bride, and to declare himself a vassal of the Khan, was willing to assist the Mongols in their abortive attempts to invade Japan.

Preceding pages, schoolgirls pass on uniforms but remain partial to hats. Left, the older and wiser. Above right, the traditional hanbok is still worn for special occasions.

As the Golden Horde weakened and receded, it was easy to blame Buddhist ascendancy in the government for Korea's national disaster. When anti-Mongol general Yi Songgye rebelled and proclaimed himself founder of a new dynasty in 1392, one of his immediate concerns was to eradicate Buddhist power at court. Confucianism, of a peculiarly orthodox and dogmatic type, was installed in power; leading to the calcification of an already rigid social system.

Korean humor among the oppressed and ignored lower classes found outlet in bawdy, grotesque folk dramas and mask dances satirizing the effete aristocrats and the worldly cynicism of Buddhist monks.

The new dynasty started off well, however, and during the reign of the fourth monarch, King Sejong the Great (1419-1450), a cultural renaissance and some attempt at administrative reforms ushered in what many Koreans like to think of as a Utopian age.

Korea's Darkest Half Century: In 1592 and 1598, though, legions of the Japanese warlord Hideyoshi launched two successive invasions of the peninsula, bent on an invasion of China from Japan via Korea. This attempt was futile and devastating to Korea for the invading armies clashed with Chinese forces on Korean soil.

Less than 40 years later Korea was ravaged

by the Manchu forces bent on overthrowing China's Ming dynasty, to which Korea maintained a tenacious loyalty.

Stunned by this double disaster into a state of near traumatic shock, Korea withdrew from all outside contacts, assuming the role of Hermit Kingdom for over 2½ centuries. Divisive feuds festered among political factions, while idealistic reformers found themselves stymied by isolation and lack of practical knowledge.

A vital new trend toward modernization and reform at the end of the 19th century achieved extent, but in trying to extirpate the very foundations of the country's national identity: the language, customs and culture of thousands of years.

Unfortunately for their plans, the Japanese were up against an elder, tougher, more tenacious race than their own – a people armed with the ancient weapons of patience, adaptability and stubbornness.

The long-dormant nationalism of Korea's intelligentsia, awakening from centuries of apathy and self-destructive bickering, arose to

too little too late to prevent Korea from becoming a pawn in the contention between a declining China and an awakening Japan, with Russia and Western powers on the sidelines.

During the Russo-Japanese War of 1904-5, Japan consolidated 20 years of creeping encroachment upon Korea's sovereignty, and in 1910 the peninsula was formally annexed as part of the island empire.

The Japanese occupation attempted not merely annexation, but complete assimilation. The usurpers behaved with unparalleled greed, arrogance and brutality, not only in exploiting Korea's resources to a ruinous defy, deceive and destroy the oppressors, in ways ranging from assassination and guerrilla warfare to non-violent demonstrations and passive sabotage. The struggle was long and bitter, since the organized police and military forces marshalled by Japan were unbeatable so close to their home islands.

When Tokyo finally surrendered to the Western allies in 1945, following defeat in the Pacific War, Korea regained her independence, only to be partitioned by outside interfer-

Above, respectful progeny gathers round at a *hwangap*, or 60th birthday party, in 1933.

The contemporary Korean wardrobe, a very Western mode influenced during the 20th century by scattered political and cultural events, is an odd assortment of imported styles – from the abundance of uniforms reminiscent of the Japanese Occupation to *très chic* designer wares that are exact copies of fashions which debuted just last month in Paris or Rome. Settled between these two extremes is the traditional Korean costume, the *hanbok*, a Mongol-influenced garment still proudly worn by young and old alike.

The contemporary *hanbok*, with its short vests, baggy pants and puffy dresses, evolved under the influence of the Mongols in the 13th century when Korea was a Mongol vassal state. Then, women wore their hair in plaits coiled on top of their heads. The waist-jacket (*chogori*) was hiked above the waist and tied at the chest with a long, wide ribbon. The sleeves of the *chogori* were curved slightly. These apparel modifications, especially in the Korean woman's costume, have remained *de rigueur* to this day.

Throughout these fashion-changing periods, the three preferred clothing fabrics were silk, cotton, and hemp. Silk was used almost exclusively for court and bureaucratic wears. Cotton and hemp, however, were Korean's fabrics of common choice, and these utilitarian fabrics, usually in plain cotton white or hemp yellow, were sewn into traditional Korean street attire. Because the Koreans have long used white as the primary color for apparel, they became known as "the white-clad people."

Western clothes were introduced in the late 1800s, and again, it was the trendsetting upper class which initiated a move to business suits and cocktail dresses. Since the Japanese were ousted from Korea after World War II, the biggest fashion influence has been an all-America blend of President John F. Kennedy and diplomatic corps pin stripes, G.I. and Peace Corps casual, and visiting industrial salary-men. Pointed Italianate shoes, and Gucci and Yves St Laurent scarves and handbags are as

common in Seoul as in Manhattan. It's not exactly Fifth Avenue or the Champs Elysée, but in the locally swank Myong-dong shopping area you'll see all types of modern Western gear being worn and voraciously purchased.

In Myong-dong, you'll also spot Koreans in traditional wear – on national holidays or at social events – with distinctly Korean overtones. In other parts of town, and in country towns, nearly all Korean *halmoni* (grandmothers) and *haraboji*

(grandfathers) wear the *ch'ima-chogori* and *paji-chogori*. A grandfather usually wears a set of dangling, amber buttons down his *chokki* and don rubber shoes with traditionally upturned toes (*komusin*).

Seldom will you see a distinguished Yi dynasty gentleman, or a *yangban* Confucian with long beard, topknot and a horsehair hat (*kat*) in Seoul. But in the villages, you'll find old men who look as if they've just walked out of a late Yi dynasty genre painting and into your line of sight.

Bride with doting relatives.

ence and, five years later, endured a civil war that proved far more cataclysmic than any earlier invasion.

Koreans still find it difficult to speak of the Japanese annexation with any degree of equanimity and they shudder at the suggestion that they resemble their island neighbors. The Japanese did influence Korea in many ways – they stepped into a vacuum in social structure, political organization, education and administration – but the price was so severe that even today, Japanese songs and movies are still banned in Korea.

During the occupation, when Christian missionaries from America, Britain, Canada and Australia offered an alternative, many Kore-

the painful memory of both the colonial period and the subsequent division of the peninsula into northern and southern halves. The pain of family division – an estimated 10 million Koreans belong to families separated by the DMZ – has remained for four decades, unrelieved by a total refusal by either side to bend and permit its people to travel to the other side. Only since 1988 has South Korea stopped penalizing Korea-Americans and other overseas Koreans who travel north for family reunions.

In some ways, this sorrow threatens the stability of the southern portion of the peninsula – students inevitably blame the current government for maintaining the status quo –

ans quickly took up the calling. The Japanese recognized the Christians as leading subversives, but did not directly seek to dismantle the churches until World War II because of their links to foreign powers.

Although there was far wider acceptance of Japanese rule than modern Koreans wish to remember, the dream of independence never died for the majority. But with the royal family and the nobility discredited by their handing over of sovereignty to Japan and the absence of strong new leadership, the independence movement fell into factionalism.

Korean anger against foreign powers and frustration over her own weakness underlie

but it also serves to strengthen the society. Koreans hold onto one another like parents do their children to fend off foreign influence and maintain their traditions. National pride and resilience results, a force far stronger than armies.

Kibun, Nunchi'i and Mot: As Dr. Paul Crane observed some years ago in his pioneer study of this people, entitled *Korean Patterns,* "Korea today shows many faces. The old ways of thinking remain strong in the minds of most people regardless of their education and rank. …a superficial overlay of Western thought patterns has changed the outward appearance of many. Because of this overlay of Western dress and manners, some mistakenly assume that the inner man has changed."

Despite the economic urgency of importing modern science and technology, Koreans still show more concern with manner than with matter. In the words of essayist Lee O-young: "In Korea, they say there is no logic . . . instead there is emotion, intuitional insight and a soulful spirit."

Korean etiquette consists of an elaborate system of formalized gestures designed to produce pleasant feelings and smooth relations. This is done by ensuring maintenance of proper *kibun* (mood or aura) through adroit employment of *nunch'i* (intuiting another's feelings through observation), and behaving

and cheerful people, the proverbial salt of the earth – an impression that usually remains, even after the strange experiences some inevitably encounter in a clash of cultural values. The whole abrasiveness of such a clash is not felt, because the foreigner is considered in the same category as classless people, or *sangnom*: "unpersons" and outcasts who are not expected to know how to behave in a proper Korean manner, and upon whom it would be pointless to waste anger or reprehension.

From the vantage point of the foreign *sangnom*, a Korean can be seen in his best light – without all the hangups he has to deal with among his compatriots – as a courteous, con-

with suitable *mot* (style or taste).

Somewhere along the line, amidst the maze of honorifics and the anxiety to determine whether one must talk up, down, or straight-from-the-shoulder to a given individual, any idea of truth, fairness, or brass-tacks agreement becomes distinctly secondary.

Despite the differences, most Occidental visitors receive a favorable impression of Koreans as a warm, friendly, sympathetic

Left, the child on his first birthday is honored with fruit, rice cakes and cash. **Above**, bus stops are common points of arrival and departure for the Koreans.

siderate, and tenaciously loyal friend. The Korean is gregarious, fun-loving, hearty, even bibulous; and yet remains a devoted family man, a hard worker, and a solid citizen. He is very likely highly cultured – taxi drivers know Beethoven symphonies, schoolboys gather tasteful wildflower bouquets – with great respect for learning and refinement. He is fiercely nationalistic, not shallowly patriotic, and exhibits a touching reverence for the natural beauties of his mountain-riven, storm-tormented land.

You may sometimes glimpse the other side of the coin: an intoxicated Korean becomes angry or tearful, not euphoric.

The seminal changes sweeping through Korean society are being felt even in the time-honored custom of matchmaking. In the autumn and spring, peak times for betrothal and marriages, the thoughts of mothers with eligible daughters and sons turn to wedlock. In the new Korea, since democratic and social changes swept the land in the wake of demonstrations in 1987, many young Koreans now want to be masters of their own destiny; they want more say in selecting

their own partners. More and more girls, particularly university graduates, are going to the hotel nightspots and nightclubs in It'aewon. A popular way of finding a suitable partner among the graduates is the "line-up" where an equal number of men and women meet up at a coffee shop and pair off.

The trend towards meeting by chance has spelt bad news for the official matchmakers, traditionally old women employed by rich families to find suitable partners for their children. But observers are quick to concede that most young Koreans still abide by the wishes of their parents and usually allow their mothers to arrange a meeting for them, the most common and popular introduction being the famous coffee shop meeting. The business of continuing the family lineage and keeping the bloodlines pure is too important to be left to romance and chance encounters.

The scenario opens as protagonists come in with their seconds and await their entrance into the ring of their intended partner. The mothers, who have already been to the fortune-teller to check the "*saju*" and "*kunghap*" of the couple, monopolize most of the conversation while sipping the customary orange or pineapple juice. "*Saju*," based upon the four pillars of year, month, day and hour of birth, is a person's chances of success in the future and "*kunghap*" is the couple's compatibility.

After the preliminary introductions, the families go to another table in the corner and the couple is left alone. Head bowed and hands demurely in lap, the young woman studiously avoids the inquiring gaze of her male companion across the table. The man, wearing his best suit and smoking nervously, does his best to go through the ritual opening gambits. Molly-cuddled by mum from birth, he is at pains to find out whether the woman plans a career. Career women are not popular as it means they will not be at home in the day to look after their lord and master, and they may be a little too independent.

The first encounter usually decides whether there will be wedding bells or not. Despite all the scheming by the families, the couple still has the final say.

Nevertheless, whether the matchmaking is done through friends or families, there is hardly a Korean man or woman in the country who has not gone through this process several times. Stories also abound of women suddenly latching on to men and getting married within a few weeks before turning 28, the bewitching age for Korean women. Fortune-tellers do a roaring trade in advising these "old maids" on the best stratagems to get married.

Facing the future together.

Like all human beings, Koreans crave the elusive goal of security; some assurance of a plausible future for themselves and their children. They have always had less than most, and are not really confident in the signs of change. That is why their songs are sad and their poems piercingly nostalgic; it is why they try so hard to be happy, to seize the fleeting moment before it is past.

Koreans have been called the Irish of the Orient, yet the burden of their history has been even longer and heavier than that of the Irish. This human family may be indissolubly united, but each link in the chain represents a unique, idiosyncratic national entity, with its own customs created or adapted to special circum-

brick wall of a Korean's home. Rather than an odd way of curing condiments, this sight proclaims the birth of a baby boy a week or less before.

Rather than simply a means of proclaiming good news (the symbolism is quite obvious; girls are announced by string of charcoal and pine, the significance of which is less apparent), the decorative peppers had a practical message to convey: a taboo on visitors. It was traditionally believed that during the first week – until the mother's lactation begins, as gynecologists point out – the newborn child was especially vulnerable, and this would include susceptibility to bad luck or evil spirits attached, known or not, to accidental visitors.

stances. And in these differences reside the main points of interest for the traveler.

In Korea, the hallmark of nationality has for a long time probably been symbolized by family ritual. The ancient Chinese called their Korean neighbors "the ceremonious people of the east," admitting that the Koreans had outdone the Sage's own people in adherence to Confucian formalities.

If a traveler strolls through a farming village, he may see a string of dried red peppers hung across the gateway in the stone or mud-

Also during this week it was practically a ritual for the mother to consume quantities of *miyok-kuk* or seaweed soup, like it or not, as a restorative.

The first birthday is celebrated with a special rice cake called *susokttok* which is flavored with mugwort.

Marriage used to occur only after the ministrations of a matchmaker who blended astrology with canny pop psychology and sociology. Nowadays the dating game is played among the young, with rather stricter rules perhaps than in the West. Traditionally, marriage occurred quite young. A girl's family sent her bedding and trousseau chest to the

Above left, Korean bus driver. **Above right**, a Korean couple taking to the hills.

boy's home and the boy's family reciprocated with gifts.

On the nuptial day the bride was carried in a palanquin to the groom's house and the couple – often meeting for the first time – shared a cup of rice wine to pledge their troth.

This ritual is now seen only in staged form at folk village shows, for the ubiquitous custom of the *yesik-chang* ("wedding hall") pervades town and country.

These marriage factories, often huge buildings with dozens of weddings going on simultaneously in various-sized chambers, provide everything from flowers to Western-style music. Crowds of friend and relatives gather in pew-like seats, with no compulsion to retain order or quiet; and children frequently scamper and shout up the aisles. The only trace of the old days remaining is the family-only room at the back where time-honored bows are performed and wine shared. The public part of the ceremony is the bridal procession, a short homily by a family and the indispensable group photography. Guests bring gifts, usually cash in white envelopes.

After marriage the birth cycle was reasonably expected to resume and keep the family busy with rituals. No further scheduled event was indicated until the 60th birthday, or *hwan'gap*, one of the most important events in any Korean's life.

The 60th birthday is celebrated with all possible pomp and ceremony. The elder sits virtually enthroned on cushions, receiving the kowtows of children and grandchildren. Behind him are low tables piled high with fruit, rice cakes, cookies, candies and other goodies set out among brass candelabra.

After the ceremony comes a feast with drinking, music, and dancing for all, including the guest of honor, to the endurance of the last one to give in.

Traditional funeral customs called for the coffined body to be placed in the house where ritual wailing went on by servants, shirt-tail relations, or paid mourners, while the family provided a convivial party resembling an Irish wake. On the third day, a procession accompanied the coffin on a bier borne by laborers, fueled by frequent stops for rice wine, to the grave site preceded by the wooden tablet (or pennant) lettered in Chinese with the name of the deceased, which would later be enshrined in the house.

The grave would probably be located on a scenic hillside deemed propitious by the fortune-teller or geomancer whose business was to select auspicious places to build or do important things. Burial would be above ground in a domed mount later planted with sod and perhaps marked by a stone stele carved with the name of the deceased.

Though such old-fashioned funerals may still be encouraged in the countryside (but should not be photographed by strangers), they are obviously impractical in big cities, where the choice is cremation for the poor.

Though the funeral completes the life cycle, it does not end the cyclical pattern of Korean family ritual, for twice a year – on the *ch'usok* autumn harvest holiday and in spring on *hansik* (or cold food) day, now coincidental with Arbor Day – the family members gather at the grave site from far and near, set up tables covered with fruits and rice cakes that are eaten later, and perform ceremonial bows. A cup of rice wine is ritually poured over the grave, and the rest goes to wash down the feast.

Taming The World: Although modern-day Koreans continue to practice the ceremonies of the past to show respect to their ancestors, they are no longer quite so superstitious. The ceremonies often provide an excuse to reminisce about those forbears whom they can recall to mind and to enjoy a few hours with their extended family. Many young people are now leaving the parental home after marriage so the traditional days of gathering are less frequent.

The streets of Seoul in this day and age look much like the streets of any international city where people wear business clothes and walk at a clip. Upon first meeting a Korean, there seems to be little mystery to his character and little contrast to the Western style. It is only after one learns to know the Korean better that his culture gradually shows through in details of behavior and thought and he will never become unapproachable. Koreans are out to tame the world and they have adapted to the 20th century without letting go their heritage.

It will take time to know Korea and her people, to recognize and appreciate what history took 5,000 years to create.

Haraboji (grandfather) with black horse-hair hat and faraway look.

...Confucianism makes love and righteousness its basis. By a life of virtue, and by keeping the Five Commands blessed thereby ... Taoism has to do with purity and by means of water and fire lifts its subject to a place of refinement where the spirit sloughs off its outer shell and guards only the essence... living in the world and yet not of the world... Buddhism dwells in the regions of silence... With all sensations of the mind and body cast aside as worthless, and zero as the objective attainment... it grows brighter and clearer in mind as the body decays.

−17th century Korean scholar
Hong Man-jong

Such was the literati's view of Korean religion 300 years ago. It was complicated to analyze then, and so it still is:

It was Easter Sunday at Seoul's Myongdong Cathedral. Elderly Korean Christians receive respectful bows from their juniors in the never-dying tradition of Confucius prior to entering the vestibule of this grand and Gothic church. Matrons dressed in brightly colored hanbok *embroidered with Taoist symbols sell Easter eggs and candy to anxious children in the plaza below. Meanwhile, the bald-headed Buddhist monks in gray robes pass by the entrance to the cathedral compound, and across the street a fortune teller consults manuals in order to advise an aging woman on her future – to the best of his shamanist knowledge.*

Most East Asian countries adhere to a spiritual mainstream, but Korea denies a simple religious label. Strong traditions of shamanism, Confucianism, Taoism, Buddhism, Christianity and other religions infuse Korean society. Though many Koreans ascribe exclusively to one religion, they also allow all of the country's spiritual beliefs to play an occasional role in their lives.

If one could peer into the souls of Korean people, one would find fascinating elements

Preceding pages, a trilingual plea for silence; a "thousand Buddhas" at Chikji-sa near Kimch'on. **Left**, Prince Yi Kyu and descendants of Yi dynasty royal families honor their ancestors in Confucian rites at Chongmyo Shrine.

of shamanism, the folk worship of a pantheon of household, village and animate and inanimate forces in nature.

Koreans, like other Asians, maintain ancient traditions such as the *kut*, or exorcising ceremonies. These practices have not been fully institutionalized into a religion but shamanism has been kept very much alive in Korea – as in the deification of Sanshin, a non-Buddhist Mountain God, who has found his way into special shrines located within the courtyards of Buddhist temple complexes.

Shamanist elements have also worked their way into Confucian ceremonies dedicated to *Sajik* ("Gods of Land and Harvest"). Indeed, until the end of the 19th century such cer-

general "of the heavens" and his female general "under the earth." These posts are placed outside of villages to repel evil spirits.

Korea's Taoist Way: Taoism has been practiced in Korea for more than 1,300 years, but active examples of its presence are rare these days. Though Taoist texts were often studied in the past, and though some of Korea's Buddhist temples temporarily served as Taoist temples, few remnants of early Taoist art survive today, save for the occasional Taoist statement on a Yi dynasty genre painting, a few ubiquitous Chinese characters for longevity (*su*) and blessing (*pok*) which serve as decorative motifs on clothing, bedding, jewelry, and other such items.

emonies took place throughout the country and even during royal rituals.

The veneration of Tan'gun, the mythical founder of Korean race and civilization, has earned government backing as a means of instilling greater patriotism. Tan'gun was the central figure in a Taejong cult which declined to near extinction by the 15th century. The cult may be generically separated from shamanism proper but in actual practice it is inseparable from the shamanist world.

The visitor to Korea will notice, sprinkled throughout the countryside, carved and painted shamanist posts depicting an ancient

Taoism achieved its greatest height in Korea during the Unified Silla dynasty (AD 668-918). Practitioners aren't so dedicated today but Taoism is experiencing something of a renaissance as a number of modern, synthesizing religions draw upon its teachings. Koreans as a group have never really been as serious about Taoism as have their Chinese neighbors to the north and west, but they have recognized the readings of Lao-tze and Chuang-tze as being complementary to Buddhist and Confucian thought.

Above, modern Chin-do *mudang* burns an offering to a restless and ancient Shaman spirit.

SHAMANISM

Part priestess and part folk therapist, the shaman has been a mainstay of Korean society for centuries.

When called on to solve spiritual or other problems plaguing a household, she may suggest practical advice mixed with some ritual lore. Wives should keep their husbands' affections by maintaining an even temper and businessmen should temper their deals with prudence.

The shaman's therapy is essentially family therapy. She considers all kinds of affliction, whether family quarrel or burglary, to be symptomatic of some deeper malaise in the house. Her job is to repair the family's relationship through the household gods.

When events have taken a turn for the worse, she will announce that the ancestors are "hungry" and that the gods "want to play." The family, she suggests, should pay for a *kut*. This noisy ceremony, featuring much clanging of gongs and shouting, is an invitation to the gods and ancestors to feast and play and thereby purge their malevolence.

The shaman dons different costumes and speaks for the gods. Participation is the name of the game. When the gods speak, the women of the household and neighbors and friends in attendance talk back. Greedy supernatural officials gorge themselves with wine and meat, make bawdy jokes and demand more and more money from the housewife. Troublesome ancestors causing prolonged illness can be exorcised with a pelting of millet grain. Angry gods are mollified with treats and tribute.

A *kut* goes on all night. By the next morning, the shaman and her assistants beat drums outside the house, do a final exorcism and cast ghosts and other bad elements away.

Chronicles of ancient dynasties record such ceremonies held for the prosperity of kingdoms as far back as the 6th century. Scholars suggest the Korean shaman's affinity with the Tungusic shaman of northern Asia.

Whatever their ancient source, shaman rituals have been shaped by several centuries of Korean history. When the country accepted Confucianism from China in the late 1300s, the shamans fell into disfavor and were denounced as lewd charlatans.

But even the most radical reformers failed to remove them from the women's quarters of the palace and homes of the aristocrats.

Sometimes they were implicated in factional power struggles and found themselves accused of practicing witchcraft to further the politcal interest of this faction or that.

In a more benign role, shamans appointed by local magistrates held rituals for the prosperity of the entire community. In times of drought, shamans would offer *kut* to the rain dragon by a well or a river. In one such ceremony several years ago near Seoul, an overly-ambitious dragon sent a mid-July hailstorm before the shamans had finished chanting.

To Catch a *Kut*: Your Korean hosts may deny the existence of shamans in present-day Korea. However, the tell-tale cacophony of drums and cymbals still resounds from urban and rural streets. If you hear the noise, follow it to the source and you will find yourself invited in.

Another possibility for *kut* seekers is to go to the Kuksadang, a public shrine in the hills above Sajik Park in Seoul. Shamans rent the shrine when clients are unable or unwilling to hold the rituals in their own homes.

In Kangnung on the east coast, shamans revel through the entire week of Tano. Tano is the fifth day of the fifth lunar month and usually falls in early June by the solar calendar. There is also a one-day Tano celebration in Seoul at a shrine on the banks of the Han River. Sometimes, colleges and folklore associations sponsor public performances of *kut*.

Intended as an entertaining and educational display of Korea's cultural heritage, these performances help preserve their original religious flavor. Inspired women from the audience make offerings and receive divinations much as they would at any ancient village ritual. ∎

Buddhist Theocracy: When it comes to the arts and innovative thought, Buddhism stands out as one of the most important of this country's cultural fountainheads. This religion stresses finding a practical and moderate way towards self-actualization while on earth. In ancient times, Buddhism split into a number of spiritual schools but the two largest – Hinayana and Mahayana – earned the most converts outside of India. The Mahayana school – which preached that any practical methods towards teaching salvation is generally acceptable – eventually entered China from the west along the ancient Silk Route. This sectarian form of Buddhism, with its easy acceptance of local deities as a means of drawing the

conquered the entire peninsula, Buddhism flourished, and a new height in Korean culture was reached under the Buddhist government of the Unified Silla (AD 668-918) period. During the following Koryo dynasty (918-1392), temples became Korea's centers of learning and Buddhist monks enjoyed privileged roles within the society. Wonhyo, one of Asia's greatest thinkers, dominated intellectual and religious arenas both inside and outside of Korea. The most important Buddhist achievement during that time was the carving of some 80,000 woodblocks to print and preserve the *Tripitaka Koreana,* one of the world's most complete collections of ancient Buddhist scriptures. The blocks are preserved today in

masses to the temples for an eventual study of more orthodox doctrines and practices, proved much to the liking of the Koreans.

Buddhism entered the northernmost of Korea's three kingdoms, Koguryo, in AD 372. Though Chinese ancestor worship had been commonly accepted for some time, Buddhism became Korea's first sophisticated, truly institutionalized religion. The Paekche kingdoms (18 BC-AD 661) to the south gradually accepted this new faith as they recognized the political, cultural and philosophical merits of a Buddhist theocracy.

It was the Kingdom of Paekche that transmitted Buddhism to Japan. Silla eventually

Haein Temple, southwest of Taegu in the Mt. Kaya National Park. These blocks are regarded as one of the greatest achievements of world Buddhism and Korean culture.

As the Koryo dynasty degenerated, the major philosophical force to emerge was Confucianism and eventually its adherents called for an all-out government reformation. In 1392 the Yi dynasty (1392-1910) was established by T'aejo or "The Great Founder." From that time on Buddhists fared poorly under the attacks of Neo-Confucian court scholars. An occasional Yi king would look favorably on the religion, but Buddhism was basically driven from Seoul's courtyards of power and into mountain retreats. The social status of monks often was degraded to that of itinerant entertainers and prostitutes. Only in recent times have the Buddhist monks and nuns been able to recover any significant gains in prestige.

While Buddhists took an active part in Korea's struggle against the Japanese occupation during the first half of this century, it was, ironically, the Japanese who encouraged the revival of modern Buddhism in Korea. However, it was definitely in Japan's interest to strenghten all cultural similarities between the two nations. And at the same time, the Japanese installed a variety of sects from Japan that allowed monks to marry and otherwise change Korean Buddhism.

Today, the traveler will regularly spot many of the more than 30,000 gray-robed monks and nuns who come from all levels of Korean society. Buddhism is Korea's largest single religion. Indeed, the religion is so strong that in 1975 the Republic of Korea government recognized Buddha's birthday as a national holiday. This popular festival is fervently and joyously observed throughout the nation.

One may find Buddhist influences in modern-day Korea subtle but pervasive. In the thought patterns of Koreans, for example, the principle of "Karma," or "cause-and-effect," allows many to take a passive view of the world. The individual who is caught by the negative effects of some past action may justify his or her problem as being out of his or her control.

Another element of Korean Buddhist psychology is "Creation, Staying, Destruction and Nothing." This concept of reincarnation, with an accompanying perspective of a cyclical nature of history and phenomena, gives Koreans an introspective view of the Universe.

A Confucian Empire: Confucianism has become a way of life in Korea. Confucius – or *Kongja*, as the Koreans refer to him – was never a breaker of traditions but a conservative reactionary who rallied for a return to China's "Golden Era," the early days of the Chou dynasty (1112 BC-256 BC). His greatest innovative moment came when he proclaimed that the ultimate measure of political success was not sheer might but a ruler's virtue and his people's contentment. Confucius was the region's first and greatest moralist.

Confucian codes, which encourage harmony in relationships – from that of the Emperor with Heaven down to that of a mother with child – became the social and cultural keystone of over 800 years of Korean history.

While there are traditions and records of various forms of Confucianism, or Confucian-like religions propagated in Korea as early as 550 BC, these initial movements were not necessarily Confucian. Confucianism never really made serious headway in staunchly Buddhist Korea until about AD 896 when it was reported that a Korean named Ch'oe Ch'i-won passed the highest Confucian examinations in Beijing.

As Buddhism became more and more corrupt under the protection of the Koryo dynasty, a call for a more moral form of government began to gain great appeal among Korea's dissident intellectuals. In AD 953 a Chinese Confucian scholar, San Gen, took office under Kwangjong, the fourth Koryo king. Under San Gen's leadership, Confucian examinations or *kwago* – exactly like those administered in China – were introduced into Korea's bureaucratic qualifications system.

Kwago became the backbone of a solidly Confucian Korean society. The system had its base in local primary schools that nearly every community of any size supported during the Yi dynasty. Through a series of examinations, any male – but actually almost always those of the aristocratic *yangban* class – could eventually rise to enter one of the four colleges. Each school admitted 100 students, but only 200 students could pass the *kwago* examinations which were held three times a year.

Secretive Examiners, Neo-Confucianists: In the beginning, according to the late religious authority Charles Allen Clark, a great deal of energy was spent on keeping these examinations free of favoritism. Upon completion of compositions, for example, a court scribe would copy the manuscript so that detection of the examinee's identity would not be possible by judges. Furthermore, a *nom de plume* was affixed to the rolled papers, and when they were delivered for evaluation, the examinations were thrown over a high wall so that the judges could not even see who was throwing the compositions. Later on, though, even this foolproof system was corrupted and success could be obtained through a secret exchange of wealth. During the later years of the *kwago* system, which ended in 1894 with the era-changing Kapo Revolution, corruption had become so widespread that the best of scholars refused to take the examinations.

During the Koryo dynasty, Buddhism and Confucianism survived side-by-side and generally complemented one another. This peaceful coexistence, however, began to change when the philosophies of the great Neo-Confucianist, Chu Hsi, entered the Koryo court in the 12th century.

The Neo-Confucianists were able to unify and synthesize various Confucian theories into a more homogeneous and dynamic form of political philosophy. They denounced Buddhist practices as wasteful and injurious to the state. Furthermore, Neo-Confucian philoso-

political circles, and this dogmatic adherence to tradition suffocated much of the Chinese thought and culture which preceded it. This was even more true in Korea. The Koreans introduced inflexible precepts of Neo-Confucianism into almost every aspect of daily life.

Today Confucianism thrives more in Korea than in any other nation. And though Confucianism has been greatly discredited since the turn of the century by both foreign and domestic intellectual movements, its basic values and premises still dominate the lives of all Koreans. Ancestor worship continues to be practiced much as it has been for more than 1,000 years. In Korea even an "old fool" is first and foremost an "elder." To rebel against the

phies found royal favor in the court of T'aejo who usurped political power from the Koryo court. He astutely recognized the necessity for a new, integral political philosophy to solidify his power. With the revolutionary support of the Neo-Confucianist he quickly gained absolute political control of Korea.

Initially, Neo-Confucian philosophies devised by Chu Hsi were innovative and dynamic. However, Chu Hsi's followers soon regarded his complete logic as more than a practical and ethical way of life; they saw his work as an all encompassing venue of truth. Soon, the following of his doctrines to the letter became the standard fare in Chinese

word of an elder is to invite social censure – a conservative and powerful force which is very effective in Korea's small and closed society.

Confucian deference to age, respect for those generically superior, and responsibility towards "family first" are all well-practiced ideals which have been only modified during "modernization" and "Westernization" of the past 50 years.

Confucianism today sits somewhat uncomfortably in the modern Korean psyche. It is admired because it is the basis for a long tradition which gives Koreans their identity. At the same time, its precepts are felt to stifle genuine, innovative thought. It is a 2,000-

year-old philosophy, lifestyle, and institution that is desperately trying to find a tolerant place in contemporary Korean society.

Christian Korea: So far this view has discussed religious forms one might expect to encounter in an Oriental country – shamanism, Taoism, Buddhism and Confucianism. However, first-time visitors to Korea often gaze with wonder at the many purely Christian church steeples and crosses that punctuate populated skylines. As with all the faiths, there is a discrepancy between claimed membership and government estimates. Over 9 million, or by government reckoning, almost half of all Koreans who follow a particular religion, are avowed Christians.

people, was frowned upon as being uncouth and Buddhism was denounced as frivolous and blamed for the demise of the previous Unified Silla and Koryo dynasties. But Confucianism in the end promised nothing more than a better society based on an ideal historical model. There was little of spiritual substance available to the masses.

Christianity entered Korea's spiritual vacuum in 1592, the date of Hideyoshi's invasion of Korea from Kyushu, Japan. One of his two generals, Konishi, was a Christian who was given the unenviable assignment of storming through Korea enroute to do battle with the Chinese Empire.

Traveling with Konishi's Christian samurai

When Yi T'aejo set up his new capitol in Seoul and instituted a new political system throughout the peninsula. Buddhism was tossed out of the spiritual picture and Neo-Confucianists began dominating Korea's royal centers of powers. As mentioned earlier in the chapter, the Neo-Confucianists had succeeded in creating an almost too ideal state which had eventually stagnated into a bureacracy.

Shamanism, the spiritual soul of the Han

Left, 1880s Presbyterian missionary, Rev Samuel Moffett with new Christians. **Above**, Sam Moffett appearing in a 1980s Korean film portrayal of his grandfather.

were two Jesuit priests – one Japanese and the other a Spaniard named Gregario de Cespedes. Because Koreans of that time were less than interested in being converted to a foreign religion, these two priests had to restrict their missionary work to as yet unconverted Japanese troops. Aided by Chinese troops, the Koreans were able to drive the invaders – and their Western religion – out of the country. Surviving Christians who made it back to Japan eventually met martyrdom or accepted apostasy during later purges of Christians by Japanese rulers.

Several scholars – those of the Sirhak (Practical School) movement – learned more of this peculiar Western faith during diplomatic missions to Beijing where emissaries of Christian nations were stationed. But only a few looked upon Christianity with anything more than casual curiosity. Eventually some studies of the religion were written in Chinese and a few of these books were brought back to Seoul as intellectual curiosities.

In 1777 a scholar named Yi Tukso joined a group of friends at a mountain temple to study various schools of thought: Among the works they brought with them was a book on Roman Catholicism. Yi appreciated the ideas espoused in this book and soon was using all his influence with the Korean court to secure other books on the religion. He quickly realized, as

to perform ancestor sacrifices, the government to take decisive action. By the end of the 18th century there were 4,000 Christians in Korea, but already hundreds had been arrested and tortured for leaving the national Confucian religion.

Later, a number of Chinese and European priests smuggled themselves into the country, but most were betrayed or gave themselves up to Korean authorities, when they attempted to stop the persecution of Christian brethren. Missionaries – both foreign and native – were allowed at various times to preach their religion but still, Christian Korea had to endure at least four major periods of persecution.

By 1849 there were 11,000 Roman Catho-

he became more committed to this new religion, that for the new faith to grow he would have to convert an influential family. This he accomplished through the conversion of the politically influential Kwon family of Yangun.

Shortly afterwards, the town of Yangun began the first Christian community in Korea. The new Christians soon learned, however, that converting a politically prominent clan was a double-edged sword. As much as this badly needed prestige helped spread the religion, it also eventually attracted the critical attention of the Confucian government. And when a number of these first Christians – influential in their own right – began to refuse

lics (led by 12 French priests) in Korea. In 1864 King Kojong advocated a reign of tolerance towards the Christians. His policy was to play Catholic France against his encroaching neighbor, Orthodox Russia. By 1866, though, the young king was forced by his staunchly conservative court to order the greatest and last of Korea's Christian persecutions. Seoul's Bishop Simeon Francois Bereneux and three French priests were seized and on 8 March 1866, led to a public execution ground above the Han River. At this spot, named Choltu-san, ("Chop Heads Mountain"), they were decapitated by sword. During the next three years about 8,000 people were put to death.

Of three surviving French priests who individually escaped to China via small boats, one, a Father Ridel, returned to Korea as an interpretor with an armada of French ships. This task force vainly tried to establish contact with the Korean government to demand explanation for the Christian slayings. When it became apparent that the royal court in Seoul was ignoring them, a force of 150 men decided to take on a badly underestimated unit of Korean tiger hunters at a monastery fortress. After suffering a severe mauling, the French forces retreated to their Chinese ports and Korea entered a reinforced – if brief – final period of isolationism.

Today a Church of the Martyrs stands next

distributed a supply of bibles among the villagers, met some local Catholics, then departed as suddenly as he had arrived.

The first substantial contact of Protestantism occurred with the arrival in Korea in 1884 of Dr. Horrace N. Allen, who also served as the U.S. Minister to Korea. Allen, was soon followed by waves of missionaries of all creeds, in particular by successful Presbyterian and Methodist groups.

The Protestant missionaries came at a most opportune time to proselytize their faith directly to the masses. Their additional knowledge of Western technology – and a dedication to establishment of schools – made them a very attractive influence.

to the Second Han Bridge in Seoul to commemorate the spot where the first French priests lost their heads. The second floor serves as an interesting museum and memorial to the thousands of Korean Christians who were killed for practicing their religion.

Missionary Waves: Protestantism first touched Korea's shores in 1832 in the guise of one Charles Gutzloff who had commissioned a British ship to take him to the south coast of Ch'ungch'ong Province. There, he quickly

<u>Left</u>, Buddhist dancers wearing stiff hemp hats perform before spectators in Seoul. <u>Above</u>, the "flying" Chin-do *mudang* lures spirits.

Missionaries – Protestant and Roman Catholic – later made substantial contributions to the Korean independence movement and the anti-Japanese resistance. Through ongoing institutions such as the Royal Asiatic Society, missionary families have done much to educate the outside world about Korea. Through the founding of several higher educational institutions such as the Ewha and Yongsei universities in Seoul, these families have contributed much to Korea's development.

Today, Christianity plays a disproportionate role in power circles, both government and opposition, considering its small percentage of the Korean population. Christian leaders can be found at the highest levels of society, probably because of their historic headstart in local education.

While one may encounter almost every brand of Christianity in Korea, Christianity here has a distinctly fundamentalist flavour. More moderate sects (such as Presbyterians and Methodists) include among their flocks large numbers of fervent devotees who would probably feel quite out of place in similar congregations in the West.

About 500,000 Koreans belong to a wide variety of "minor" religions. The most well-known internationally is the Unification Church, a movement started by Moon Sun-myung, a North Korean refugee, in 1954.

Unlike other Korean-born faiths, Moon's church has a wide following overseas with missionaries, many underground, in almost every country in the world and a wide variety of affiliated businesses and organizations abroad and in Korea. Since 1989, the church has published a major national daily.

Perhaps the best known of the native religions is Ch'ondokyo, founded in the 19th century by an impoverished scholar called Ch'oe Che-u, who experienced a vision calling upon him to lead mankind in the ways of heaven. Ch'oe's followers' belief in *Hananim* (God) and the use of magical symbols caused the government to suspect that they were part of the Catholic movement. Ch'oe argued that his was not of the Sohak (Western Learning or Catholicism) School but of the Tonghak (Eastern Learning) School. In 1866 the government decided otherwise and Ch'oe was executed along with the Catholic martyrs.

Nevertheless, Ch'oe's religion continued to gather strength among Korea's southern peasantry as their only viable form of representation to the declining Yi government. In 1893 a band of "Tonghaks" approached the court in Seoul and petitioned the government to remove its ban on their religion. If this was not done, the delegation said, its followers would slay all foreigners responsible for the confusion which led to the Ch'ondo-kyo persecution.

Shortly afterwards, a man named Chon *Noktu* ("Little Beans") Pong Chon captured the leadership of this religion. The Tonghaks organized a revolt that quickly spread through much of the southern third of the nation and a panicked court requested military aid from China. The Chinese responded as requested, but they were in violation of a treaty with Japan that required prior notification before any movement of Chinese troops into Korea. The Japanese seized this opportunity to send troops into Korea, crushed the rebellion in the south and moved northward to engage the Chinese. In a short time, Japan was recognized as a world power because of its victory in the Japanese-Chinese War.

Today, the religion continues its synthesized faith by adhering to a goal of, in the words of the founder, "fusing into one the ethics of Confucianism, the awakening to nature taught in Buddhism, and the cultivation of energy as espoused by Taoism."

One recent development in modern Korea has been the introduction of Islam. There are 35,000 Korean Muslims today. The teachings of Muhammad never made a real impact until 1950 when Turkish troops arrived to fight for U.N. forces. In 1955 a teacher and a handful of Korean followers formed the nucleus of a Korean Muslim movement, and in 1960 the Korean Muslim Federation was founded with a Korean as its leader. Today, statistics for the number of Korean Muslims varies greatly but the group is attracting attention for its efforts to establish a true Muslim community.

Above, nuns stroll in Botanic Gardens, Seoul. Right, Easter egg baskets at Seoul's Myongdong cathedral.

For insights into a nation's character, look at its art, particularly its architecture. For example, in the three principal East Asian countries – China, Korea and Japan – the eaves of buildings have curved upwards for centuries. A subtle difference, however, exists in the manner of these upturns.

China's traditional architecture is vertical in feeling, elevated on high stone platforms above ground, with somewhat pinched-in edges to the roof; her roofs reflect a nation out to conquer or control nature. Even China's delicate porcelains express a determined struggle for perfection, an ethos of man-over-nature.

In contrast, Korean roofs form soft curves which float ever so gently heaven-ward, flowing with nature's rhythms. And Korean ceramics appear less perfected, warmer and more approachable, so that the viewer touches the potter's hand in spirit.

Noticeable and striking patterns, meanwhile, seem to be a major characteristic of Japanese art. Japanese roofs, even when turning upwards, appear more diagonal, their shallower curves making them more earthbound than those in China or Korea. Japanese ceramicists came to greatly admire the warm naturalness of Korean pieces, but in designing their own teaware they developed a "contrived" effect. Some Japanese intentionally made pieces "as though careless."

"Sky Blue After Rain": In homes of the wealthy today a few pieces of Korean 12th- or 13th-century celadons repose on shelves, along with white porcelains of the more recent Yi dynasty. Almost every museum in the Western world has a few treasured pieces of Korean celadon too. The outer silhouette of a Koryo-period celadon teapot or a Buddhist ritual vessel for holy water (*kundika*) may resemble a melon, a pumpkin or some other growing form, with a handle twisted into a simulated vine or a spout suggesting bamboo.

Korean celadon pieces for use by nobility were shaped into ducks, tortoises, geese, and even lion-dogs. One surviving wine pot was formed in the shape of a serving maid, and a tripod incense burner was placed on three tiny feet in the shape of long-eared bunnies.

A granite-sculpted mother and her children grace a suburban Seoul Park.

No matter which of nature's shapes is suggested, the Korean potter created beautiful elongated curves which soar with controlled energy. These unknown craftsmen decorated their porcelains with a pale, gray-green celadon glaze which sometimes became "kingfisher," a bluish-green considered "a secret color." More than 60 shades can be distinguished by the attuned eye, but the most highly admired are "sky blue after rain," and "sea water washed by rain and wind."

Around AD 1150 Koreans began using inlay techniques in their porcelain production. The potter took a bamboo knife and cut designs in the leather-hard piece, then filled the recesses with an extremely thick, white slip of diluted clay. When the excess was wiped off and the piece was covered with celadon glaze and fired in kiln, creamy white pictures appeared where the slip had been pressed into the concavities. Again these designs speak of Korean closeness to nature: two- or three-winged cranes flying in white pattern over a sea of celadon green, or weeping willow trees with a pair of Mandarin ducks floating in water. If the knife entirely penetrated to the clay surface, a reticulated design resulted so that delicate shades of the celadon glaze filled the openwork.

A new type of ceramics came to be favored with the suppression of Buddhism in AD 1392. This Yi-dynasty ware forsook the delicate and intricate to produce the unpretentious and spontaneous. A glaze made partly from pine needle ashes was decorated with stamped designs of chrysanthemums, key frets and other abstractions. Sixteenth-century Japanese tea masters came to value certain unselfconscious Korean peasant rice bowls as the most ideal tea bowl for their "refined poverty aesthetic." Today the best pieces have been bought or taken by Japanese to their homeland.

Meanwhile, white porcelains were developed for upper class use. Upon large jars, artisans painted sparsely, creating simple designs with iron-impregnated copper or malachite containing copper oxide or cobalt, "Mohammedan blue." Unlike Ming dynasty blue-and-white ware potters, the Korean craftsman never went to the same excess of treating his pot's surface as though it were an easel for painting. Rather, he limited his decorations to hints of nature – such as a single, blossoming spray, a pair of fish, a dragon, or curving leaves with grapes. The underglaze painting with iron is casual rather than pretentious and so suggests an earthy Korean spirit.

Today Korean traditional homes of the upper class tend to exhibit not only Koryo-period celadons and Yi dynasty white wares but also ancient 5th- and 6th-century Silla dynasty gray stoneware and even earlier Kaya pieces. For many centuries the Koreans preferred their own stoneware to the glazed ceramics of China. Korean ceramics has since been considered functional rather than a major art. Yet its very simplicity and unpretentiousness has increased its appeal to outsiders.

The Apollos and Dianas of Asia: When Buddhism swept out of India and all over Central and Eastern Asia, the artists of each of a dozen countries responded by creating cave sculptures, free-standing images of Buddhas, and temples. They represented the human body thinly disguised as a deity with certain "sacred marks" such as long earlobes, a depression between the eyes and a pronounced "protuberance of wisdom" on top of the head. Figures of the Buddhist pantheon were anthropomorphic, following India's example. The features and repose of Buddhas in each Asian country differed although the basic iconography is the same.

Some art history books concentrate on tracing an "International Buddhist Style" in sculpture, but it is like grouping together all early Christian and medieval Christs and madonnas into a "Pan-European International Style." In Asia, as well as in Europe, each country developed its own particular marks of charm, revealing both national proclivities and also the inherent qualities within the various materials most frequently used in each region.

Korean Buddhist art was no more a subsidiary to China than French medieval art was to Italy, or British art to France. The story of early Japanese art stands as an exception since she lay at the remote end of this Buddhist wave and converted to it later. Countless numbers of Koreans went to Japan over a period of some 150 years to assist in erecting Buddhist temples, sculpting "Golden images" in wood and in bronze, and painting religious icons.

Buddhism dominated art in China for about 1,000 years but it became a minor force after AD 1368. Korea also was influenced in art by Buddhism until the Yi government suppressed it in 1392. In Japan Buddhism ceased to be a meaningful force around 1600 when temples there became mere census indicators for the shoguns and produced little original art. Japanese Zen ideals had by this time been absorbed into the culture through the tea ceremony, gardens, ink painting, flower arrangement and the martial arts.

In creating Buddha statues the Chinese carved solemn images out of sandstone and limestone, while Koreans used granite from their mountains and the Japanese favored wood. China's sculptured deities were at first basically reflective of her preoccupation with calligraphy, so her images appear linear and fairly two dimensional. Later, by AD 600, Chinese Buddhist figures gradually became more naturalistic, three-dimensional and modeled in plastic. By the 8th century they had become excessively fat-faced, even jowled.

Korea's earliest bronze statuettes appear relatively flat and linear, also inspired by the calligraphic line: but soon her natural genius in metallurgy and her skilled stone chiselers initiated their own directions. By the 7th century, Korean Buddhist art attained a peak of spiritual expression.

According to most art critics, China's apex of Buddhist sculptural expression lies in the stone images of the T'ien-lung-shan caves. Yet even at that spot there is evidence that the Chinese artisan had become so naturalistic and earthy that the aura of spirituality had lessened. As for Korea's development, two artistic peaks are the remarkable meditating Maitreya (in Korean, *Miruk*) figures in the Seoul National Museum, and the Sokkuram cave-grotto at Kyongju which date as late as the middle 8th century. They have not lost their religious thrust. The cave-grotto has numerous relief carvings of deities sculpted on rectangular blocks which express the apogee of the Buddhist tradition. In addition Sokkuram contains a giant central image which actualized in a single piece of free-standing sculpture, representing the quintessence of Buddhism's spiritual momentum in the Far East.

The above evaluation does not preclude Japan's exquisite Asuka period (552-645), her own peak Buddhist art. Yet much of the Asuka art work should be attributed to Korea since it was created by Koreans and then exported, or else made in Japan by Korean immigrant artists. Japan's purely native Buddhist sculpture became important only after AD 700. It adopted the fat-faced, sensual archetypes of T'ang China, which go so far towards realistic detail and voluptuousness that worldly overtones mask their spirituality.

Heavenly Bells, Dolmens, Dancing Spirits: No one disputes that Korean artisans created the most intricate, the most melodious and most beautiful temple bells that the world was ever to hear or see. The earliest dated one was cast in 725 and now hangs at Sangwon-sa in the Odae-san National Park area. The most famous is the "divine bell," or the Emille Bell (cast in 771), now kept in a special pavilion at the right of the entrance to the Kyongju National Museum. It is said that the sonorous notes of this 12-foot (3.6-metre) high bell could be heard

The Korean peninsula is dotted with Buddhist figures carved in rocks in the mountains. Korea excels in granite sculptural work. Perhaps due to the fact that their terrain is 70 percent mountainous, Koreans developed a special love for stone and a skill in using it both as building material and for sculptural pieces. Huge dolmens of early times speak of the strength and dexterity of unknown Neolithic inhabitants on the peninsula.

By the 4th century AD, Korean architects were erecting tombs half the size of the Egyptian pyramids. They used dressed granite blocks so perfectly engineered that they survive today as well as the frescoes on their walls.

In these Korean tombs one can view genre

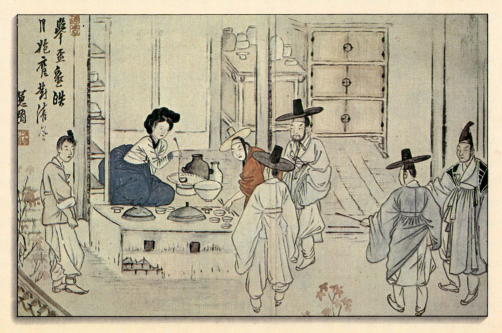

40 miles (64 kilometers) away on a clear day. The sound chamber at the top took the form of a dragon, but the most spectacular decoration consisted of two pairs of Buddhist angels or devas, holding censers of incense and floating on lotus pods amidst wisps of vegetation and gossamer-thin garments which swirled heavenward and took the place of actual wings. These bells played a major role in ritual and worship. They should be regarded as major works of bronze sculpture inspired by Buddhism at its peak.

Yi dynasty painting of a *kisaeng* house.

scenes on the walls and decorative symbols on the ceilings and understand the old beliefs about death. Ancient musicians and dancing girls in frescoes are strikingly reminiscent of modern shaman dances. Considering that it is tomb art, these frescoes are extremely lively and cheerful, suggesting a flow of spirits. Perhaps this "flow of spirits" derives from the faster beat and blood through Korean veins! It shows in many of their art forms. This "faster blood" can be traced to the time of their migrations across the whole of north Asia when their culture was based on a belief in countless "spirits." Each mountain, river, tree, the sun and moon, the constellations, had "spirit" – as did dead ancestors. Any one of them might become angry if neglected. Shaman priests (*mudang*) possessed special skills of communication with these "spirits," largely through dance, and might go into trance. They could appease the angry spirits and send good fortune to those who made food offerings and other donations.

Silla's Shaman-Kings: Even as late as the early 6th century, when the rest of the Korean peninsula had adopted Buddhism as a state religion, the southeastern and relatively remote region of Silla was still ruled by shaman kings. The people's belief in spirits, coupled with the custom of cairn-type tomb burial in which shaman royalty went to their graves in full

as golden girdles, ornate belts, elaborate earrings, silver and gold goblets, necklaces, bracelets, finger rings and ceramics.

Of the golden crowns discovered so far, among the most intriguing was one unearthed in 1973 at the excavation of Tomb #155 in the heart of Kyongju city. When viewing it one first sees its outer circle of hammered, beaten gold with saw-tooth or wave designs representing the nether world. (This lower region was associated with water.) An inner golden cap fits the head. Fifty-eight tiger claws carved of jade were suspended from the crown. In the shaman religion, the tiger is associated principally with three things: a strong power to destroy evil forces, human fertility and male

religious regalia, made the Silla capital, Kyongju, Asia's single most spectacular archaeological site. Hundreds of tombs are yet to be explored in this city which already has become a veritable "outdoor museum" of the 5th and 6th centuries.

Breathtaking crowns designed for monarchial use were buried in Kyongju's mounded graves. It is not just the precious materials used, although jade is much worshiped in the Orient, but the intricate fabrication of these crowns. So far, 10 slightly different "gold crowns of Silla" have been brought to light. Alongside the crowns, other royal possessions have been discovered, such

virility. These curved pieces carved from jade formed a major part of the symbolism when these crowns were worn. They were suspended loosely with thin, twisted gold wires, and several hundred tiny golden spangles, suggesting golden raindrops, were affixed onto the crown with the same type of thin gold wires. If the ruler, who symbolized the power of the sun as well as other forms of nature's energy, moved his head ever so slightly, he created a dazzling sight and vibrating sounds, unforgettably impressive upon his audience. Pendants – thick ropes of golden leaf-shaped droplets – hung on each side of the crown. Some golden crowns were more than two feet high. This profusely rich burial of objects proclaims the divine power of the old Silla rulers and their right to the wealth of the country and expertise of her jewelers.

The key to understanding the meaning behind all this magnificence lies in the three unusual upright pieces attached to each of the major crowns. These are 17 inches (40 centimeters) high and shaped in three forms: deer antlers, stylized trees, and pairs of wings.

Since shamanism is considered a superstition by today's government, native archaeologists have been rather timid about discussing the shamanistic symbolism in these relics. However, clues indicating shamanistic influences in the design of the crown abound. Among the Tungus people from whom the Koreans descended, for example, climbing a tree is a shaman initiation rite; a three-branched tree represented the "three spirits" of shamanism – the heavenly world, which holds the "spirits" of sun, moon and constellations; the earthly world of "spirits," such as mountains, rivers and trees; and the human world with ancestral "spirits."

The curving wing pieces suggest the shaman's power to levitate or to fly. The golden fabricated stag antlers of these crowns substituted for Siberian reindeer, whose fleetness the shaman-king acquired by wearing their horns. On the Tungus plains of Central Asia, shamans used to wear reindeer horns, fabricated from iron, in the headdress. The Silla people were rich enough to create these talismen out of pure gold.

The Magical Flying Horse Tomb: After Tomb #155 had been excavated in 1973, archaeologists and museum men examined over 10,000 ancient pieces; most of them went to the Kyongju National Museum. The tomb was restored to its original shape with one exception – half of it was supported by a steel framework so that visitors could enter the area. A glass wall was erected across the midsection so that tourists could enter the tomb and look at the exact position in which the crown, sword, girdle, pottery and many other objects were buried.

Also when Tomb #155 was excavated, at the head of the tomb where the shaman-ruler was buried, a "treasure box" was discovered;

on this spot an actual royal horse had been offered in sacrifice. This recalls the traditional importance of horseriding to these people, former nomads of northwest Asia. Elaborate horse burials were not unknown in Siberia.

A special horse belonging to the shaman-king was believed to be a flying horse. This creature could levitate just as a powerful shaman could. When the horse was killed, his saddle guards made of laminated birch bark, sewn together with deer leather trimmings, were buried in the grave along with other horse trappings and treasures. Six of these saddle flaps have been found and they are as amazing as the golden crowns. The outer edges of the flaps have bands of floral patterns in red, blue,

green and white. Centered on one of these birch bark saddle flaps is a painting which shows a magical flying horse at full gallop – a "heavenly horse" as it were. His mane streams out behind, his hoofs are winged, and his long, curving tongue suggests enormous exertion.

Horsemen were depicted on other flaps, and on another is a phoenix symbol of immortality in ancient China, with outstretched feathers of yellow and vermillion. In tribute to the vivacity of this ancient painting, Tomb #155 was renamed the "Heavenly Tomb."

It might be noted that Silla's worship of white horses and their association with divine royalty passed over to Japan, which kept its shaman ways through Shintoism. As recently as pre-war times, Emperor Hirohito owned a white horse which was considered sacred until the end of World War II when it was surrendered to General MacArthur.

Backed by mountains rich in metals, such as silver and gold, artisans of old Silla became extraordinarily skilled in metallurgy. Thus its shaman-kings were able to maintain and retain their ancient animistic religion against the encroachments of Buddhism until AD 527. After that shaman-type symbolism disappeared from Korean art objects (it did manage to survive in folk art though) and Buddhism was taken up by the court.

Japan has uncovered a few small, simple nese paintings" but the paintings reflect Northern Sung works in style, when Buddhism's influence was deep. Korean artists carried the lines of gold and the brilliant areas of clothing (scarlet, malachite green and sapphire blue) into further refinement and grace as well as complexity.

This fine, delicate and intricate work in Koryo Buddhist icons disappeared when the Yi government suppressed Buddhism in 1392 and encouraged a Confucian attitude. This "attitude" recognized only "the three excellencies" – poetry, calligraphy and ink painting – as created by the amateur scholar-artist. Having been educated in "nobility" by his constant reading of Confucian-approved clas-

crowns of bronze, but none of gold.

Koryo Paintings: Almost as remarkable as uncovering the rich treasures of golden crowns from Korea's 5th and 6th century and rediscovering her 12th- and 13th-century pale green celadon wares has been the unveiling (in 1978-79) of 93 Koryo period paintings – Buddhist icons of unsurpassed beauty. It was thought that such art had vanished. Sad to say, though, all these beautiful Korean art works are now owned by Japanese. The same slender, refined curves of the best celadon pieces are seen in these Buddhist deities. Tucked away in various temples and shrines, these rarely seen paintings on silk were largely labeled "Chi-

sics, he could also use his hand, trained in calligraphy, to create landscapes in his leisure. These were not to be actual scenes, but rather "landscapes of his noble mind," and so they became rather abstract ink play.

Yi Genre Glimpses: During the Yi dynasty (1392-1910) an official "Painting Bureau" did exist, supported by the court for its own purposes. Professional painters were hired to do portraits. By the 18th century Korean artists had begun to paint genre scenes which revealed insights into the mores of common folk doing ordinary things. Today, these genre glimpses are more appreciated than the scholars' ink play.

An entirely different approach to art is revealed in Yi dynasty folk paintings. Charmingly naive and unpretentious, they reflect the actual life, customs and beliefs of the Korean people. Today they are still relegated to special museums, such as Emille Museum at Songni-san, because the national museums are perpetuated by a Confucian-type bureaucracy. Yet collectors, both native and Western, have "discovered" them, and the value of such works has escalated. Yi folk paintings appear mundane and combine the symbolism of shamanism, Taoism and Buddhism, but they transcend class lines and their domestic use. Even Confucian-influenced court art was colored by symbolism, such as *The Four No-*

rin ducks swimming in pairs, or with *Hundred Babies Screen*, since Yi dynasty marriage was pre-arranged and for the main purpose of progeny. Fertility symbols were legion. Among the most commonly used flora and fauna were those which represented happiness, longevity and positive energy.

Korean folk art with its blue dragons, white tigers and magical fungi is based on symbolism which developed and evolved over a long period of time and were understood by all the people. Even today, a basic understanding of this complex system is essential to appreciate this lively art.

The Zodiac, Yang and Um, and the Fungus of Immortality: In the mists of China's remote

ble Gentlemen themes or *The Three Friends of Winter*.

Due to a great respect for calligraphy among the scholarly class, auspicious ideographs were used for decorative themes in painting folding screens for the home. Important anniversaries were celebrated by the creation of new folding screens with motifs of longevity or good omen. Weddings also stimulated art activity; designs emphasized conjugal happiness with Manda-

<u>Left</u>, temple judges determine final afterlife judgements. <u>Right</u>, the swastika door ornament graces a temple at Andong.

antiquity, symbolic directions arose as part of a cosmology derived either from Taoism or an even more ancient shamanistic system of concepts. Among the most important were the correlatives of heaven and earth, *yang* and *yin*, male and female, along with five directions (north, south, east, west and center), five colors (black, red, white, blue and yellow), and five material elements (water, fire, metal, wood and earth).

Such ideas, which originated in prehistoric times, gained increased popularity during the Han dynasty (200 BC-AD 200), which gave rise to a number of Taoism-inclined emperors searching for the elixir of immortality.

Cosmological symbols passed into Korean traditions and have remained ingrained there ever since.

During the peak of Buddhist influence, cosmological symbolism played a minor role in Korean art. The lotus, the official religious flower, and other such Buddhist symbols dominated art. However, with the suppression of Buddhism in 1392, Taoism, Buddhism and shamanism had become homogenized so that they were hardly separable in popular thought. For example, it is difficult to determine the exact origin of the 12 zodiacal images used in art. They usually relate to time and astrologers still use these animals to foretell suitability in marriage. The zodiac

also was associated with *yang* and *yin* (in Korean, *yang* and *um*). It read, in clockwise order: rat, ox, tiger, rabbit, dragon, snake, horse, sheep, monkey, chicken, dog and wild boar (or pig). Furthermore, the Korean astrological animals represented the 12 points of the compass.

Thus folk painting created for the home was based on the effects of such symbolism as accepted through centuries of use. Folk painting, furniture, linens, clothes, all accessories, even hairpins, are decorated with it. All things, including outside walls, are full of the five elements, the 10 symbols of longevity, the four directional animals, the 12 zodiacal animals and propitious ideographs; all have become art motifs for old painting and other minor arts. Flowers and birds are not represented accidentally or casually selected, but reflect an associated meaning. Even the educated put some measure of faith in these emblems, somewhat convinced that such symbols can repel evil and attract good fortune.

Even Confucian-influenced artists occasionally turned to folk painting themes. In approaching any of these works today, the viewer should be familiar with their basic symbolic meanings or associations in order to participate in a greater appreciation of them.

The major symbols used and their meanings are as follows:

Four Sacred Animals of Good Luck: Turtle, dragon, unicorn, and phoenix.

Ten Symbols of Longevity: deer, crane, turtle, rocks, clouds, sun, water, bamboo, pine and the fungus of immortality *(pullocho)*.

Auspicious Ideograms: *bok* (good fortune), *su* (longevity), *yong* (peace) and *kang* (health).

Fertility Symbols: pomegranate, jumping carp, 100 babies and "Buddha's hand citron."

Special Guardians: tiger (front gate or front door), dragon (gate or roof), *haet'ae* (fire or kitchen), rooster (front door) and dog (storage door).

Four Noble Gentlemen: orchid, chrysanthemum, bambon and plum.

Three Friends of Winter: pine, plum and bamboo.

Individual Associations: peach (longevity), pomegranate (wealth), orchid (scholar, cultural refinement), lotus (Buddhist truth, purity), bat (happiness), butterfly (love, romance), bamboo (durability), peony (noble gentleman, wealth) and plum (wisdom of age, hardiness or independence, beauty, loftiness).

The list could go on and on. No one sat down and wrote a formal list; it was simply a part of Korean tradition, familiar to everyone from the itinerant painter to the "drunken master," or a member of the court's Bureau of Painting.

Above left, Koryo origins dot the countryside. **Right,** *Kwanseum-posal with Willow Branch* was painted with mineral colors on silk by Sogubang, a 14th-century Koryo artist.

Walking down one of the winding back alleys of Korea's cities, you may hear, emanating from the window of a local tavern, the sounds of hearty, and perhaps slightly inebriated, voices singing to the clickety-clack of chopsticks being beaten against the edge of a table. The singing will probably be punctuated by boisterous cries of "*Chotha*!" and "*Olssiguna*!" (variously translated as anything from "Bravo!" to "Right on!")

Nowadays the song will be a modern one written in a style imitative of the contemporary Western popular idiom, or an older one reminiscent of the Japanese songs of earlier decades, called *ppongtchak norae* here.

A hiking trip to a popular mountain spot will treat you to more of the same with the added element of dance. Korean picnickers, especially older ones, often bring along such traditional Korean percussion instruments as the *changgu*, an hourglass-shaped drum, and the *kkwaenggwari*, a small, ear-shattering gong, to use on their way back down the mountain when they stop to eat, drink, and be merry – being merry in Korea inevitably means singing and dancing.

All of this is just a small indication of the important place music and dance play in the cultural lives of Koreans. For the traditional Korean, the enjoyment of these art forms is in the participation and not in merely watching the polished choreographed versions so commonly seen on stage.

Shouting calls of encouragement and rising briefly to move to the rhythm of the music have, perhaps for the worse, been banned from modern auditoriums such as the National Theater. On more than one occasion, the innocent country fellow who attends one of these performances in Seoul has been shushed or asked to leave if he persists in his delighted grunts and cheers. Get yourself to a performance outside in a tent for a true taste of the flavor of an old-time show.

Music and dance are by far the most highly developed of the performing arts in Korea, including, of course, the modern Western

introductions, which have a great appeal to Koreans of the younger generation. There are no traditional dramatic forms except those that appear as forms of dance. Acrobatics, juggling, and other circus-type entertainments exist but in a very limited and unevolved variety. The puppet days, of which the only one widely known is the *Kkoktu Gaksi Norum*, are lively and interesting, but the puppets are crudely made – rustic, at best – and the techniques of manipulation are primitive.

Music and dance, by contrast, exist in a great variety and are of all levels of sophistication – from the simplest improvisations

of country grannies on an outing to the most subtle, intricate movements of skilled professional folk dancers. And they are of all types – from the ethereal Confucian ceremonial music to the raucous thumps of a farmers' band. They are a source of unending delight and joyful surprise to the foreigner who comes to them with open ears and eyes.

Hung and Mot: Korean dancers move with a total lack of emphasis on what Westerners call "technique." There is a complete absence of movements like those of ballet that require years of vigorous physical training. For the Korean those years are spent teaching the body to express outwardly the inner mood of the dance he wishes to perform.

This brings us to two concepts that are never

Left, a *Hwagwan-mu* (Flower Crown) dancer whirls. <u>Above right</u>, a jazz celebrity.

left out of any discussion of Korean dance. One is a state of mind called *hung*. It is *joie de vivre;* it is how you feel when the spirit moves you and the "feeling" in "once more with feeling." It is essential to all dance, not just that of Korea, but it is fairly easy to come by. The other is an elusive spiritual quality called *mot*. As applied to a person's dress or the appearance of an object, to have *mot* is simply to be very good-looking. But when used about a person's behavior, personality, way of speaking, or more important here, his or her way of dancing, the term defies direct translation. It is charm, grace, that certain something – even a bit of sexuality – all rolled into one. Without *mot*, even the most perfectly executed dance is

to the upper back. This creates the straight-back posture peculiar to Korean dance. The chest almost appears concave.

Virtually all movement is curvilinear, and angular articulation of the body parts is somehow made to appear curved as well. The cut of the traditional Korean costume worn for dancing helps produce this effect of jointlessness. The sole exception of this is the foot which is turned sharply towards; stepping and turning are done mostly on the heel.

In many women's dances the foot is rarely seen at all, being hidden beneath the floor-length Korean skirt. In certain dances the invisibility of the foot gives the dancer the appearance of floating smoothly from place to

but a pretty piece of choreography.

The more tangible aspects of Korean dance movement are described in terms of the way the dancer feels he is moving and of the effect he wishes to create, rather than of the actual physical movements he executes.

The dancer uses the body as a fluid unit without isolating parts. The upper part of the torso is the nucleus from which most movement originates. The arms usually float out at the sides as extensions of the upper chest, while the legs extend downwards to *relate* the torso to the ground, not to support the body weight. The body is supported as though from above by an invisible thread which is attached

place on air cushions.

Korean dance does not use posturing or intricate hand motions to tell a story, as is so prevalently done in other parts of the Orient and in Oceania. The hand is merely an extension of the arm, with the fingers held in a natural position. Korean dance in itself never tells a story; it strives only to communicate its mood. Whatever stories emerge are told verbally or through acting that is supplemental to the dance, as in the masked dance dramas. True posturing is a no-no: A Korean dancer never moves into or out of a position – he moves through it. Even when the dancer appears to halt for a moment, he is never static;

his whole body "breathes" in a slightly undulating movement.

Subtle Microtones, Startling Vibratos: While it is quite easy to learn to enjoy almost any kind of dance with a few exposures, it is another matter altogether to learn to appreciate the music of a culture different from one's own. Korean music poses a number of formidable problems here.

Most of the music uses a five-note scale rather than the more familiar seven notes. Different arrangements of the scale, called modes, are available, however, to enrich tonal resources. Except for the octave, the intervals between pitches are not the same as we are used to hearing.

many different ways, instruments and voices simultaneously stressing different portions of the 12-beat phrase produce a rich rhythmic counterpoint.

Korean instruments are primitive compared to the multi-valved, steel-stringed, complex-action Western instruments; but they are exactly suited to their task. They are traditionally divided up into classes according to the material of which they are made: skin, silk, bamboo, metal, earth, stone, gourd and wood. Representative of the skin instruments is the *changgu*, the hourglass-shaped drum mentioned earlier, which is seen everywhere Korean music is performed. The *kayagum* is the most commonly heard of the

No system of harmony is used, but this lack is more than made up for by melodic ornamentation including unusual attacks and decays, subtle microtones, startling vibratos, unexpected changes of the timbre of the instruments when changing registers, and highly complex rhythms. The rhythm especially is to be noticed.

In Korean indigenous music each rhythmic phrase contains 12 or nine beats, or some other multiple of three. Because 12 can be divided in

Left, female dancers perform in an ancestral ritual. **Above**, *changgu* (hourglass drum) musician marks time in a Korean classical setting.

silk category, so classified because the strings are of silk. It is a versatile zither having 12 courses, which are plucked with the fingers. Among the bamboo instruments, the *p'iri* has a double-reed mouthpiece and its sound reminds one of that instrument, though the *p'iri* is much shriller. The sound of the *taegum* might be said to be *the* sound of Korea – the wanderer's flute heard in the woods on a misty morning. In the metal category are the bells that hang in their frame at the back of the full Korean orchestra balanced by the stone chimes on the other side.

There are more than 12 different genres of Korean music, though the repertory of all but the folk song is somewhat limited. Dates and places of performances of Korean music and dance cannot be predicted but are very frequent. Korean lunar holidays are a good time to look for outdoor performances that capture some of the atmosphere of the old Korea. These outdoor shows include farmers' music and dance, folk singing, and various kinds of folk dance such as masked dance drama. For other performances check the schedules of large theaters and university auditoriums.

Ancient Court Dances: Just as Korean dance as a whole can be divided into two main types, court and folk, so can court dance itself be put into two classes: *ilmu* and *chongjae*.

Ilmu is by far the smaller of the two classes,

meaning "display of talent," were performed as entertainment for the king and his court; commoners who had no access to the inner court never saw these dances. Although there were dozens of *chongjae* dances during the Yi Dynasty, fewer than a score can be reconstructed with any confidence and, in fact, only half a dozen have come down to use in an unbroken line.

Hwagwan-mu, the Flower-Crown Dance, is by far the most commonly seen of the court dances. It precedes almost every performance of Korean dance. The name derives from the tiny sparkling crown perched on each dancer's head. As in all court dances, the dancers wear sleeve extensions (*hansam*) over the hands.

comprising only the dances done at the Sunggyungwan Confucian Ceremony and the Ch'ongmyo Royal Ancestral Shrine. The dance, performed in rigid lines, involves very little movement from place to place and consists primarily of circular arm movements and bows to the cardinal points. The dance is in two sections, recognizable by the dancers' change in attire and symbolized by the objects they carry: For the civilian portion of the dance, each carries a feathered stick in his right hand and a flute in his left; in the military portion, the right hand holds an axe and the left, a shield.

The court dances you will see on stage belong to the *chongjae* class. *Chongjae*,

The sleeves were originally just long enough to cover the hands but gradually became longer and longer as it was realized that the swirling motions added color and excitement to the otherwise slow, refined movements. Other common court dances are *Ch'oyong-mu*, *Mugo*, *Ch'unaeng-mu* and *P'ogurak*.

Ch'oyong-mu is one of the oldest extant Korean dances, having come down to us from the Silla period. The dance celebrates the life of Ch'oyong, a man who came to live in Silla from a distant land.

Mugo is done by eight dancers around a large horizontal drum. Four of the dancers have drumsticks hidden in their *hansam*, and the other four carry flowers. The climax of the dance is the beating of the drum.

Ch'unaeng-mu is the Dance of the Spring Nightingale. The dance is by a solo performer entirely within the area of a long reed mat and is characterized by extremely slow, delicate movements.

P'ogurak must have added a big chunk of hilarity to the solemn atmosphere of the court. In the middle of the stage stands a high wooden screen with a hole at the top. Each dancer has two balls which she attempts to throw through the hole while dancing. If she manages to make at least one "basket," she is awarded a flower. The dancer who fails, gets a healthy swatch of black ink across her face.

the commoners to release their frustrations about the treatment accorded them by the upper classes and the clergy, as well as to learn to laugh at themselves.

In Seoul you're most likely to get a chance to see either the Bongsan Masked Dance or the Yangju Pyol Sandae Nori. Of the two the Bongsan is a more widely known – the Bongsan Players have even made a very successful tour of the United States and received rave reviews everywhere they went. The Bongsan dancing style is vigorous with lots of leaps and squats and broad body movements. The masks are humorously grotesque, though less so than in the past.

The Yangju dance style is more subtle and

Sting with Satire: No-one knows exactly where the masked dance drama originated, but they must have come from a single source because the story of the drama is the same everywhere. It is a series of satirical vignettes portraying the foibles and misadventures of a group of apostate Buddhist monks, a lecherous old gentleman with one-too-many concubines, a stupid nobleman and his smart servant, a traveling merchant, and a charlatan shaman. Masked dance drama was a way for

<u>Left</u>, masked dancer pokes fun with his bizarre presentation. <u>Above</u>, flutist plays in royal costume.

elegant, but less broad in its humor. The masks, too, are subdued by comparison.

Farmers' Dance, Shamanist Acrobatics and Bobs: Farmers' Dance is both the oldest and newest form of Korean music and dance. According to Chinese records of the 5th century, percussion and dancing were part of the agricultural rituals of the Korean village people. It is the newest in the sense that it is constantly being added to through the improvisations of the expert players.

There are two major types of Farmers' Dance: *Chwado-kut* and *Udu-kut*. *Chwado-kut* is faster paced and the dancing is more acrobatic. *Udo-kut* is somewhat slower and the rhythms can be more intricate and contrapuntal. Nowadays the two styles are often mixed: *Udo* music with *chwado* dancing.

Besides being a great form of entertainment, Farmers' music and dance are still considered by many to be efficacious shamanistic tools. They are performed to purify the village well, protect houses from thieves and fire, appease the mountain spirit in exchange for his blessing, ensure a bumper crop, etc.

P'ansori Storytelling: *P'ansori* is the art of the dramatic song. Developed out of the folk-singing style of the Southwest, *p'ansori* is done solo to the accompaniment of a barrel drum. The singer's voice must be extremely versatile: he sings all the roles and recites the

explanatory narrative between songs, as well. It must be durable, too. for one complete *p'ansori* can last for up to six hours.

Of the original 12 *p'ansori* stories, only five are still performed. They are *Ch'uinbyang-ga*, the Cinderella story of a country *kisaeng*'s daughter and her prince charming from Seoul; *Hungbo-ga*, the story of two brothers, one rich and evil and the other poor but good; *Sugung-ga*, a charming funny story of the King of the Sea, who has fallen ill with a strange disease that requires a rabbit's liver as a cure, and of how the rabbit saves its own life; *Simch'ong-ga*, the story of a devoted daughter who offers her life so that her blind father's eyesight may

be restored; and *Chokpyok-ka*, the adventures of a Chinese general.

P'ansori performances are given frequently on Saturday afternoons in the Small Auditorium of the National Theater on Nam-san. The Society for the Preservation of *P'ansori* sponsors other performances done in various theaters and auditoriums around town. To get the fullest enjoyment out of the performance, it is wise to read an English translation of the story first.

Of all the Korean folk dances, the two that carry the expression of *mot* to its pinnacle are *Sungmu*, the Priest's Dance, and *Salp'uri*, a dance of spiritual cleansing.

Sungmu is done in a hooded robe with floor-length sleeves that make the dancer appear somehow larger than life. A single drum stands in its frame at the back of the stage. There are various opinions as to what the drum represents; some say it is the ecstasy of enlightenment; others relate it to the temptation of worldly pleasure. The dancer's own interpretation affects the mood he tries to convey through the dance.

The first section of the dance shows the priest vacillating between giving in to the call of the drum and ignoring it. Tension builds as he is alternately drawn to the drum and repelled from it. Finally, unable to resist, he draws his drumsticks out of the long sleeves and plays breathtaking solo on the drum. When the rhythms are played well, the audience actually gets rushes in the chest and throat at climactic points. The speed builds until the drummer gives up in exhaustion. He leaves the stage with a dreamy, faraway look on his face and only the drum is left. Performances by the best specialist in this dance are known to leave audiences in tears.

Through the *Salp'uri* the dancer strives to free her spirit from trouble and anguish. A long white scarf her only prop, the dancer carries herself and the audience through a series of emotions from sad quietude to invigorating joy in the space of five minutes. When done without true emotion, this dance is nothing but a sequence of rote movements with a scarf. With *mot*, however, it is the epitome of Korean dance, enough in itself to convince you that this is a field truly worth exploring.

Spicy. Fiery. Earthy. Cool. Korean food is diverse and provocative. Its bold and subtle tastes, textures, and aromas are sure to elicit comments, sighs, and even tears at every meal.

Most foreigners associate pungent garlic and hot chili pepper with Korean cuisine. It is true that garlic-eating has been heartily appreciated by Koreans since the race's first breath, but little is it known – even in Korea – that the chili pepper did not even exist in this country until the 16th century when it

autumn *kimch'i* making. At *kimjang* time, women gather in groups throughout the country to cut, wash, and salt veritable hills of cabbage and white radish. The prepared *kimch'i* is stored in large, thick earthenware crocks and then buried in the backyard to keep it from fermenting during the winter months. Throughout the dark and cold winter, these red-peppered, garlicked and pickled vegetables are a good source of much-needed vitamin C.

During other eating seasons, a variety of

was introduced by Portuguese traders.

However these two ingredients may have reached Korean plates and palates, they are now used in many dishes – most liberally and notoriously in *kimch'i*. For the newcomer, learning to eat this dish is the first step to becoming a connoisseur of Korean food.

Kimch'i Culture: *Kimch'i* is *the* dish that has made Korean food famous. Next to rice (*pap*), it is the most important component in any Korean meal. It is not known when or how *kimch'i* originated, but like curry in India it's in Korea to stay. So institutionalized is *kimch'i* that one of Korea's most important annual social events is *kimjang*, or

vegetables such as chives, pumpkin and eggplant are used to make more exotic types of *kimch'i*. The summer heat makes it necessary to prepare a fresh batch almost daily, often in a cool, light brine. Raw seafood, such as fish, crab and oysters are "*kimch'i*ed" too, and indeed, in Korea, a woman's culinary prowess is often determined first and foremost by how good her *kimch'i* tastes.

Exotic Herbs: Not all Korean food ingredients are quite so passionate as the garlic and chili pepper. In actuality, the earliest Korean dishes consist of understated ingredients. To Koreans, almost every plant and animal in their diet has a herbal or medicinal quality and certain dishes are purposely eaten to warm or cool the head and body.

Wild aster, royal fern bracken, marsh plant, day lily, aralia shoots and broad bell-flowers are just a few of the many wild and exotic plants included in the typical Korean's diet. Others, such as mugwort, shepherd's purse, and sowthistle, are also seasonally picked and eaten.

More common table vegetables – such as black sesame leaves, spinach, lettuce and mung and soybeans – are typically grown in the backyard, but others are found only in the wild. All are collectively called *namul* when they are individually parboiled, then lightly seasoned with sesame oil, garlic, soy sauce,

(*miyok-guk*). The latter is said to be beneficial to lactating mothers.

A seafood dish of some kind is usually included with various "side dishes" which are called *panch'an*. This may be a dried, salted and charbroiled fish or a hearty and spicy hot seafood soup called *mae-un-t'ang*. A delicious *mae-un-t'ang* usually includes firm, white fish, vegetables, soybean curd (*tubu*), red pepper powder, and an optional poached egg.

Bulgogi and Kalbi: Probably the most popular Korean entré ordered or automatically served to Westerners is *pulgogi* (barbecued beef). Most beefeaters – whether Texans or Koreans – are unanimous in their apprecia-

and ground and toasted sesame seeds.

Another vital part of the Korean meal is soup (*guk*), which is said to be one of Korea's earliest culinary techniques. Soup will always be found at a proper table setting. Especially popular is *twoenjang-guk*, a fermented soybean paste soup with shortnecked clams stirred into its broth. Also popular are a light broth boiled from dried anchovies, and vegetable soups rendered from dried spinach, sliced radish or dried seaweed

tion of this dish which is essentially strips of red beef marinated and then grilled over a charcoal brazier. Another popular meat dish is tender and marbled *kalbi* short ribs which are marinated and barbecued in the same way as *bulgogi*.

To Koreans, however, rice – not meat – is considered to be the main dish of the meal. In fact, one of the most common street greetings, "*Pam mogoss-o-yo?*" literally means "Have you eaten rice?"

When Koreans sit down to a traditional meal, they relax on a clean lacquered paper floor. The meal comes to them on a low table. Usually the food is served in a collection of

<u>Left</u>, dinner for two. <u>Above</u>, cabbage and turnip vendors during annual autumn *kimjang*.

small metal bowls which are neatly arranged. The utensils used are a pair of chopsticks and a flat soup spoon.

Westerners may be surprised to find that Koreans often will eat a bowl of rice and maybe have an extra helping even though tastier side dishes remain unfinished. Don't let this preference for rice bother you; if you run out of a particular item, the lady of the house will bring more. When you've had enough to eat, place your chopsticks and soup spoon to the right of your bowl; do not leave them stuck in the rice or resting on any of the bowls.

A dish of sliced and chilled fruit is usually served as a dessert. Depending on the season, tent rice *makkolli* is excellent, so *kul-jip* never lack customers.

There are only a few other bomb-shelter winehouses in Seoul but there are many places to drink – probably more per capita than in most other countries. Within a few minutes' walk of *kul-jip* are a beer hall with draft and bottled beer, a market wine shop serving several alcoholic beverages, and a roadside drinking cart, where passersby can duck in for a quick snort on their way home.

Drinking is an important part of Korean culture. There are few proscriptions against alcohol here and many social reasons for imbibing, so most Korean men – and a growing number of women – drink.

muskmelon, strawberries, apples, pears and watermelon are among the fresh and sweet selections. At major celebrations, steamed rice cakes *(ttok)* are presented as tasty ritual food.

Toasting the Spirits: Deep within a cave beneath a hill in northern Seoul, four men sit around a low round table, drinking small bowls of a milky white liquor they pour from a battered aluminium teapot.

Welcome to *kul-jip* ("cave-house") one of Seoul's most unusual drinking spots. A bomb shelter during the Korean War three decades ago, today it is operated as a wine-house by several aging ladies. The quality of the po-

Drinking with Koreans provides one of the easiest opportunities for a foreigner to penetrate Korean culture. This is partly because of the salience of drinking in the culture and partly because, like anywhere else, alcohol removes inhibitions and speeds social and cultural interaction.

On Floating Cups and Kisaeng: History doesn't reveal when Koreans first discovered fermentation, but drinking was an important part of the culture even in Korea's early dynasties.

During the Silla dynasty, the king and his court relaxed at *P'o-Sok-jong* drinking bower outside Kyongju. Here a spring bubbled up into an abalone-shaped stone channel. The drinkers set their cups afloat in the channel and competed to compose poems before the cups drifted all the way round.

Later Korean dynasties continued drinking. Probably the most popular surroundings were what is today known as the *kisaeng* party. *Kisaeng* were female entertainers who played musical instruments, sang, danced, composed poetry and practiced calligraphy to amuse the male aristocracy at palace parties. They also poured drinks, served the men food, and flirted. According to tradition, high class *kisaeng* took lovers but weren't promiscuous. At one point in the Yi dynasty, says a historian, there were more than 20,000 *kisaeng*.

The most famous heroine in classical Korean history was the *kisaeng* Non-gae, who lived in the late 15th century when the Japanese invaded Korea. Forced to entertain a victorious Japanese general, the forlorn Non-gae beguiled the man into walking with her along the steep cliffs overlooking the Nam River. While locked in embrace, she managed to lure him near the brink and forced him over the edge, sacrificing her own life to kill the hated enemy conqueror.

Today, few *kisaeng* can play classical instruments, compose poetry or write with a brush. Instead, most *kisaeng* parties include a band with drums and electric guitar, and the *kisaeng* and their guests a-go-go dance around the table after eating. The main patrons are Korean businessmen who are more than willing to pay large sums to entertain customers, and Japanese tourists who pay even more in the hope of bringing the girls back to their hotel for the night.

In Confucian Cups: Conservative Confucians would be distressed to find what has happened to drinking today. They would be particularly aghast to find college co-eds and other supposedly respectable women drinking freely in public establishments.

But with a little attention, the Confucians would find that not all of the old practices have vanished. There are still traditional weddings where the groom consumes rice wine and the celebration afterward also includes drinking.

According to an old custom, the guests may hang the groom upside down and beat him if the alcohol runs out.

At memorial services for ancestors, filial Koreans still customarily set a bowl of wine among offerings on the altar. After the rites are completed, the living consumes the wine, toasting the spirits and strengthening the bond between them. Funerals and wakes also involve drinking – to help the living forget their grief. Friends and relatives will usually drink, sing and gamble all night at the home of someone who has just died.

Never Drink Alone: Confucians also might be surprised to find that although bowing while drinking has been largely forgotten,

other elements of traditional etiquette still remain. The cardinal rule is that one doesn't drink alone. Furthermore, a drinker doesn't pour his own glass, but waits until his companion fills it for him. In this tradition, to serve oneself would be an act of arrogance and greed.

Generally, in a gesture of respect and friendship, a drinker will give his cup another, conveying it politely with both hands. His companion receives the cup with both hands and holds it thus while it is filled to the brim. He may then drink. After emptying the cup, he again uses both hands to return it to the owner. Then, grasping the wine vessel with

Left, a Korean businessman's lunch. **Above right**, local beer and spirits.

both hands, he refills the cup for the owner, returning the favor.

In a group, several drinkers in succession may offer their cups to a single person, leaving an array of brimming cups before him. A person who has given up his cup can't drink until the recipient returns it or someone else gives him his. So whoever has received a cup has an obligation to empty it and pass it on without inordinate delay.

The custom of forcing drinks on each other hardly encourages moderation, which is probably why most drinkers in Korea go home rather tipsy. Drunkenness carries no social stigma. To the contrary, when most Koreans drink, they do so until they are drunk. The rise in car ownership has reduced this tendency to some extent, but Koreans remain heavy social drinkers. In keeping with the camaraderie that Korean drinking fosters, the members of a party who are least under the influence make an effort to ensure that their companions get home alright. During the late hours of the night, the streets are filled with drinkers putting their inebriated friends into taxis or onto buses and telling the driver or conductor where they should disembark. Somehow, there is always somebody who stays sober enough to do this.

The Working Man's Brew: A popular Korean brew is *makkolli*, a milky liquor that most rural households ferment at home from rice. Reputed to be highly nutritious, farmers found that a few cups during the long working day helped stave off hunger.

Makkolli was inexpensive in the cities as well, making it the working man's drink. For many people, until the early 1970s, going drinking usually meant going to a *makkolli-jip*, an establishment that served *makkolli*.

Makkolli-jip vary in style and quality, but are generally comfortable unpretentious places where nobody can put on airs. The *makkolli* is dipped out of a hug tub or vat into cheap teapots or bottles, and any old bowl may serve as a cup.

The two most important factors about any *makkolli-jip* are the quality of the *makkolli*, and the kinds of side dishes, *anju*, that it serves since all drinking in Korea involves eating.

The things that go best with *makkolli* range from fresh oysters, peppery octopus, dried fish, squid or cuttlefish, to soybean curd, soups, bean pancakes, scallion pancakes and omelettes.

The other beverage with long-standing popularity is *soju*, a cheap distilled liquor of around 25 percent alcoholic content, with a quality somewhere between gin and kerosene. Price and the high alcoholic content make it Korea's cheapest drink. While far from smooth, a bottle of *soju* goes down very well with certain foods, such as pigs' feet, barbecued pork, Korean sausage and other meat dishes.

But these days, Korean drinking tastes are changing. Beer, popular for many years, has now overtaken its rivals to become the top drink, especially with the younger generation. Once a rich man's drink, it is now the ordinary man's choice.

Higher Class Spirits: Western liquors like scotch and bourbon have always had high import duties in Korea. Since the mid-1970s, Korea has been importing, in bulk, scotch and other spirits and bottling their own brands. The resulting Korean scotch, gin, vodka, rum and brandy are much cheaper than imported brands and sales of these liquors increase each year. As Korea has increased in economic power, so has pressure increased for the Koreans to open markets to foreign imports. Protection of the whiskey market has been a source of friction between Korea and Britain for several years, but the government timetable now promises open competition by the mid-1990s.

Where should the foreigner visiting Korea go drinking? To get a feeling for what remains of the traditional, the best place would be a *makkolli-jip*. Korea also has plenty of beer halls. Try the Mugyo-dong district in downtown Seoul or the area around Sinch'on Rotary in western Seoul. (Note: During your visit to Korea, don't be surprised if you meet acquaintances who may well bring you out to drinking parties.)

If you are dining at Korean or Chinese restaurants, beer or traditional spirits may complement the meal. Restaurants usually don't serve *makkolli*, but they will have beer, *soju* or *chongjong*, Korean *sake*.

If you are eating Western food, you might wish to try a Korean wine called *majuang*. Most hotel restaurants stock it, as do the grocery stores.

Enticing food display at a *hwangap*, or 60th-birthday feast.

According to Korean legend and history, a she-bear and a tigress who wished to be incarnated as human beings were once granted a herbal prescription by Hwan-ung, the heavenly king. Each was given a bunch of mugwort and 20 bulbs of garlic and told to retire from the sunlight for 100 days. Only the she-bear carefully followed the king's advice, and emerged from her cave as a woman. She was then married by Hwan-ung and gave birth to Tan'gun Waggom, the great ancestor of Choson (Korea).

pharmacopoeia. Some knowledge of Chinese herbal medicine had been previously transmitted to Japan when, as early as 414, a Silla doctor named Kim Pa-chin was sent to cure Japan's King Inkyo and was given a large reward for his medical favors.

Around the middle of the Three Kingdoms Period (57 BC-AD 936), Korea started to publish its own pharmacopoeia with original prescriptions which combined Korean and Chinese medical knowledge. The use of indigenous herbs came into prominence dur-

This tale illustrates the close bond Koreans have with nature and also their belief in the power of herbs. Mugwort and garlic have long been vital ingredients in the Korean diet and other basic herbs have for centuries been recognized as preventives and curatives for human illnesses.

Chinese herbal medicine and acupuncture were officially introduced in AD 561 to the Koguryo court by a Han named Chih Tsung. Chih's knowledge dramatically expanded the possibilities in the field of Korean medicine. This knowledge was carried to the neighboring kingdoms of Paekche and Silla, and was assimilated with ancient Korean

ing the Koryo (936-1392) and Yi (1392-1910) dynasties. More than 150 medical manuals were published during the Yi dynasty, and one of the most valuable of these, the *Uibang Uch'wi*, was stolen by a Japanese warlord Kato Kiyomasa, during one of the Hideyoshi invasions of the 1590s. This pharmaceutical manual is still retained in Japan as a national treasure.

A Choice of Hanyak or Yak-guk: In 1880, Western medicine was introduced by doctors from China and Japan. However, despite the pervasiveness of 20th-century medicine, *hanyak*, traditional Korean medicine, remains extremely popular. Western-style pharmacies (*yak-guk*), replete with men dressed in starched white gowns and waiting behind drug counters, can be found on just about any modern, commercial street in Korea.

Hanyak shops are also visible almost everywhere – many of them distinguished by their fascinating window displays of snakes, enormous, human-shaped white ginseng roots pickling in belljars full of Korean wine, and a random collection of deer antlers, dried reptiles and insects. There are numerous *hanyak* shops in Seoul along Chong-no 5-ka and in Taegu on "Yak-chong Kol-mok," the city's famous "herb street." Raw herbs are also sold at most marketplaces. In addition, Korean-style pressure-point massage, *chi ap*,

t'ang) and snake wine (*paem sul*) are commonly prescribed potions – albino snake for longevity, yellow python for a cure-all, and viper for neuralgia and tuberculosis. Dog meat soup (*posin t'ang*; *posin ha-da* means to build up one's strength) is also a very popular body rejuvenator, especially when it's prepared from the meat of white and black dogs. Many small shops and cafes specialize in these reptile and canine soups, but Westerners may find a more palatable tonic in an *insam ch'at chip*, a ginseng teahouse.

Homemade, aromatic and delicious: The cozy herb teahouse is usually identified by white, anthropomorphic ginseng roots painted on

and acupuncture, *ch'im*, and a variety of other traditional healing techniques are still practiced.

Some of the common ingredients used in prescriptions are iris root for feeble-mindedness, snakeberry leaves to help regulate the menstrual cycle, and chrysanthemum roots to cure headaches. Not all of the antidotes are vegetarian, though. Snake meat soup (*paem*

Korean herb vendors display their medicinal wares in numerous colorful ways. Left, the window of a herb shop in Seoul. Above, an array of herb vats at Taegu.

its door and by the pungent aroma of hot cinnamon and ginger tea. Inside the shop, belljars of foreign, dried herbs line the shelf. More than just homemade ginseng tea is served.

There are, to name a few delicious concoctions, aromatic ginger tea (*saeng kang ch'a*) made with boiled and strained ginger root and raw sugar; *t'ang*, fresh white ginseng root blended with water and sugar; and porridges such as *chat chuk*, made of pine nuts, water, rice flour and salt or sugar to taste; and *kkae chuk*, toasted black sesame seeds, water, rice flour and salt or sugar. (Beware, however, of large heapings of sugar.) Herbs are steeped in earthenware pots (metal is said to deplete herbal potency) over a low-burning *yont'an* (coal briquette) for at least an hour or two until an essence is thus extracted. Besides teas and porridges, fresh fruit juices and fruits, such as sliced persimmons, strawberries and tangerines soaked in *soju* (25 percent to 50 percent proof drinking alcohol), are also served.

Panax Ginseng, the Cure-all Wonder: Among the herbs in Korea, *panax ginseng*, referred to as *insam* in Korean, is by far the most popular. As far back as the 3rd millennium BC in China, herbal potions and poultices were used to maintain and restore the internal *um-yang* (i.e. the positive-negative, acid-base, male-female) forces to proper balance by stimulating or repressing either aspect. Ginseng, which originally grew wild along ravines and in the forests of Korea and Manchuria, was found to be bursting with *yang* energy. It became a vital ingredient used in medications prescribed in the first Chinese pharmacopoeia.

The exchange of medical knowledge with China encouraged trade in herbs. Ginseng flowed into China until the Koryo dynasty, when supplies began to diminish, and was exported during the Yi dynasty as a tribute to Chinese royalty. To boost the supply, ginseng cultivation was encouraged in the Kyongsang and then in the Cholla provinces. The herb was first processed into ultra-potent "red ginseng" and exported to China during the reign of King Chongjo (1776-1800).

Modern Korean ginseng cultivators have been able to raise superior grade ginseng. Ideal climatic conditions, especially between northern 36° to 38° latitudes where optimum mountain-forest simulated environment is maintained, have produced a cultivated root that is considered to be the international standard.

Extreme care is administered in nurturing the root. In the preparation of *yakt'o* (soil for herbs), only a moderately rich mulch of

deciduous chestnut or oak leaves is used. Hand-thatched mats are erected to shade slopes of ginseng from direct sunlight. The main ginseng-growing areas are on Kanghwa Island, and in the Kimp'o, Puyo, and Kunsan districts. Once used, the land is not cultivated with ginseng again for at least another 10 to 15 years.

The growth and maturation cycle of Korean ginseng takes from four to six years depending on the intended use of the root. In mid-May, the plant flowers. Seeds of the strongest, most mature, five-year-old plants are selected in mid-July and planted in late October. After harvest, the roots are washed, peeled, steamed, and dried. They are then produced in two grades – white (*paek*) and red (*hong*). Approximately 60 percent of the best ginseng is selected for the red variety which is further processed to preserve the potency of its chemical components.

The "elixir of life": Although *panax ginseng* is also cultivated in neighboring China, Russia and North Korea, only the Republic of Korea exports the product on a grand scale. Valued more precious than gold in ancient times, Korean ginseng today is still considered a costly commodity and is sold in the *hanyak* shops at varying rates, depending on the grade of the product. While white ginseng is readily accessible, only about one

ennial radix plant of the *Araliaceae family*. Active components detected thus far in Korean, Chinese, and Russian ginseng (which differ pharmaceutically from the North American *panax quinquefolius* variety) are glycosides, saccharides, fatty substances, volatile substances, inorganic elements, B-vitamins, enzymes, and alkaline substances.

If consumed regularly in small doses, scientists claim the root will help stimulate the central nervous system. Larger doses, however, depress the nervous system by buffering out physical and chemical stress, and by promoting cell production which counteracts anaemia and hypertension. Ginseng thus reportedly increases physical and mental ef-

percent of the better-quality red ginseng product is marketed domestically by the government Office of Monopoly (which also exclusively controls the production of all ginseng-related commodities).

Modern, scientific analysis and extensive research of ginseng's mystic efficacy for the past several decades has helped fan the herb's worldwide popularity. To the Western world, *panax ginseng* has been identified as a per-

ficiency, and enhances gastrointestinal motility and tone.

It is also a common Western notion that ginseng virilizes one's libido. The Koreans, however, rely on much more potent aphrodisiacs, such as powdered deer antlers and dog or snake soup.

And perhaps to placate Western consumers who are seeking an "elixir of life," ginseng comes conveniently packaged in 20th-century pill form as well as in capsules, extracts, jellies, instant tea forms, soft drinks, body creams, jams, candies, chewing gums, and – would you believe – even in cigarettes and shampoos?

Left, perhaps nothing is more symbolic of Korea than preserved ginseng roots. **Above**, medicine shops are intriguing sidewalk purveyors of *hanyak*, traditional Korean medicine.

From morning calm to economic miracle: A new culture has emerged in the 5,000-year history of the Land of the Morning Calm. Along with the rich cultural heritage that intrigues the three million visitors who visit Korea annually, a unique business culture has developed.

For anyone seeking to understand the modern Korea, it is essential to examine the "economic miracle," and its central character – the businessman. Much of the rising national confidence that is freeing Koreans from a heritage of being looked down upon by the regional bully boys is due to the success of Korea's export machine which has turned the nation into one of Asia's industrial powerhouses.

The backbone of this astonishing success story has been the *chaebol* or business conglomerates and the industrial chiefs who have run them. These mighty warlords and their successors have seen per capita GNP grow from US$100 to US$600 in one generation. By the end of the century it should have passed the US$10,000 mark.

From years of deficit, Korea turned in three years of more than double digit growth in the late 1980s – the height of its economic power – to record surpluses. Now, because of rapid wage increases caused by democratic reforms which spilled over into the economic sector, the *chaebol* have lost their competitive edge. Korea has been replaced by other Asian countries as the home of cheap labor.

But, in true Korean fashion, the *chaebol* are recovering from the blow and moving into the next stage of the nation's economic growth. Ambitious plans to develop hi-tech industries are being laid out to help close the gap between Japanese and Korean products, always the yardstick for judging Seoul's development.

The industrial tycoons of the last three decades have been modeled on the elder Confucian statesmen of the past. Most of the former top chairmen, espousing Confucian ideals, have always regarded their employees as "family." Although insisting on obedience, they have always tried to look after their staff. But, although in relative terms, for a developing nation, the difference between worker and manager was not great, labor unions in recent years have pushed wage increases in an effort to close the gap.

Korea was still a nation of farmers just a generation ago, but now, because of its economic success, two thirds claim to be members of the urbanized middle class.

The challenge facing the next generation of *chaebol* tycoons is to balance the still-strong Confucian background of Koreans with its transition into the modern world. Economic success, and the successful hosting of the Olympics, have pulled the once-closed doors of the Hermit Kingdom off their hinges.

Business leaders now realize that they have to give middle managers a greater say in how their working livers are run. Despite greater emphasis on leisure these days, with Koreans able to travel freely overseas, most white-collar workers are still in the office from 9 p.m. to 8 p.m. and only have Sunday for a holiday.

With the top 30 *chaebol* accounting for over 50 percent of GNP – and over 70 percent of exports – it is virtually impossible to examine the industrial success without exploring the contribution of the *chaebol*. Similar in structure to the mighty Japanese conglomerates, the Korean *chaebol* still retain many of the unique cultural characteristics of Korea.

Since the late 1950s and 1960s, when men such as Chung Ju-yung of car giant Hyundai and the late Lee Byung-chul of electronics giant Samsung ruled with the iron rod, the first industrial barons were masters of all they surveyed.

Now, in line with the winds of change sweeping the country, many of the second-generation chairmen educated in the United States tend to be more open to advice. Nowadays, senior executives or "advisers," who often wield more power than managing directors of some of the subsidiaries of the *chaebol*, are often school friends or army colleagues of the chairman. An aide in the chairman's office of Hyundai, although technically not having the same rank as the managing director of Hyundai Heavy Industries (one of the country's biggest shipbuilders), may have more influence on the overall running of the group.

Many of these advisers are major figures in their own right and it is not uncommon for them to be former prime ministers of ex four-star generals. They tend to work in the chairman's office, secretariat or are the heads of "think-tanks." According to business analyst Lee Keum-hyun, the research outfits in the top groups hold much more power than is generally realized. "When the presidential office, the Blue House, wants to contact the *chaebol* heads, the officials there always ring up the think-tank directors," she said. "The men in charge are often the right-hand men of the conglomerate owners."

The think-tank referred to is usually the planning and coordination office (*kijoshil*), the chairman's office (*hwaejangshil*) or even the secretaries' office *(beesoshil)*. These offices are charged with collecting and processing information which may be useful to the business. They can be interpreted as having the

function of a group intelligence agency.

Business Etiquette: The foreign businessman approaching these key conglomerate offices or simply meeting Korean counterparts is advised to seek some minimal guidance on etiquette. For, if the Korean businessman is something of a modern day Atlas, bearing the burdens of the nation on his shoulders, he is also as sensitive as a poet and may react to the mildest perceived slight.

The initial meeting is the most important and is taken very seriously by Korean businessmen. Although business is not usually

Waiting game: businessman tries to hail a taxi.

conducted on the first meeting, he may decide to end the relationship there and then on the basis of a poor first impression. Such a setback may be caused by one of several innocent "mistakes" such as arriving unannounced, meeting the wrong person, being introduced by someone the targeted contact does not trust or respect, or failing to produce a name-card.

The foreign businessman should consider whether he has done everything to ensure that his targeted contact can trust him. The best way to ensure this is to have a go-between, such as a consultant or mutual acquaintance. Do not bring your lawyer. It implies lack of trust and, anyway, there will be no detailed business agreed on in the first meeting.

These subtleties come naturally to most Asians and even to some Europeans, but Americans, used to back-slapping and first names, frequently find themselves in trouble on these points. The name-card is to be treated with respect. It should be received with decorum and read, not just taken casually and slipped into the pocket. Your own card should be given to the most senior person first.

You should always bring your own interpreter. Larger firms may decline as they usually have good English speakers on their staffer.

Just because an executive speaks English, do not assume that everything you say is understood. Language teaching in Korea is not geared towards conversation and, although your contact may read *TIME* magazine, he may have trouble following what you are saying.

One of the great sources of misunderstanding is the Korean use of the word "yes." It may often mean "I heard you" rather than "I agree with you" and sometimes it can even mean "I don't understand what you're saying but keep talking." The foreigner is advised to speak non-colloquial English slowly and clearly.

Koreans are very warm and emotional, but at the same time they are extremely formal. Informality only exists between close friends. Never use first names unless invited to do so.

Be prepared for questions about your age, marital status and religion. Your contact is trying to place you socially and characterize your relationship.

Perhaps the final piece of advice is that, after having digested the etiquette guide books, forget them and be your natural self. Koreans are far more familiar with the west than vice versa. They expect you to be a courteous foreigner, not a pretend-Korean.

Republic of Korea

Sea of Japan

Yellow Sea

Kosŏng
Sariwŏn
Kimhwa
Sibyŏn
P'yŏnggang
NORTH
SOUTH
Ch'ŏrwŏn
Kansŏng
Sinhŭng-sa
Naksan-sa
Hwach'ŏn-chŏsuji
Sokch'o
Haeju
Kaesŏng
Ongjin
Kyŏnggi-man
Kangnŭng
Yongmun-sa
Ch'unch'ŏn
Soyang-chŏsuji
1577
Kyebang-san
Uijŏngbu
Chongp'yong-chŏsuji
Sangwŏn-sa
Samch'ŏk
Inch'ŏn
Seoul
Anyang
Sŏngnam-si
Yongju-sa
Wŏnju
Yŏyang-ni
TŎKCHŎK-KUNDO
Suwŏn
Wŏlchŏng-sa
P'yŏngt'aek
Chech'on
Uljin
Sindŏk
Ch'ŏnan
Kap-sa
Pusŏk-sa
T'aean
Yŏngju
Choch'iwŏn
Ch'ŏngju
Andong-chŏsuji
Andong
Taech'ŏn
Chongmim-sa
Kongju
Sangju
Pŏpju-sa
Yŏngdŏk
Taejŏn
Chikji-sa
Changhang
Kwanchok-sa
Kimch'ŏn
Tongwŏn-sa
P'ohang
Mirŭk-sa
Kunsan
Songgwang-sa
Tŏgyu-san
Taegu
Kyŏngju
Kumsan-sa
Chŏnju
1608
Yongyon-sa
Pulguk-sa
Haein-sa
Tongdo-sa
Ulsan
Chŏngŭn
Namwŏn
Miryang
Chii-sah
Hwaŏm-sa
1915
Ssanggye-sa
Naktong-gang
Pomo-sa
Songjŏng
Kwangju
Chinju
Masan
Chinhae
Pusan
Songgwang-sa
Sunch'ŏn
Samch'ŏnp'o
KŎJE-DO
Western Channel
Mokp'o
Ch'ungmu
Changhŭng
Yŏsu
KAMINO-SHIMA
Chindo
Kohŭng
Kaedo-ri
TSUSHIMA
CHIN-DO
Wando
SHIMONO-SHIMA
POGIL-TO
CHŎNGSAN-DO
SOAN-DO

Halla-san
1950
CHEJU-DO

80 km / 50 miles

To see Korea, whether through a camera lens or in person, is to want to touch her. She's tough, fiery and independent but she's also gentle and warm, rich in colors and textures which flit and freeze in her golden light like luminescent butterflies a-dance over cliffs of granite.

Called the "Land of the Morning Calm," Korea offers 5,000 years of art and culture, historic places, spectacular scenery, splendid shopping malls, fine hotels and friendly people who have a traditionally warm welcome for tourists. This preview is, however, only the tip of the iceberg, and Korea is waiting to be explored.

Like most places, Korea has to be discovered while one travels on improbable and serendipitous courses. Except for the time of arrival and the first few days in Seoul (the magnetic center of this land between the Pacific, Russian Siberia and Chinese Manchuria) all other travels in Korea are the result of considered and curious decisions.

With that pure traveling spirit in mind, move along and explore the charming "back streets" of Korean culture. Join ancient travelers in the search for early plum blossoms in the snow. Wink at a 1,000-year-old *Miruk-bul*, "Buddha of the Future." Rest and drink sweet rice wine in a wayside tavern, and then, in an outrageous finale, marvel at the Yangju mask dancer who looks like a red beetle recently emerged from a phosphorescent cave.

The formal provinces of modern Korea, like the constantly shifting powers and borders of the ancient kingdoms of Choson, defy traveling logic. They are serpentine units of space and time which appear merely as flashing roadsigns on highway blurs. Fly on past Kyonggi-do, Kangwon-do, and the north and south sectors of Ch'ungch'ong-do, Kyongsang-do and Cholla-do. Explore the gnarled pines, rocky headlands, combed burial mounds and sculpted treasures that frame this ancient Asian queen "of 10,000 peaks, 10,000 islands, and 10,000 waterfalls."

But most importantly, pause now and then for long looks – and feelings – of people, places and things which are Korean; as such unexpected, but definitely visible and touchable.

119

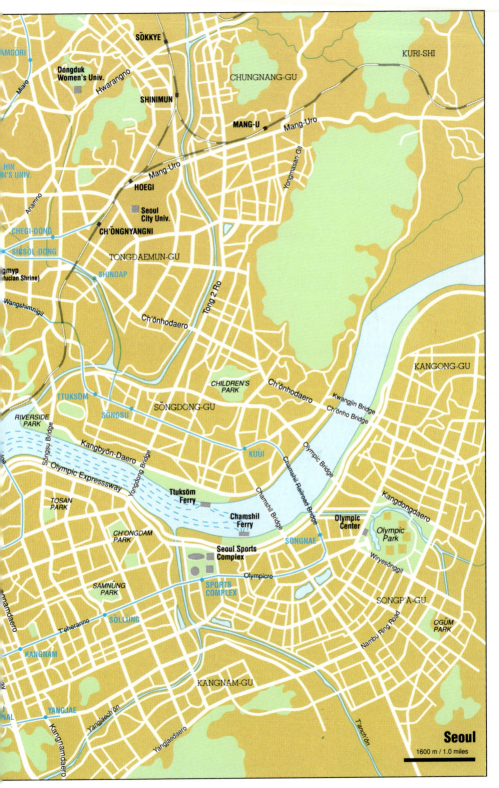

Seoul

1600 m / 1.0 miles

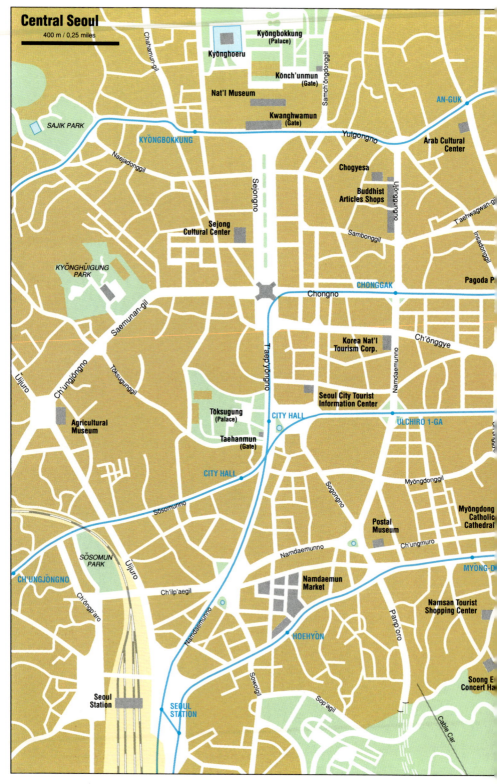

Central Seoul

400 m / 0,25 miles

Kyŏngbokkung
(Palace)

Kyŏnghoeru

Kŏnch'unmun
(Gate)

Nat'l Museum

Kwanghwamun
(Gate)

AN-GUK

SAJIK PARK

KYŎNGBOKKUNG

Yulgongno

Arab Cultural
Center

Naejadonggil

Chogyesa

Buddhist
Articles Shops

Sejong
Cultural Center

Sejong

Sambonggil

T'aehwagwan-gil

Insadonggil

KYŎNGHŬIGUNG
PARK

CHONGGAK

Pagoda P

Chongno

Chongno

Saemunan-gil

Korea Nat'l
Tourism Corp.

Ch'ŏnggye

Uijuro

Ch'ungjŏngno

Tŏksugungil

T'aep'yŏngno

Namdaemunno

Seoul City Tourist
Information Center

Agricultural
Museum

Tŏksugung
(Palace)

CITY HALL

ÜLCHIRO 1-GA

Taehanmun
(Gate)

CITY HALL

Sŏsomunno

Sogongno

Myŏngdonggil

Myŏngdong
Catholic
Cathedral

Postal
Museum

Ch'ungmuro

SŎSOMUN
PARK

Uijuro

CH'UNGJŎNGNO

MYŎNG-D

Ch'ŏngp'aro

Ch'ilp'aegil

Namdaemun
Market

Namsan Tourist
Shopping Center

Namdaemunno

Namdaemunno

Panp'oro

HOEHYŎN

Sowŏlgi

Soong E
Concert Ha

Seoul
Station

SEOUL
STATION

Sop'agil

Cable Car

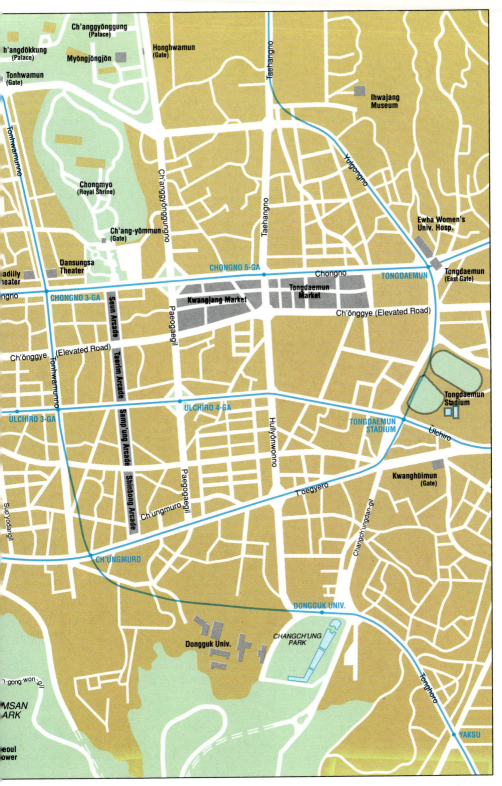

Ch'anggyŏnggung
(Palace)

h'angdŏkkung
(Palace)

Myŏngjŏngjŏn

Honghwamun
(Gate)

Tonhwamun
(Gate)

Tonhwamunno

Ihwajang
Museum

Taehangno

Chongmyo
(Royal Shrine)

Ch'anggyŏnggungno

Ch'ang-yŏmmun
(Gate)

Dansungsa
Theater

adilly
heater

ngno

CHONGNO 3-GA

CHONGNO 5-GA

Chongno

TONGDAEMUN

Tongdaemun
(East Gate)

Ewha Women's
Univ. Hosp.

Taehangno

Yulgongno

Seun Arcade

Kwangjang Market

Tongdaemun
Market

Paegogaegil

Ch'ŏnggye (Elevated Road)

Ch'ŏnggye (Elevated Road)

Tonhwamunno

Taerim Arcade

ŬLCHIRO 4-GA

Samp'ung Arcade

ŬLCHIRO 3-GA

Shinsong Arcade

Hullyŏnwonno

TONGDAEMUN
STADIUM

Tongdaemun
Stadium

TONGDAEMUN
STADIUM

Ŭlchiro

Paegogaegil

Kwanghŭimun
(Gate)

Sup'yodarigil

Ch'ungmuro

T'oegyero

Changch'ungdan-gil

CH'UNGMURO

DONGGUK UNIV.

-gong-won-gil

Dongguk Univ.

CHANGCH'UNG
PARK

Tonghoro

MSAN
ARK

eoul
ower

YAKSU

SEOUL: THE CAPITAL

"If you have a horse, send it to Cheju Island; if you have a son, send him to Seoul." So an old Korean saying advises. Send a horse to Cheju Island where the grass is green and lush. Send a son to Seoul to go to school: the city swarms with thousands of students attending its 18 universities and 15 colleges. Send him to Seoul to get a job: all the head offices of any enterprise – commercial, financial, governmental – are in Seoul. Send him to Seoul for a chance at the best opportunities.

That's what Seoul is: the center of the nation, the heart of the country to which everything else is drawn. It's as if Seoul were a giant magnet attracting to itself filings of trade and commerce, education, culture and the arts, government, politics – all the occupations of any nation. So many people, both sons and daughters, have responded to Seoul's pull that the city is now home to one quarter of the country's population. Its residents now number over 10 million. If you were in downtown Seoul at 6 or 7 p.m., you would feel yourself caught up in the all too tangible and audible force field of a city at rush hour. Seoul is *the* central city and has been the capital for more than 5,000 years (the word *Seoul* means capital), the eye, as it were, of the Korean vortex. And what better place to begin exploring such a city than at its epicenter?

Centers of the Vortex: Topographically, that center is wooded **Nam-san** (South Mountain), a 900-foot (274-meter) elevation that gazes across mid-town at conically shaped **Pugak-san** (North Peak Mountain). Between these peaks sprawled the old walled city. A 10-mile (16-kilometer) encircling wall made of earth and dressed stone is gone, but a few crumbling stretches on Pugak-san and Nam-san, and other restored patches that were rebuilt for tourist visibility, have survived. The original wall, however, was pierced by nine gates. Five still stand, and the two largest – **Namdae-mun**

(Great South Gate) and **Tongdae-mun** (Great East Gate) – are regal presences in the midst of the modern city's swirl. They are reminders of the capital as it was once laid out.

Some think the center of the city is **City Hall Plaza**, the fountain square bounded on the north by **City Hall**, on the south by the **Plaza Hotel**, on the east by the entrance to **Ulchi-ro** (one of the main east-west streets), and on the west by **Toksu Palace** (a remnant of the old dynasty that founded the city). Running under the plaza are two subway lines. Traffic running in and out of the square from three major arteries swings round the fountain; pedestrians descend underground to cross the square through its underpasses; and, if traffic allows, you can stand in the middle of the north-south street, **T'aep'yong-no**, and look south to Namdae-mun and north to **Kwanghwa-mun** (Gate of Transformation by Light), the reconstructed gate in front of the 20th-century capitol building. This is City Hall Plaza – a link between the old and new.

Other centrists claim that the Kwanghwa-mun intersection is Seoul's center. This is the next crossing north of City Hall Plaza and it's dominated by a looming **statue of Yi Sun-sin**, Korea's great 16th-century naval hero.

From that intersection, T'aep'yong-no runs south, **Sejong-no** north, **Sinmun-no** west and **Chong-no** east – yes, the streets change name as they cross. Even more perplexing is that the Kwanghwa-mun intersection is not directly in front of the Kwanghwa-mun gate for which it is named. That's another long block north of here! People who believe that this intersection is *the* center of the city probably think so because it is the entrance to Chong-no, or Bell Street, the city's original main commercial street. When he established Seoul as the capital in 1394, Yi dynasty founder Yi Song-gye, whose royal name was T'aejo, hung a bell there. The bell was rung at dawn and dusk to signal the official opening and closing of the city gates. The bell hanging inside the Poshin-gak belfry at Chong-no intersection today was rebuilt in 1984 and is rung only on special holidays.

Namdae-mun-no, Seoul.

The governmental heart of the old walled city was **Kyongbok Palace** (Palace of Shining Happiness); which was T'aejo's residence and seat of power, and was used by him and his successors until 1592 when it was burned during warfare with Japan. If you inquire more minutely, you will discover that Kyongbok's throne hall, the **Kunjongjon** (Hall of Government by Restraint), rebuilt in 1867, was the very center of Taejo's governmental heart. Here the king sat to receive ministers ranged in orderly ranks before him, made judgements, and issued proclamations. The hall faces south down Sejong-no and once commanded an unobstructed view through Kwanghwa-mun to Namdaemun. This vista is now blocked by the old Capitol Building, now the **National Museum**, built in 1926 by the Japanese colonial rulers. In June 1991, the government launched a 10-year project to restore the palace, rebuilding some buildings such as the **Kangnyongjon** (residence of the king) and **Kyotaejon** (residence of the queen), destroyed by the

Japanese, and removing some pagodas which the Japanese built. Flanking the palace gate are two stone *haet'ae*, mythical animals from Korean lore, which have witnessed Seoul's changes and additions ever since they were carved and placed here in the 15th century to guard the old palace from fire.

The exact geographical center of the old city can be definitely placed, but in the name of progress it's now almost impossible to find. Just off **Insa-dong,** an area east of Kwanghwa-mun known for its art galleries, art supply stores and antique dealers, there used to be a square granite marker enclosed by short octagonal pillars. That square of granite marked the geographical center of the old walled city. Typically enough, this particular piece of Yi dynasty history was ignored: neither the stone itself nor any signboard proclaimed what this spot was. This remnant of history was carted off during construction in the mid-1980s. A new office block stands in its place. Just by this spot is the former house of a Yi dynasty prince, a building where leaders

Kyonghoeru Pavilion in Kyongbok Palace grounds.

of the 1919 independence uprising planned their protest against the Japanese rulers. This building is marked by a plaque.

Seoul Chic: Many people think Seoul's real center today is modern **Myong-dong,** an area of narrow alleys that starts a 10-minute walk southeast from City Hall Plaza directly across from **Midopa Department Store**. Myong-dong's main thoroughfare, a one-way street, is lined on both sides with swanky shops that sell chic clothes and accessories, and it ends at the top of a low hill before **Myong-dong Cathedral**. The grand center of Catholicism used to be one of the largest buildings in the city decades ago. Now it is dwarfed by large hotels and office buildings, but it still remains a landmark. In recent years it has become a rallying point for anti-government demonstrators.

Not only has the Catholic faith attracted politically-active converts through its human rights stance, but many protesters ranging from the homeless to radical students have sought ref-

uge within its hallowed grounds. Even in the 1990s, the pungent smell of teargas lingering from a recent demonstration often hangs over the area around the cathedral.

Myong-dong alleyways come alive in the evening when they are crowded with after-work strollers window-shopping – "eye-shopping" in Korean – past the fancy displays of shoes and handbags, tailor-made suits and custom-made shirts, dresses in the latest fashions, handcrafted modern jewelry, and cosmetics. But these are only the surface attractions of Myong-dong. The district was famous during the Park Chung-hee era for its tiny upstairs and hideaway drinking houses which used to serve cheap liquor up until curfew time. These have been largely replaced by fashionable, and pricey, coffee shops packed with young Koreans.

Nam-san, City Hall Plaza, Kwanghwamun, Myong-dong. Perhaps the visitor should think of Seoul as having more than one center: it's certainly a city big enough and old enough for more than one special center of interest.

Midora Department Store in central Seoul.

Korea's capital has literally risen from the ashes of its wartime desolation and is now rushing into the mainstream of international activity. Independent Korea has bred a people determined to improve the homeland and to gain recognition and values all the while. Seoul's noise and congestion is living proof of Korea's capability; its calm and grandeur attest to the strength of Korean culture. As you walk around the city you will feel the push of the future and the pull of the past: the essence of a soul which pumps through every artery. Indeed, Seoul is Korea's soul.

Getting around: Administratively, Seoul is divided into 22 wards (*ku*), with each *ku* again segmented into various precincts (*dong*). A *dong* is an area of considerable size, but the term is often used simply to identify where you live or where you're going. People hoping to share a taxi ride, for example, stand at the side of the street shouting, "*Hannam-dong!*", "*Tonam-dong!*", "*Yaksu-dong!*" and other *dongs* at passing taxis.

Only downtown, in fact, will you hear the names of certain streets used regularly. It's handy, however, to have some idea of which streets these are. The east-west streets include: **T'oegye-ro** which runs east from Seoul Railway Station and follows the northern foot of Namsan until it joins Ulchi-ro beyond Seoul Stadium; **Ulchi-ro** which runs east from City Hall Plaza (west from City Hall Plaza runs another main artery, Seosomun-ro); **Chong-no**, which runs east from Kwanghwa-mun intersection to Tongdae-mun and beyond; **Sinmun-no** which runs west to **Sodaemun** (this is the West Gate, but no gate stands there now); and a block south of Kwanghwa-mun intersection is **Ch'onggyech'on**, which runs east in the shadow of the elevated **Samil-lo** expressway.

The north-south streets are: **Namdaemun-no** which curves northeast from Namdae-mun until it intersects Chong-no (where its name becomes An'gukdong-no); and **T'aep'yong-no**, which runs from Namdae-mun north to the Kwanghwa-mun intersection where its name becomes **Sejong-no**. (A word to

those who may be confused: The Chinese character for "road" is romanized to -*no*, -*ro*, or -*lo* according to the ending of the preceding word to reflect how it is properly pronounced.)

To say to a taxi driver that you want to go to Chong-no is not enough, however. Each of these thoroughfares is longitudinally divided into areas roughly corresponding to blocks, called -*ka*; each -*ka*, in turn, is numbered sequentially from where the street begins. Chong-no 1-ka, for example, is an area extending from Chong-no's beginning at Kwanghwa-mun intersection to the next major crossing where it meets Namdae-mun-no and where the great bell that used to signal the closing and opening of the city gates now hangs.

With increasing traffic congestion, however, the subway is the handiest means of transport in Seoul. Four lines are currently in operation with three more under construction. These lines connect to the national railroad lines to nearby cities such as Inch'on, Uijongbu and Suwon. Visitors will be happy to hear that signs and maps at subway stations are clearly marked in English which makes doing the city underground relatively simple. Line No. 1 is marked red on subway maps and, predictably for the first subway line, begins at Seoul Railway Station.

The first stop from here is City Hall which brings you right out onto the city plaza and within easy reach of Toksu Palace, the Plaza, President, Westin Chosun and Lotte Hotels, the British Embassy and the American Cultural Center. Shoppers going to **Tongdae-mun Market** or movie-goers heading for the **Hollywood**, **Piccadilly** and **Danseongsa** theaters should get off at stops further down the line.

Outside the downtown area, the name of a *dong* is necessary to identify where you live or where you want to go. Although each *dong* is further divided into units of a few households called *pan*, people living in a particular neighborhood often refer to it as "our village," a concept not necessarily identical to the government's *pan* or *dong*.

The urban neighborhood village is

Components of a Yi Dynasty structure.

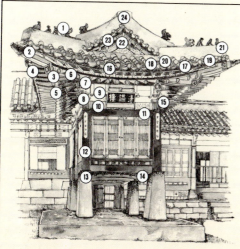

Chagyŏng Hall,
Kyŏngbok Palace,
Seoul

1 Clay *chapsang* animal "guardians" or "ridge beasts".

2 A false hip rafter which gives an upward curve to the eaves.

3 A true hip rafter.

4 False rafters accentuate roof curves.

5 True rafters.

6 "Jack rafters" rise to the hip rafter.

7 Girders, also called header plates or purlins, support the rafters.

8 The echindus, a square, round, or polygonal moulding that caps a post or column.

9 An architrave beam.

10 Tie-beams, or header beams, connect and bind post tops.

11 The lintel.

12 Post or column, usually of wood

13 A "one bay"

14 Raised floor to help provide air circulation.

15 Eave bracketting system in which the girder is supported by a cantilevered truss.

16 Clay and straw mortar covering wood or bamboo subsurfacing supported by the rafters.

17 Flat antefix tiles.

18 Flat tiles.

19 Round antefix tiles.

20 Round tiles covering seams between flat tile rows.

21 Decorative vertical tiles called finial plates.

22 The gablet.

23 False rafters.

24 The main gablet ridge, which accentuates this gambrel or half-hipped Korean roof.

typically a maze of small alleyways and side streets. A visiting western urbanologist once wrote, "If you imagine pouring some water onto a pile of large rocks, the pathway found by the water between the rocks, as it flows to the ground, is somewhat similar to the way streets exist in Korean neighborhoods." Partly for this reason, knowing the address of a particular house does not guarantee that you will find it - at least, not quickly. Addresses are given as such-and-such *ku*, *ku*-and such-and-such *dong*, and a house number. And house numbers seldom follow in numerical sequence; rather, they are assigned according to when the house was built. For these reasons, all Koreans get a lot of practice in drawing maps.

"Virtuous Longevity": For "modern" and exploratory openers, begin your tour of Seoul at the central and historical **Toksu Palace** (Palace of Virtuous Longevity), whose gate faces City Hall Plaza. Toksu is not the oldest of the surviving palaces – it was built as a villa toward the end of the 15th century – but it is impor-

tant for its role at the unhappy end of the Yi dynasty. King Kojong, who was forced to abdicate in favor of his son Sunjong in 1907, lived in retirement and died here in 1919 after having seen his country annexed by the Japanese in 1910 and his family's dynasty snuffed out after 500 years.

Among the most conspicuous structures on the palace grounds, regularly open to the public, is a **statue of Sejong**, the great 15th-century king who commissioned scholars to develop a distinctive Korean writing system, different from the traditional Chinese characters, and officially promulgated it in 1446. There's also a royal audience hall and two startlingly European-style stone buildings, with Ionic and Corinthian columns designed by an Englishman in 1909, which used to house the **National Museum of Modern Art**, now re-located south of the city. The palace grounds offer a welcome relief from the modern bustle, especially in the fall when its aisle of gingko trees are aflame in gold.

When school's in and the weather is

National Folklore Museum at Kyongbok Palace.

good, lines of schoolchildren stream through the gate of nearby Kyongbok Palace. They scatter around the grounds where, with paint brush and palette in hand, and canvas on easel, they work intently to capture the color of the flowers and leaves, and the charm of interior vistas once seen only by royalty and their attendants. A favorite subject is **Kyonghoeru** (Hall of Happy Meetings), a two-story banquet hall that was built in 1412, burned down in 1592, and rebuilt in 1867 when the ruling regent had the entire palace renovated for his son, King Kojong. The hall extends over one end of a spacious square pond. Swans glide over the water and, in winter, skaters glide over the pond's frozen surface. But in July, from the shallow waters of another pond surrounding the much smaller but more charming **Hyangwon pavilion** in the northeast corner of the palace grounds, giant pink Indonesian lotus do rise on long quivering stems above dinner-plate-sized leaves.

In front of Kyongbok Palace is the **National Museum of Korea**, the largest museum in the country, displaying over 100,000 items from ancient times through the Choson Kingdom period. These include Paekche tiles, Silla pottery, gilt Buddhas, Koryo celadons and Yi calligraphy and paintings. The building, once the central government offices, boasts the largest and finest collection of Korean art in the world. Inside the palace grounds stands the **National Folklore Museum** of Korea which houses artifacts of everyday use and dioramas showing how they were used.

Round a Secret Garden: About a block east of Kyongbok lies **Ch'angdok Palace** (Palace of Illustrious Virtue), built in 1405 as a detached palace, burned down in 1592, rebuilt in 1611 and used since then as the official residence of various Yi kings, including the last one Sunjong, until the latter's death in 1926. The best preserved of Seoul's palaces, Ch'angdok has a throne room hall surrounded by long drafty corridors leading past reception rooms furnished with heavy upholstered European chairs and sofas. In private living quarters, the furnishings are

National Assembly Building in Yoido in Seoul.

those of traditional Korea: low, slatted beds, lacquered chests and tables.

Nakson-jae, a small complex of buildings within Ch'angdok's grounds, is still the residence of descendants of the royal family: Ensconced there are an elderly aunt of Sunjong; the wife of the last crown prince, Sunjong's son (who never ruled); her son; and his wife. In the formal back gardens of Nakson-jae, a series of stair-stepped granite-faced tiers planted with azaleas, it is possible to feel totally isolated from the sounds of modern Seoul. From within a small raised octagonal pavilion at the top of this garden, you can imagine the royal family sitting here, gazing out over the curved roofs of the palace buildings and the arabesque walls encircling them. Under leafy tree-tops that stretch towards Nam-san in the distance, you can hear court whispers and imagine the turbulence and intrigues of Korea's late Yi dynasty.

Behind Ch'angdok lies the extensive acreage of **Piwon**, the Secret Garden, so called because it was formerly a private park for the royal family. In wooded and hilly terrain, footpaths meander past ponds and pavilions and over small bridges. The most picturesque of these sites is **Pando-ji** (Peninsula Pond) shaped like the outline of the Korean peninsula. From its shore extending out over the water stands a small, exquisite fan-shaped pavilion from which Injo, the 16th king, could cast a line for a bit of quiet fishing. Piwon and portions of Ch'angdok Palace may be visited by joining one of several daily guided tours at the Piwon entrance. Nakson-jae is open to the public twice a year for royal ceremonies.

One block east from Ch'angdok lies **Ch'anggyongwon**, another ancient palace grounds now open to the public. Visitors may wander on their own here, the largest public park within Seoul. Young couples seek out nooks to proceed with their courtship, families bring picnics, and elderly folk in traditional dress or new-fangled hiking gear take long, silent strolls.

Across the street from Ch'anggyongwon, lies **Ch'ongmyo**, the Royal Ancestral Shrine. This walled complex includes

Chogye-sa devotees, Buddha's birthday.

134

two long pillared buildings housing, according to Confucian requirement, ancestral tablets listing the names and accomplishments of the 27 Yi kings and their queens. Ch'ongmyo is open to the public and is a favorite strolling ground for young couples. Once a year on the first Sunday in May, a traditional ceremony honoring the spirits of kings and queens is held here. Ancient court music, not otherwise heard, rings eerily over flagstones and beyond cedar pillars as Confucian celebrants pay appropriate respects and offer proper foods and wine to each of the enshrined spirits in a ritual lasting six hours.

Honoring the sage: Strangely, the teachings of the great sage Confucius, who lived in China about 2,500 years ago, became more deeply rooted in Korea than in their native land, especially during the Choson dynasty (1392-1910) when they formed the basis of Korean society. Even today, many aspects of Confucianism live on in Korean society such as the emphasis placed on education, respect for one's elders and ancestral worship.

Twice a year in the second and eighth lunar months, many people still gather at the **Songgyun'gwan** shrine located on the grounds of **Songgyun'gwan University** to the northeast of Piwon. The Sokchon honors the spirit of Kongja (Confucius), the man whose principles formed the basis of government and code of behavior in Yi Korea.

Songgyun'gwan University is in fact a modern transformation of the old Songgyun'gwan, a national institute sponsored and supported by the Yi Court where Korea's best scholars pursued the Confucius Classics and instructed those who aspired to pass government examinations in order to receive official appointments.

According to the *Hangnyong*, the rules governing students' lives, "Any student guilty of violating human obligations (prince and minister, father and son, husband and wife, brothers or friends), of faulty deportment, or of damaging his body or his reputation, will be denounced, with drumbeats, by the other students. Extreme cases may be reported to the

onfucian
ancers,
ongg-
ung'wan
hrine.

Ministry of Rites and barred from academic circles for life."

After all, the aim of the school was – as its name says – *song*, "to perfect human nature," and *kyun*, "to build a good society." This is the dual purpose of a good Confucian education.

Buddhism's Hub: The Confucian Yi court tried hard to extinguish the spirit of the Buddha throughout the country but it failed miserably. Buddhist temples abound. City temples, though, are hardly places of quiet retreat. **Chogye-sa**, founded in 1910 and the headquarters of the official sect of Buddhism in Korea, is right downtown off **An'guk-dong-no**. As the center of Buddhism in the country, it hums with activity, and on the occasion of Buddha's birthday, on the 8th day of the 4th lunar month, it becomes the hub – and hubbub – of Buddhist festivities in Korea.

On this day, in common with all Buddhist temples in the country, the courtyard in front of Chogye-sa's main hall is strung with parallel strands of wires on support poles. As dusk falls, worshipers come to the temple to buy a paper lantern and candle. The names of all the members of the worshiper's family are written on a tag dangling from the bottom of the lantern. The worshiper fixes the candle into the lantern, lights it, hangs the lantern on one of the wires, and bows and murmurs a prayer when she's finished. Row after row of flickering candle flames illuminate the courtyard as darkness deepens. If in some stray gust of wind a lantern catches fire and burns, everyone stands aghast and mute at this stroke of ill fortune – an evil omen for the year to come. Meanwhile, within the main hall, devotees light incense on the altar before the Buddha's golden image, bow to the floor three times in reverence and offer prayers. Everywhere the temple is thick with people. Anyone may buy and hang a lantern; so many non-Buddhist foreign residents do. Some even march in a long lantern parade that winds through downtown Seoul – an elaborate affair with floats and bands. It's a good way to try to ensure good luck for a year.

Besides these and other surviving

Candid lanterns, Chogye-sa.

Buddha's
birthday
celebrations,
Toson-sa.

pockets of history connected to the old dynasty, other sections of the city are interesting for more specialized reasons.

Foreigners, the Waeguk Saram: When the first Western foreigners appeared in significant numbers in Korea, they were not allowed to live within the city walls. In the 1880s, however, King Kojong permitted foreign missionaries, traders and legations to buy land in **Chong-dong** just inside the western wall and behind and to the north of Toksu Palace. Many of the structures they built still stand and are still in use: the **Chong Dong Methodist Church**, which Korea's first modern president Syngman Rhee attended, and the **Ewha Girls' High School**, founded by Methodist missionaries. All that remains of the **Russian Legation** is the ruins of a white tower near the present Kyonghyang Shinmun (newspaper) building, but the **American ambassador's residence**, the **British Embassy** and an adjoining **Anglican Cathedral** are still in active use. The Cathedral is a graceful Italianate building, its square belfry visible from City Hall Plaza over the intervening walls. The British Embassy, a red brick structure dating from 1890, was in 1990-91 being given a US$6 million face-lift and expansion.

The American ambassador's residence, behind walls and a heavy gate emblazoned with a red-white-and-blue American seal, is a low one-story Korean-style house. Its most recent renovation added a replica of P'osok-jong, a channel in the shape of an outsized abalone shell carved from stone. In ancient times, a Silla king and his courtiers sat around the contours of the real P'osok-jong (in Kyongju) which was filled with running water. Through the channel floated wine cups. When a bobbing cup hesitated in front of king or courtier, it was his turn either to compose an impromptu poem or down the hesitant wine as a fine for lack of instant inspiration. A frequent result was a tipsy king and an equally tipsy court. It is not known if successive American ambassadors have continued this tradition.

Many early foreigners never left Korea, and it is the prim **Seoul Foreigners'**

Cemetery that keeps and guards their bones. At the northern end of the **Second Han River Bridge**, across from the **Church of Martyrs**, it is a place for history and feeling. Some of the graves are American, others are English, Canadian, French, even Russian – these last marked by Orthodox crosses and Cyrillic epitaphs. Not all were missionaries. There is Arthur Gorman, born Yokohama 9 April 1884, died Seoul 3 March 1929, served in the Royal Dublin Fusileers 1915-1919. Lying now with this early foreign soldier are American servicemen from the late 1960s and early 1970s, several of them sergeants who probably retired from service here. There are also many small headstones marking children's graves.

Cruising It'aewon: It'aewon is an urban area that runs down from the southern flank of Nam-san and eastward from the fenced edge of **Yongsan Garrison**, the site of the headquarters of the 8th U.S. Army. The main thoroughfare that bisects the army base into north-south posts similarly bisects It'aewon into an uphill-Nam-san side and a downhill toward-the-Han-River side. For years, that flank of Nam-san has been one of the main housing areas for Westerners because the Korea Housing Corporation, a government agency, built and maintained Western-style houses there. That idea is perpetuated, but foreigners, not all of them Western, now occupy multi-story apartment buildings higher up the mountain – a location that gives them a sweeping view of the **Han River** and mountain ridges south of the city.

Imagine, however, the look of astonishment on the faces of the Buddhist monks who, for some 500 years, kept a free hostel for travelers near here. What if they could return for a brief glimpse at the **Hyatt Regency Hotel**'s mirrored facade reflecting a setting sun and passing clouds? And their reaction if they turned and caught sight of the twin minarets of an onion-domed mosque below? What would they make of the *muezzin*'s call to afternoon prayer?

Centuries back, It'aewon was used as a stopover point for visitors to the capital. Then, during the Japanese Occupation,

Suburban Seoul City snowscapes.

Japanese troops were housed here. These soldiers were replaced after the Korean War with American soldiers stationed at the adjacent Yongsan base and Korean merchants moved into the thoroughfare to cater to soldierly needs.

Today, It'aewon merchants attract shoppers from civilian ranks as well, and visitors hail from all over the world. By day, bargain-hunters swarm through the hundreds of clothing, eelskin, brassware, shoe and antique stores where they stock up on Korean-made goods.

By night, It'aewon attracts more young Koreans than foreigners. Higher prices and more varied entertainment elsewhere has drawn away much of the foreign custom. The It'aewon strip has now doubled in length with many new discotheques and restaurants catering to the new generation of Koreans. In former times the hundreds of bars and discos used to rock until the break of day. The alcohol flowed and many a cross-cultural marriage had its beginnings in one of the packed clubs.

But now It'aewon is a mere shadow of its former self. By day, new department stores cast long shadows over the street stalls; by night, a midnight closing time, strictly enforced since its introduction in 1990 to combat drunk-driving and rising crime, has forced many of the small establishments to close down.

Chinatown: For years there was a special section of the city for the Chinese – as there is in almost any sizable city outside of China. This "Chinatown" was behind the Plaza Hotel, but the construction of that hotel and other forms of city renovation razed much of the old area and scattered the Chinese around the city. Nowadays what remain as parts of a Chinese "section" are the **Embassy of the Republic of China**, Chinese middle and high schools, and, in a side valley on the fringe of Myong-dong, a Chinese temple.

Once a year on a spring day determined by the lunar calendar, Chinese residents offer an all-day performance of Chinese opera here in the temple. The day celebrates the birth of the Chinese goddess of progeny. The performers are

h'anggyongwon in winter.

amateurs who practice weeks to produce the high-pitched voices required by his kind of music. The audience is Chinese (few Koreans know about this piece of Chinese culture in their midst), and sometimes you can even glimpse an elderly woman with bound feet.

Of course, there are Chinese restaurants everywhere in Seoul – with fare ranging from awful to delicious, usually depending upon the cheap to very expensive price. Latest reports say, however, that these days many young Korean-born Chinese are leaving Korea, where they face restrictions as "foreigners," to go to Taiwan where they go to college and pursue careers.

During the Japanese colonial rule, Seoul was called Kyongsong. After World War II, the old name of Hanyang was resurrected. But for centuries the city had been popularly known as "Seoul," a Korean word meaning the center of everything. In 1948, when South Korea was officially founded, separate from North Korea, as the Republic of Korea, Seoul officially become Seoul.

By government designation Seoul is officially a T'ukpyol-si or Special City. Other provincial capitals are referred to as Chikhal-si, or self-governing city, which entitles them to administer their affairs separate from the provincial government. Despite its seemingly large land area, the city is everywhere crowded. In 1968, Patricia Bartz reported in her book, *South Korea*, that the population density of the city in certain areas is up to 77,500 persons per square mile in the most crowded area, Map'o-ku.

Everything You Want: The life of an urban villager, especially that of the housewife, revolves around the local market. Though Korean households have refrigerators these days, the housewife (or housemaid) still shops everyday for the basic ingredients.

Tonam-dong market is typical. This market lies along both sides of a roadway which shoppers on foot share with bicycles, handcarts and an occasional motorcycle delivering goods. The shops are more like open stalls because few of them have fixed doors. In the morning, a shop-

A shop in Joongang market.

keeper pulls down his metal shutters and sets out platforms displaying his goods. Sellers of one commodity tend to cluster together, so you'll find a neat segregation of products: fruit sellers are ranged in a double row down on roadway, then all the fish dealers, all the grain stores, all the vegetable stalls, all the umbrellas, all the dresses and skirts and so on.

The Tonam-dong market also includes a large two-story building which on the first floor features open shops selling ready-to-wear clothes, household goods; accessories, cosmetics, kitchenware, plastic goods, textiles in a rainbow of colors, and a whirl of patterns. The proprietress of a textile shop is often a seamstress who, after you've picked out the material you want, will whip out her tape measure and measure you up, down and around for a set of *hanbok,* traditional Korean clothes, that will be ready in a few days. The second floor of the building, meanwhile, is quarters for the shopkeepers and their families. For the shopkeepers don't just work here in the market; they also live here with spouses and children. Preschool children scamper underfoot intent on their games in the midst of shoppers and bicycles and handcarts. And they become fascinated spectators if a shopper happens to be a foreigner strange to the neighborhood.

The local *sul-jip*: In the evening, another aspect of market life unfolds; the *sul-jip* or drinking house. A *sul-jip* should not be thought of as a bar, cocktail lounge, or beer hall, though those too certainly abound in the city. Rather, a *sul-jip* is a mini-restaurant and social hall. Indeed, a stranger could pass through the market unaware that behind a tiny sliding door is a narrow room with four small oil drum tables, a cluster of tiny stools, and space for 16 customers sitting (and up to three standing at a counter).

Here the men who live and work in the market gather for a few after-work snacks and bowls of *makkolli* rice wine. A certain amount of *makkolli*-sipping leads to loud singing (accompanied by banging metal chopsticks against the edge of a table) – and so unwinds another working day in a Seoul marketplace.

Marketplaces specialize in everything from food to clothing.

In the late fall, special neighborhood markets are set up to sell the ingredients necessary for that staple of the Korean diet, *kimch'i*. A foreigner wandering through one of these markets would be amazed at the mountains of Chinese cabbage, towering stacks of giant white radish, bins of powdered red pepper and anchovy sauce, and the fierce bargaining going on over the price of enough ingredients to make *kimch'i* to last a family through the winter.

To carry her considerable load of vegetables home, the proper Seoul housewife hires a *chige* man, a figure not yet vanished from the Seoul scene. He carries strapped to his back a *chige*, a large wooden frame in the shape of an A which is well-designed for transporting large, cumbersome loads. The housewife leads the way home, *chige* man following, and then begins the timeless Korean task of chopping her ingredients up and pickling them in brine – a process that transforms cabbage, radish, garlic and red pepper into *kimch'i*.

If you're really into fish, try the fish market in **Noryangjin**, south of the Han River. Fresh fish on ice, crabs waving their claws about, squid trying to slither away, and fat and succulent shrimp all promise gourmet experiences. But you'll have to get there in the wee morning hours before dawn if you want to compete with those who have come here to get supplies for their own fish stalls in neighborhood markets.

Any foreign visitor to Seoul should venture into a proper market, if not one of the neighborhood markets, then certainly into one or both of the great central markets downtown. Take the previous description of Tonam-dong market, multiply it by 50, and you have **Namdae-mun Sijang** (Great South Gate Market, located east of the gate itself); then take **Namdae-mun** Sijang, multiply it by another 50 and you have **Tongdae-mun Sijang** (Great East Gate Market), a large area that stretches south of Chong-no 5-ka and 6-ka.

At either place you can find almost anything you want, and, perhaps, many things you'd rather not find.

Feast your eyes on the silk market in Tongdae-mun Sijang – stall after stall of brilliantly colored silk and synthetic brocades, a truly dazzling display. The history of this market goes back to the 14th century and the roots of the Yi dynasty. In more recent years, many refugees from North Korea, escaping the communist regime, rebuilt their lives by taking work at the market. In addition to silks they sell Korean bedding, kitchenware, handicrafts and sports goods.

The most modern of the markets in Seoul is the **Yongsan Electronic Arcade** where all kinds of computers and home appliances are available. Visitors may also like to try the **Soch'o-dong Flower Market**, the **Chang-anp'yong Antique Market**, the **Hwanghak-dong Flea Market**, the **Kyong-dong Oriental Medicine Market** and the **Chungbu Dried Fish Market**.

The more adventurous need to travel a few miles south of the city to **Songnam**. There at a market, dogs, live and dead, are bought for restaurants specializing in *posin-t'ang*, a spicy dog meat soup.

Labyrinthine Arcades: Although the

Seoul station, at Namdae-mun-no.

142

markets undoubtedly contain anything you'd want to buy and would find if you searched long enough, the city offers other somewhat more convenient if less colorful shopping place: modern department stores – **Midopa** on Namdaemun-no and right next door to the **Lotte**. Just up the road is **Sinsegye** opposite the old Bank of Korea building. On Samil-lo, by **Ch'onggyech** on 2-ka, is the swish new store, **Printemps**.

There are long streets of shops underground, along **Chong-no** and **Ulchi-ro**, and smaller and more pricey arcades underneath the **Westin Chosun**, **Lotte** and **Plaza** hotels. Above ground there is the **Nagwon Arcade** at Chong-no 2-ka and a four-block arcade running north-south from Chong-no 3-ka to T'oegye-ro 3-ka.

Underground labyrinthine shopping arcades lie invisibly beneath some of the city streets: the **Sogong Arcade** runs from under the corner of the Plaza Hotel, turns left at the Chosun Hotel and continues between the Lotte and Midopa department stores to the edge of Myong-

dong; the **Hoehyon Arcade** starts in front of the **Central Post Office** and runs up to T'oegye-ro; and other mini-arcades exist where pedestrian underpasses allow room for a few stores. These arcades offer clothes, jewelry, calculators, typewriters, cameras, and souvenir items, including reproductions of antique porcelain.

"Mary's Alley": Above ground, specialized shops tend to run along together in a row – a hangover from market days, perhaps. Barbells, volleyballs and other sporting goods can be found at any one of the half dozen stores under the shadow of **Seoul Stadium** (what could be a more appropriate location?) at Ulchi-ro 7-ka; Buddhist rosaries at the shops near the entrance to Ch'ogye-sa; and puppies and brightly painted dog houses along T'oegye-ro 4-ka and 5-ka. Hub caps and car seat covers? On a street connecting Ch'ong-gyech'on 5-ka with Ulchi-ro 5-ka. Men's tailored suits? Along Namdaemun-no north of Ulchi-ro, in an area called Kwang-kyo.

And antiques? Ah, antiques.

The time-honored location for antique dealers is **Insa-dong** along a narrow street called by foreigners "**Mary's Alley**" that leads south from **An'guk-dong Rotary** to **Pagoda Park**. (Who Mary was nobody remembers now.) Some shops offering fine Koryó celadon, Silla pottery and Yi furniture are still flourishing there, but many have fled to other sections of the city, notably to **Ch'onggyech'on 8-ka**. Ch'onggyech'on is well worth a visit even by someone who isn't in the market for antiques. It's actually part of **P'yonghwa Sijang** (Peace Market), itself an extension of Tongdae-mun Sijang.

Although some of the antique stores face the street, others lurk in back alleys snuggled between tiny restaurants, junk dealers, and blaring tape and record stores. Some vendors spread their wares on blankets on the ground. It's a real bargain hunter's challenge. Who knows, the hunter may even *find* a bargain. Other favorite antique haunts are Ahyon-dong and It'aewon.

Korean Alpiners: Shopping can be a recreation, but Koreans enjoy many other forms of play, too. For instance, sports. Most Korean men and boys are sports buffs, and to further stress the point, Seoul has three sports arenas to satisfy their lust for organized athletic competitions: Seoul Stadium for baseball and soccer, **Ch'angch'ung Gymnasium** for volleyball and boxing, and the **Olympic Sports Complex** in Chamsil, south of the river. When a Korean athlete or team competes in a televised international event, traffic in the city virtually comes to a halt. People are indoors or congregated in front of a TV shop window watching – and cheering or moaning. Sports gained in popularity with the staging of the Olympics in 1988.

Age-old Korean martial arts such as *t'aekwon-do*, *hapki-do*, and *yu-do* are taught in schools and centers nationally, and these days around the world. A favorite *t'aekwon-do* viewing spot is the **Yuksamdong World T'aekwon-do Headquarters** across the Third Han River Bridge.

Korea's unofficial sport for young and

Outdoors and indoors: a baseball game at Chamsil Stadium...

old alike is hiking and trekking year-round, probably because 70 percent of the country is mountainous. In the fall, hikers wearing alpine gear can be seen lined up to board buses out of the city to assault the nearby mountain peaks on Sunday mornings. They are a strikingly colorful and eager lot decked in hiking boots, long colorful socks, sturdy pants and windbreakers, and backpacks stuffed with the makings of a cook-out lunch. A hat or cap with a jaunty feather tops off the costume. (Koreans are among the greatest hat wearers in the world. The members of almost any group out on an excursion can be readily recognized by their identical caps.)

A favorite and easy peak to scale among Seoulites is **Tobong-san**, which is just northeast of Seoul. Once on top the mountain, hikers let loose with not-so-alpine-like haloos and yahoos vaguely akin to a yodel.

Other forms of Recreation: While hiking may be the most popular outdoor recreation, tennis is not far behind. Tennis courts can be found all over the city, and Kore-ans play not just in the summer but on into the winter.

Picnicking elsewhere in the world usually involves just a leisurely meal. In Korea, however, it is a recreation especially popular during the spring and fall. Friends, fellow office workers, and family carry with them not only food and drink but also, if the picnic grounds permit, a *changgu* (an hourglass-shaped drum) to set the rhythm for singing and dancing – essential entertainment to rouse the spirit. (However, modern youths display a tendency toward guitars with portable amplifiers). Among the few picnic grounds in the city limits, those on the slopes of Nam-san and **Chong-nung Valley** in the northern part of Seoul draw the most people. It is common to see a club of middle-aged women in long flowing Korean dresses out for an afternoon. At some point, they will relax and form a circle and dance to their *changgu*, waving their arms gracefully and turning slowly and rhythmically. With their full skirts billowing, they look like pastel flowers blowing in a passing breeze.

At the end of the day, everyone wends home. Some, not yet surfeited, dance down the mountainside. The dancer could well be a grandma. Once past her 60th birthday, a woman is freed of many Confucian restraints and, at this age, she can drink and smoke in public. And dance.

Seoul After Dark: After the sun sets, Seoul's pleasure seekers have a considerable amount of entertainment at their disposal. They can go to the movies. A theater-goer can choose a locally produced feature (either a historical drama or a modern melodrama) or a subtitled American or European film (though some imported films are from Hong Kong's prolific studios). Although the censors are more lenient these days, nudity on the screen is either blurred or cut.

In addition to the many movie houses, Seoul boasts about a dozen little theater groups. Many of them rise and fall rapidly, but a few – notably the Silhom, Minye, Munyae and Space Theater troupes – have managed an existence of some years; a couple even have their own small theaters. These groups produce works by both Korean playwrights and plays in translation by such writers as diverse as Woody Allen, Neil Simon, Harold Printer, and Ionesco.

A music lover can have his fill in Seoul. Today's typical Korean likes Occidental music most whether his tastes are classical or popular. Korean preference in Western classical music tends to the tried and true – Beethoven, Brahms, Tchaikovsky – and opera. Someone once said that the country appears to be made up of thousands of aspiring Italian tenors. Truly, Koreans are often splendid musicians as the international successes of such people as concert violinists Chung Kyung-wha and Kim Young-uck or the Kim Sisters, a pop vocal group, attest. Concert goers will pay high prices to hear these artists or touring foreign performers but tend to neglect the talent of local performers – except for Korean pop singers who are popular among the young.

These artists can perform in either of two luxurious concert and theater halls: the **National Theater** on the slopes of Nam-san, the **Sejong Cultural Center** opposite the **American Embassy** on Sejong-no, or the new **Seoul Arts Center** in Socho-ku, south of the river.

The National Theater, supported by the government, is the home not only of its own drama group but also of the National Symphony, the National Ballet, the National Opera Troupe, and the National Traditional Performing Arts Troupe. The National Classical Music Institute is also located there. It offers scholarships to children through high school to study and perform traditional Korean music and dance. Foreigners also enroll here for special classes. The Institute's faculty and students perform at important ceremonies and traditional rituals. Thus, there are many stages presenting a variety of cross-cultural performances. The Sejong Center, which opened in 1978, is a true musical and architectural marvel. It even houses a 99-rank organ, the first of its kind in Korea and one of very few in Asia. The new Seoul Arts Center is a modern arts complex south of the river. Its location reflects efforts by the city authorities to move many key facilities out of the congested downtown area.

Nightlife: If the pleasure seeker is of a somewhat different stripe, he can indulge himself in other kinds of music and dance at Western-style nightclubs and discotheques. Many first-class hotels have discos but so many similar establishments have opened nearer residential areas that their popularity has declined. One exception is the Hyatt Regency Hotel's **J.J. Mahoney's** bar-and-disco complex which features a dance floor, darts, snooker, and an American jazz group. It'aewon is still the main area for night-time romping, despite the introduction of midnight closing time – the "new curfew" as some foreign residents call it.

If the pleasure seeker is a tippler (some do say the national sport is not hiking but drinking), where he goes to tipple depends on his pocketbook. Most will choose the *sul-jip* where life is convivial and the drink cheap. More expensive is the beer hall where a demure hostess may, or may not, sit down with him and his friends to pour the beer, light cigarettes, and engage in *repartee*. In a cabaret (a beer hall with a live band), a hostess is available for a fee and will do all of the above plus dance with the customer.

If our night wanderer is especially well-heeled, he may, with a group of friends or, more likely, a group of business acquaintances, seek out a *kisaeng* house. These luxurious establishments, the equivalent of Japan's geisha houses, are located mostly in side streets or suburbs. Here, too, female companionship comes with the fee, which will of course be exorbitant, but the food, decor and costuming – though not always the entertainment – tend to be authentically traditional. The girls in a *kisaeng* house these days are seldom the highly cultivated *artistes* of the old days, but they have developed comparable skills in helping the tired businessman relax.

A step between the *kisaeng* house and the cabaret is a kind of small, discreet place you wouldn't know was there unless you already know. Inside are rooms furnished with chairs and sofas and large central coffee tables to hold bottles and glasses and plates of *anju*. Again the female companions come with the fee, but the dress and drink (Scotch, usually) and decor are Western – perhaps an adaptation of the old to modern times.

Until recently the truly determined drinker was able to find one last watering-hole on the way home: the *pojangmacha*, a mobile tent lit by a carbide lamp or kerosene taper, offering cheap drinks and *anju* of clams, eels, homemade sausage, or, in winter, whole broiled sparrows. With government restrictions of street traders, however, these one-man mobile pubs have been banished from most downtown alleyways, but some can still be sighted near suburban subway stops. These cozy tents appear like magic only late at night and, a few minutes before dawn, fold up and trundle away.

After-work Soap Operas: Of course, the city male may not be a pleasure seeker at all. He may merely go home right after work, though going home right after work is not the common practice for the male office worker or businessman. (One could suspect that if he is home early it's because he's broke and all his friends are

broke, too.) But if he does go straight home, he and his wife and his children probably settle in front of the TV set to choose from among four channels – five, if anyone wants to practice English by watching the American military station, AFKN-TV.

Korean programs include sports, game shows, variety shows (Korean comedians are among the world's best at slapstick), historical drama and tear-jerker "home dramas" – the equivalent of the West's soap opera adapted to modern Korean family life. It's possible, say some foreign residents, to get quite caught up in the ups and downs of the Kim family as it struggles with the problems generated by all the personalities in a large extended family: grandpa, grandma, married son who's failing in business, his long-suffering wife (no children yet), their married daughter and ne'er-do-well husband (at least one cute grandson, though), a rebellious unmarried son in college (he's in love with an unsuitable girl), a pert unmarried daughter in high school (she had better not be in love with anybody), and the nosy neighbors and poor relations from the country who have come to visit for a month or so.

The New Seoul: Since the Olympic "clean-up" of street traders, deemed by the city fathers to be unsightly and unhygienic, Seoul's pavements have certainly been easier to negotiate, but the city has lost some of its spontaneous charm. Amid the rising forests of multi-story apartment complexes south of the river, you can find, lit at night by carbide flames, the ubiquitous handcarts loaded with tangerines and chewing gum, dried cuttlefish and peanuts. And even here the *yont'an* man pulls his cartload of coal briquettes through the streets to deliver a family's household heating fuel supply.

Yont'an is a major item in any household; it's the main fuel for heating the *ondul* lacquer floor with flumes underneath it and it used to be the source of heat for cooking (new Seoul apartments use liquid propane gas). Even off duty, the *yont'an* man's occupation is clearly visible: black dust clings to his hands and swipes across his face.

Below left, Seoul Tower. Below right, modern buildings abound in Seoul.

In contrast to the older residential sections of Seoul on the north side of the river, the old neighborhoods of diverging alleyways, the southern section of the city, spreading out from the foot of bridges newly constructed across the Han, are carefully grid-ironed, their streets ruled into right angles. Here dwellers buy everyday necessities in "proper" stores – modern supermarkets where onions come prepackaged in plastic bags. To some, the beige and gray complexes (**Chamsil, Hyondae, Yongdong, Yoido**) lack in color and charm; yet, even they offer a kind of beauty, a beauty revealed at night by a drive east along the north bank of the Han River from the First Bridge. Across the black water, these facades of tall apartment buildings make a wall of patterned light that shimmers in the reflecting river. The bridges become ribbons of light flung across the water as streamers of automobile headlights mark the passage of traffic between the old center of the city and its new southern sector.

Kids find balconies and stairwells the best part of modern apartments.

City Streets: Many of those automobiles are driven by that exemplar of the city: the taxi driver. One rapidly develops ambivalent feelings toward taxi drivers. Frustration and hostility are easily aroused when a taxi driver won't pick you up or take you where you want to go, especially if it's rush hour.

But if you're a foreign passenger and you speak a little Korean or the driver speaks a little English, watch out. You're in for a torrent of questions about your place of origin, how long you've been in Korea, your age, your marital status, what you do for a living, when you plan to leave the country. One young American woman, married for six years and childless, has been told by no fewer than five taxi drivers that it's time she had a baby!

Sometimes all a foreigner has to do is get in a cab, answer the question, "*Odiekaseyo?*" ("Where are you going?") with a three-syllable response, "*Hannam-dong*," and then told, "*Han'guk-mal-ul chal hasimnida!*" ("You speak Korean very well!") – an opinion delivered in tones of pleased surprise. Then he's deluged with questions and comments in Korean that he

can't understand. The attitude of the driver who finally realizes that his passenger knows no more than those three syllables is very likely to be one of injured disappointment.

Another feature on the city streets is a fleet of butterscotch-colored "call" taxis which one can phone for service. The fare is higher than that of the ordinary taxi, but call taxis are air-conditioned.

An increase in the number of automobiles, especially private sedans, in the city has been far too rapid during recent years for the streets to accommodate them, and this press of vehicles creates traffic jams most foreigners groan about. Like, most large cities, Seoul is congested. Traffic snarls at the slightest excuse – such as an eighth of an inch of rain. And snow. The Korean driver is much maligned and, indeed, Korea reports one of the highest accident injury and death rates in the world, but it is possible to learn to cope with the traffic – whether as a driver or as a pedestrian. Just watch everything all the time.

Streets Abloom on Holidays: Among the people passing on the street, men will usually be dressed in western clothes; so will most of the women. Only a few wear Korean dress except on traditional holidays (Ch'usok – the Autumn Moon Festival – and Lunar New Year's holiday) when the streets seem to bloom with the sheen of silky reds, greens, yellows, blues, pinks and purples. Modern Koreans, especially the women, are highly style-conscious and tend to dress carefully and well, even for casual outings. Acceptable dress standards, however, remain conservative – no shorts (except on workmen and children) or backless dresses on the summer sidewalks.

A stroller around Seoul is sure to be detoured by some busy construction project: a mammoth office building or hotel, repairs to the street or to the flagstone sidewalk, excavations for new underground shopping centers, walkovers, underpasses or elevated highways. The city changes shape rapidly around the old palaces and gates.

Tabang Society: Congestion is a problem even indoors. Try sitting in a *tabang*, (tearoom), for instance. Although there are literally thousands of *tabang* of various sizes in the city, finding a seat in a popular one will be the first hurdle.

Tabang, where more coffee than tea is served, are popular for their convenience as meeting places. Here friends meet friends to spend an hour or so in talk or as a preliminary to going somewhere else, business associates meet to negotiate a deal, prospective bride-and-groom couples meet under the eye of their family and friends. Each *tabang* tends to specialize in a certain clientele – university students gravitate toward some, businessmen to others – largely in response to the kind of music the tearoom offers. A disc jockey in a glassed-in-booth, often labeled the "Music Box," will play customers' requests through a typically excellent stereo loudspeaker system. The mix of loud conversation and loud music can be cacophonous.

The central government, responding to complaints about overcrowding, noise and pollution, is pushing for decentralization, ordering the universities to find themselves new campuses south of the river, flinging new bridges across the Han at almost every bend. It has even moved itself out of the city to a certain extent – the ministries of justice, science and several others have relocated to areas outside of Seoul.

All the complaints about the city are well-taken, yet . . . Yet it is alive, it is invigorating, it is exuberant. There's an almost palpable air of well-being, expanding prosperity, swelling confidence. You can feel it in the pace of the city. Koreans seldom take strolls in the city streets; their steps are brisk and purposeful – thus the bumping and jostling. When a signal light turns from red to green, the driver in the car behind you impatiently honks his horn. He wants to move *now*! Lights burn late in office buildings; businessmen work 10- or 11-hour days then jet off to Tokyo, New York, or Abu Dhabi. Even Seoul's little children – beneficiaries of growing affluence – have little idle time; they literally swarm through the streets after school on their way to music, painting or swimming lessons.

Seoul, the city, is vibrantly alive.

Going fishing: Han River shore, Seoul City.

150

SEOUL AREA DAYTRIPS

Beyond Seoul's secure city walls there are numerous day outings one can go on to get away from the hustle and bustle of urban life. Stroll down to any bus, subway or train terminal, set off in virtually any direction from Seoul, and you'll be amazed at the classical intrigues which await you only minutes outside this sprawling city.

Ancient castles, artworks, massive mounded tombs, hot springs, charming pine glens, moon-watching pavilions, strawberry fields, pottery villages, and even a lion and flamingo park "for the kids" pop up like apparitions at improbable bends in a country road. Do as Koreans do: simply follow a travel instinct until it leads you to a stream filled with plum blossoms, or a meadow bursting with pink cosmos blossoms and singing grandmothers. The following Seoul trips are but a few fun and educational excursions recommended as worth your time, energy and enjoyment.

Historic Battlements: Namhansansong, the **South Han Mountain Fortress**, is a popular weekend hiking area about 18 miles (30 kilometers) southeast of Seoul proper. This grand highland redoubt – with 5 miles (8 kilometers) of stone walls, some of them 4 miles (7 kilometers) high in places – was originally built about 2,000 years ago during Korea's Paekche dynasty. Most of the fort's now visible structures, however, date to the 17th and 18th centuries, when the fortress served Yi kings of that period as a retreat from invading Chinese armies. In 1637, Namhansonsong was the site, following a six-week-long siege, where King Injo, the 16th Yi monarch, surrendered himself, some 14,000 of his men, and in the end, Korea, to a huge Manchu invasion force.

This spectacular place is located just east of **Songnam**, and may be reached via National route 3 (enroute to Kwangju), or through Songnam off the Seoul-Pusan Expressway.

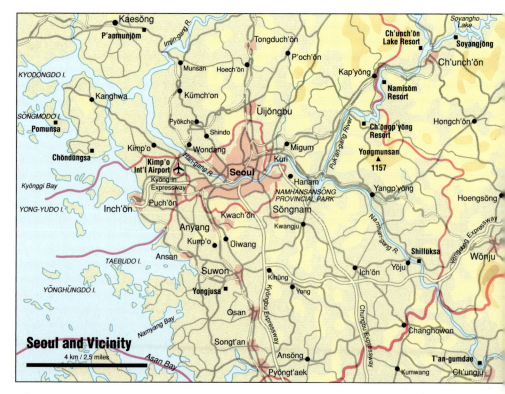

Seoul and Vicinity
4 km / 2.5 miles

Pukhansansong, the **North Han Mountain Fortress** and Namhansansong, are the two major ancient fortresses in the Seoul area. This one, similar in design and setting to Namhansansong, is located above the sprawling northeast suburbs of Seoul along the high ridges of **Pukhan Mountain**.

Pukhansansong was first built during the early Paekche period and at various times fell into martial disuse. Following severe attacks during the 16th century by armies of Ch'ing China, the Yi King Sukchong refurbished its battlements. These same walls were partially destroyed during the Korean War, but have since been restored to honor their historic importance. A neat village has bloomed alongside a stream in the crater-like center of the fortress, and meadows and small forests on its less-populated fringes are favored picnic sites. On the road back to Seoul, if you take the northern access highway, look carefully to your left and right. You may see shamanistic spirit posts (a rarity these days) peeking out at you through the brush and pines.

Rolling Dice, Tomb-Hopping: Thousands of miles away from country idylls, but nevertheless a lovely spot from which to view Seoul over a proper martini, is the well-known **Walker Hill Resort** complex. This nightlife area of Las Vegas-style revues, gambling (in the **Sheraton Walker Hill Casino**), and resort amenities is located above Seoul's eastern suburbs and overlooks a picturesque bend in the Han River. From Walker Hill's glittering lounges and gardens, you can see Seoul's city lights twinkling in the urban west. Walker Hill was named after Gen. Walton H. Walker, former Commanding General of the U.S. Eighth Army, who was killed in a traffic mishap during the Korean War.

Kwangnung: The impressive Confucian-style burial tombs of King Sejo (1456-1468), the 7th Yi king, and his wife, Queen Yun Chon-hi, are probably the most aesthetically and idyllically located tombs in the Seoul area. These monumental mounds are located about 17 miles (28 kilometers) northeast of Seoul and just past Uijongbu (a town and military

camp made famous in the American movie and television serial *MASH)*. The tombs are hidden in the thick of a forest of old trees which shade trickling streams and wide greens ideal for a picnic.

Honnung and Honinnung: These tombs of the 3rd and 24th Yi kings lie in the southeast skirts of Seoul in Naekok-dong and near a green belt area where melons, strawberries, eggplant, peppers, corn and rice are cultivated. In late spring, summer and autumn, shady fruit stands are set up in fields so people can sit and enjoy refreshing breezes, sunshine and fresh-from-the-earth fruit before hiking up to the nearby Honnung, the tombs of King T'aejong (1367-1422) and Queen Wonkyong (1364-1420), and Innung, the tombs of King Sunjo (1790-1834) and Queen Sunwon (1789-1837). All the tombs are guarded by granite statues and by fantastic animal sentries. If you are in Korea on 8 May, you may want to attend a *chesa* (ancestor worship) ceremony conducted annually at Honnung by Yi dynasty descendants.

The grounds at Honinnung are well-manicured, and the area's classical tomb settings make this a popular area for the filming of historical movies.

An African safari, American zoo, and Korean amusement park come improbably together at **Yong-in Farmland**, a recreation complex on the north side of National Highway 4 (enroute to Kwang-nung) about 21 miles (34 kilometers) southeast of Seoul. Behind a 1,634-acre (661-hectare) curtain of pine, chestnut, walnut, paulownia and other hardy trees, you can find some excitement in the Korean-style lion safari; a 163-acre (66-hectare) nursery with 1,200 kinds of rare plants; a 41-acre (17-hectare) tree park of apples, plums, pears, peaches, grapes and 14 other fruits; and the advertised "fancy performances of wild pigs and flamingoes." If that range of rural fantasies doesn't suit you, try the 1,000-meter jet coaster ride, a fishing pond, and other such thrills.

Shopping for Pots: The soulful pottery kilns of two of Korea's finest potters are about 43 miles (70 kilometers) south of Seoul near **Ich'on** (also just north of National Highway 4). In **Sukwang-ni**,

Sindung-myon, 2½ miles (4 kilometers) north of Ich'on proper, you can observe Koryo celadons being created by ceramics master **Yu Kun-hung**, or you can marvel at **Ahn Dong-o**'s Yi dynasty whiteware as they're pulled hot from his traditional kilns. These gentlemen's fine work can be purchased on the spot or in prominent ceramic art galleries in Seoul. At the other end of the potting spectrum, you will find, here and there in the great Ich'on area, row upon row of the ubiquitous shiny, brown, tall and oblong *kimch'i* pots. These utilitarian wares are hand-thrown and fired in adobe huts.

If after visiting all the above and pent up energy has you wanting to climb up mountains, consider scaling **Tobong-san**, a pleasant peak just 3½ miles (5½ kilometers) north of Seoul. The hike to this summit takes an hour or longer, depending on your serendipitous pace. You may want to linger enroute next to a clear stream or pool, or, if you're a camera buff, photograph the odd rock formations up there. Or – if Buddhist spirits move you – you may wish to trek along one of several diverting paths in and around Tobong-san to the temples of **Mangwol**, **Chonjuk**, and **Hweryong.**

The Yangju *Pyol Sandae* masked dance-drama is performed in this small village just north of Uijongbu. Traditional performance times are during *Tano* (a spring festival held during the 5th lunar month), and sometimes for the conve-nience of visiting cultural groups. This particular folk drama originated in Kyonggi Province. According to Yangju villagers, about 200 years ago, a troupe from Seoul was invited to perform in Yangju, but broke their engagements several times to perform elsewhere. Instead of enduring more cultural disappointments, the villagers decided to produce their own show and patterned it after the Seoul masked dance-drama. Since then, Yangju's versions have become extremely popular, and now people from Seoul travel to this village to enjoy its semi-annual performances.

Such *Sandae* plays originally were performed only for Yi dynasty royalty. But about 1634, during the reign of Yi King Injo, this masked dance-drama was discontinued in the court and became entertainment for commoners. To this effect, the entertainment draws heavily from the villagers' perspective of life.

The performance begins with a parade around the village by the various characters dressed in full costume and mask (made of paper or gourd). It's a rather colorful and surreal sight to see a monk, a lotus leaf "spirit of heaven," a winking spirit of earth, an acupuncturist, a shaman witch, an aristocrat's concubine, a monkey, police inspector, and 14 other characters (who play some 32 roles using 22 masks) parading past the turkey coops and vegetable gardens in this rural town.

A sacrifice to the spirits is conducted shortly after the parade ends at the dance site. Offerings of wine, fruits of three colors, rice cakes (*ttok*), pig's legs, and an ox head are presented and then eaten by the performers – to set them in the right, jolly mood. Then the day's play begins in an open-air, grassy area beneath a mountain north of the village. It lasts for several hours. The play satirizes an apostate monk, the *yangban* (aristocrats), corrupt government officials, and other lofty and fallen people while weaving in contemporary editorial comments. This performance has become a type of "gridiron" show in which persons and institutions worthy of skewering and grilling are roasted with satire that often evokes howls of laughter. There is also audience participation. Metal bowls of *makkolli* rice wine and *ttok* rice cakes are passed around in the audience (which sits in a broad circle around the performers), and when the various characters say something the audience agrees with, the audience calls out, "*Olch'i, chalhamnida!*" (or "That's right. Well said!") It is advisable to attend these masked dance-dramas with a Korean friend who can translate the jokes for you.

A morning excursion 28 miles (45 kilometers) south of Seoul to the **Korean Folk Village** near Suwon will give you a full day to tour the 240 homes, shops and other attractions in this authentically rendered Yi-dynasty village. Visit ceramic and bamboo shops, drink rice wines in a wayside tavern, then join the staged wed-

itsch
endor,
ijongbu.

ding procession of a traditionally costumed (and transported via palanquin) bride and groom who are trailed by a colorful, whirling farmers' dance band. Even in a day you may not be able to view all the fascinating exhibits in this sprawling museum. The privately funded folk village is open 10 a.m. to 5 p.m. daily.

If you have time to spare, consider one of the following day trips which involve longer distances and time, but which provide experiences equal to the effort.

The "Flower Fortress": Suwon, the capital of **Kyonggi Province**, is an old fortress-city 31 miles (51 kilometers) south of Seoul in the vicinity of **Mt. Paltal**. Suwon's name, which means "water-source" or "water-field," derives from its location in an area which was traditionally known for its fine artesian wells.

These days, Suwon is renowned for its recently restored castle walls and support structures, and – in a tastier realm – for its luscious strawberries (called *ttalgi* in Korean). The city is also famous for its *kalbi*, or barbequed short ribs, but it's the late spring through summer strawberries that come to most Korean minds when you mention the word Suwon.

The city can be quickly and easily reached by regular buses from the Soch'o Nambu Terminal in Soch'o-dong.

The first thing you'll notice about the city are its massive fortress walls, gates, and other historic architectural facilities which meander for 6,040 yards (5,520 meters) around the old city proper. Construction of these structures began during the reign of King Chongjo (1794-1796), the 22nd Yi monarch, who established the Suwon fortress in memory of his father, the Yi Crown Prince Changjo.

Prince Changjo had been the innocent victim of a mid-18th century court conspiracy in which his father, a senile, disillusioned king, unjustly condemned him to be locked in a rice box until death. Years later, this king died and his grandson, Chongjo, proceeded to prove his father's innocence and to honor his memory with the building of Suwon fortress.

Chongjo wanted to move the Korean capital from Seoul to this new Suwon site, but because of various personal and

Stylized "spirit post" guardian, Korean Folk Village.

156

political problems, he was never able to accomplish that kingly feat.

Chongjo created a beautiful fortified city here – complete with proper parapets and embrasures, floodgates, observation platforms and domes, parade grounds, command bunkers, cannon stands and an archery range. Chongjo's original fortress, known as the "Flower Fortress," was heavily damaged by the weather and by bombing during the Korean War, but in 1975 the Korean government undertook a major restoration of his dream city. The project took four years and cost several millions of dollars.

These impressive refurbished walls and other structures still look a tad too new, but even so they are a fascinating redoubt and an invitation to a city stroll. One particularly lovely spot near the North Gate, Changan-mun, is a strikingly landscaped reflecting pond, **Yong-yon**, which sits below an octagonal moon-watching pavilion called **Panghwasuryu-jong**.

This meditative spot was ordered to be created by the aesthetically inclined King Chongjo when he initiated his Suwon fortress-city master plan in 1794. These days it's a gem of a place much-favored by neighborhood *haraboji* (grandfathers), who sit inside its gabled cupola lighting long-stemmed pipes, drinking sweet rice wine, and bouncing patriarchal thoughts off nearby castle walls. The whole classical effect is officially labeled "The Northern Turret."

If, after a hike around the "Flower Fortress," it's fresh strawberries and cooling wine you crave, take a bus or taxi to the popular **Agricultural Green Belt area** in Suwon's west suburbs near the modern **Agricultural College of Seoul National University**. There you can eat baskets-ful of blood-red and juicy sweet strawberries – and grapes during the summer and fall – at umbrellaed tables next to the patches and vineyards from whence they came, before visiting one of the other Suwon area sites.

Yongju-sa, a Buddhist temple which, like the Suwon fortress, was also built by King Chongjo in his father's memory. Yongju-sa, "The Dragon Jewel," rests in a rural, piney area about a 20-minute bus

Suwon's southside city gate.

ride south of Suwon's mid-town South Gate. Built in 1790 on the site of an earlier Silla dynasty temple (dating from 854), Yongju-sa's grounds boast, among other attractions, a seven-story stone pagoda, a 3,300-lb (1,500-kilogram) Koryo-era brass bell, and in its main hall, a superb Buddhist painting by the Yi genre painting master Danwon Kim Hong-do.

Yongju-sa is a popular place to visit at the time of Buddha's birthday (celebrated on the 8th day of the 4th lunar month, usually in late April), when pilgrims from afar arrive here bearing candle-lit paper lanterns and prayers for good fortune.

Just west of the temple, in a properly serene setting, are the mounded tombs of King Chongjo and his beloved father the Crown Prince Changjo (Sado Seja, the "Ricebox Prince"). Chongjo posthumously awarded his father the title "King Changjo," and according to his wishes, he is laid to rest here forever with him.

Sogni-san National Park, a mountain retreat in North Ch'ungch'ong Province, is superb any time of the year, but is most favored by discriminating Korean week-enders in the autumn when its trees are aflame with color. Oaks, maples and gingkos try to outdo each other in their autumnal radiance. As one romantic Korean travel writer once wrote of Sognisan: "The tender green for spring, abundance of forests for summer, yellow leaves for autumn, and snow for winter – all deserve appreciation."

Indeed, since ancient times Sogni has been a preferred resort area, and appropriately, the word "Sogni" means "escape from the vulgar." To achieve this Sogni escape, travel from Seoul to **Taechon City** by train, then transfer by bus or car through **Okch'on** to the Sogni area. Alternatively, you can also motor directly by car or bus from Seoul via Ch'ongju City. It's about a three-hour motorcar journey one-way.

After passing through Ch'ongju City and beginning an ascent to idyllic Sogni, you will enter the steep **Malti Pass** which serves as an unwinding transition from urbanity to nature at its crispiest.

Just beyond a glassy reservoir, on your final approach to the Sogni highlands and Sogni village, your local guide will no **Yongju-sa.**

doubt point out the most distinguished tree in Korea. This is an old pine on the left side of the road called the **Chong-ip'um Pine**, so named because the Yi King Sejo (1456-1468) granted this hoary fellow the official bureaucratic title of Chong-ip'um, a rank equivalent to that of a cabinet minister.

Legend and history note that this humble tree was granted that distinction because it lifted its boughs in respect one day as King Sejo and a royal entourage passed by. The pine's politeness was duly rewarded by the flattered king.

Just beyond this ministerial pine is the final approach to **Sogni-dong**, a mountain village famous for the semi-wild tree mushrooms cultivated in this area and sold in roadside stands. Seoulites who know try to arrive in Sogni village at lunchtime, when they can enjoy a fabled Sogni mushroom lunch. Such a lunch can feature as many as six completely different mushroom dishes served with a dizzying array of side dishes, *kimch'i* and rice. Be sure to buy a bag of these tender air-dried morsels for later munching at home.

"The Biggest Buddha": Following this mushroom overdose, proceed uphill to Sogni-san's biggest attraction, **Popju-sa**, a large temple complex dominated by a massive **Miruk Buddha of the Future** fashioned of modern poured cement. This 88-foot (27-meter) image, completed in 1964, is often identified by tour guides as "the biggest Buddha in Korea."

This sprawling temple complex was first built at the base of Mt. Sogni in the 6th century, shortly after Buddhism had been carried into Korea from China. Records note that work began in 553 during the 14th year in the reign of the Silla king Chinhung. The original founder and spiritual master was the high priest Uisang, who had returned home from studies in India. Uisang contributed several Buddhist scriptural books to Popju-sa's first library.

Author-historian Han Ki-hyung, a former assistant editor of the *Korea Journal*, writes that this temple, "one of Korea's oldest," was reportedly "renovated during the reigns of Kings Songdok and Hyegong (702-780)." This can be

Monk farmers of Popju-sa.

confirmed by observing the stone buildings of the temple surviving to date.

"The temple was protected," Han says, "by the monarchs of not only the Silla dynasty but also the Koryo and Yi dynasties. In the 6th year (1101) of King Sukjong's reign (in the Koryo era), the king gathered 30,000 priests from all over the country to pray for the health of ailing Royal Priest Uich'on. In the Yi era, King Sejo (1456-1468) presented the temple with large tracts of paddy fields, grains and slaves, and Kings Injo (1623-1649), Ch'oljong (1849-1863) and Kojong (1864-1906) had the temple renovated."

Remnants of this favored temple's days of spiritual grandeur can be found on all parts of the compound. Consider for practical openers the famed **Ch'olhwak**, a massive iron rice pot which was cast in 720, during the reign of Silla King Songdong, when some 3,000 priests were living – and eating – here. This grand mass facility is 4 feet (1.2 meters) high, 9 feet (2.7 meters) in diameter, and 35 feet (10.8 meters) in circumference. These days you'll find perhaps only two per cent of that number of gray-robed, sutra-chanting monks, so the pot's utilitarian purpose is no more.

Perhaps the most celebrated historical treasure at Popju-sa is the five-story **P'alsang-jon**, or **Eight Image Hall**, which rises in symmetrical splendor above the complex's roomy main courtyard. As Han notes: "This five-story building, presumably reconstructed during the second year of King Injo's reign (1624) in the Yi era, is a rare architectural work for Buddhism not only in Korea but also in China, and can be compared with a similar five-story pagoda at Nara, Japan."

Other Popju-sa curiosities include a large *deva* lantern surrounded with relief *bodhisattvas*, a second stone lantern supported by two carved lions, and, outside the temple, a large "ablution trough" carved in the shape of a lotus. To the left side of the main entrance you'll also find a huge boulder that has come to life with a serene Buddha sculpted into a wide and flat facade.

Popju-sa and her concrete Buddha.

If such art boggles your mind, head for the surrounding hills which are laced with excellent hiking trails. A view of the Popju-sa complex from one of Sognisan's upper ridges is just reward for any huffing and puffing it takes to get up there.

Plum Blossoms in the Snow: Cornelius Choy, who for several years conducted countryside tours for the Royal Asiatic Society before leaving Korea in the mid-1980s, would always tell visitors and Seoulites alike they should spend at least one late winter day in the area north of Seoul which he dubbed the "Realm of the Immortals." His advice still stands.

If possible, you should try to go when plum blossoms – the year's first flowers – begin to bloom in forests and ravines that are still dusty with snow. Or as the ancients advise: "Do as amused immortals do: Whenever the boredom and frustration of a long winter indoors becomes too much for them, they put on their cape and hat, tell the attendant to saddle the donkey, and go out in the snow looking for plum blossoms."

This journey through a painted screen will take you on Highway 43 north of Seoul between two popular hiking mountains: **Tobong-san** and **Suraksan.** Tobong-san, the rocky, harsh-looking mountain on the west side of the road, is said to represent the male gender, while the curved and flowing Suraksan on the east side is supposed to personify female qualities. Beyond this broad pass, your vehicle will take you through **Uijongbu**, the "City of Ever Righteousness."

Further north, the terrain becomes yawning canyons and ravines. Beyond **Tong-du-ch'on**, turn at the highway into the **Soyo Mountains** and make the short hike to **Chachae-am temple**, a place famed as the testing ground for a monk's celibacy. Ornately carved dragons – snarling out from each corner of this quaint temple's eaves – may seduce you inside, where you'll find a pair of tempestuous carved dragons writhing on the ceiling. A spouting waterfall and narrow gorge with a stream complement this little canyon.

An even more exciting waterfalls and river scene is located much further north in the **Sinch'olwon** area. (Because there are several military checkpoints in this area close to the 38th parallel, it is advisable that foreign visitors join the Royal Asiatic Society's tour where possible.) A massive granite boulder, **Kosok**, nicknamed "**The Lonely Rock**," sits in the **Imjin River** and invites clambering up to its pine-studded brow. Legend says that this rock rolled in from the East Coast and decided to rest at this lovely turn in the fast-flowing river. A pleasure pavilion overlooks the rock and the river's noisy rapids, and local boatmen may be hired for a ride through the narrow river canyons which jut to the north.

A Feisty Carp: Due south of this "Lonely Rock" – in a deep canyon and off a steep dirt road – is the little known **Sambuyon** or "**Dragon Waterfall**." You'll see local villagers fishing for carp in pools above the falls. This is an appropriate pastime, because in these parts – and in oriental mythology – the carp and dragon are distant and legendary relatives.

The carp is regarded by Koreans as a symbol of strength and perseverance, and one famous story in national lore is about a carp who persistently tried to climb up this strong waterfall. On the 100th day of his attempt, this feisty carp succeeded (with the help of the gods) to scale Sambuyon and as a reward he was magically turned into a powerful dragon. These falls, however, are rather easy to climb (a well-trodden path runs through a stone tunnel to the right side of the falls). And, of course, you don't have to worry about being turned into a dragon once you get to the top.

On your return journey to Seoul, you may want to picnic and recuperate at **Sanjong Lake**, an artificial lake resort built by Japanese engineers during Japan's colonial occupation of Korea. The lake is a popular skating spot in wintertime, and for most part of the year, it's a splendid area for hiking and relaxation. Look out for the large colorful tents which serve as dance halls, and while hiking round this picture-perfect reservoir, don't hesitate to sip wine or sample the many tasty goods being sold by lakeside vendors.

INCH'ON, PORT-OF-ENTRY

Inch'on – which until the 1880s was a fishing village called Chemulp'o – was for a long time the only Korean place foreigners were allowed to visit. Today, it is a booming harbor and Korea's fourth largest city. The number of trading ships calling at Inch'on has increased with every passing year, and consequently the 24-mile (39-kilometer) stretch between Seoul proper and the Port of Inch'on has become the most important sea, road and rail supply route in Korea.

In the current century, Inch'on has become most well-known as the place where Gen. Douglas MacArthur, Commander of U.S. Pacific Forces, directed a brilliant amphibious landing which turned the bitter Korean War around for southern Korea and its allies. That landing, code-named Operation CHROMITE, began at dawn on 15 September 1950. Historian David Rees writes in his important book *Korea: The Limited War* that "the successive objectives of the operation called for the neutralization of Wolmi-do, the island controlling Inch'on harbor, a landing in the city, seizure of Kimpo Airfield, and the capture of Seoul." Despite fierce objections from his subordinates, MacArthur's strategy proved to have that winning element of surprise.

On D-Day, the 5th Marines poured ashore at Inch'on, as Rees writes, "to meet only scattered shots. The flag was raised on Radio Hill, dominating Inch'on harbor, at 0655, and the whole of this 114-yard (105-meter) high feature which had caused the planners so much worry was taken by 0800." U.S. Marines began a bloody advance towards Seoul and, after 12 more days of hellish fighting, took that devastated capital. Today, Radio Hill is known as **Freedom Hill** and looms over an earnest seaport abustle with international trade. Atop the hill, jaunty in sculpted khakis, is a 32-foot (10-meter) high statue of Gen. MacArthur, gripping a pair of binoculars in his right hand.

The fastest and easiest way to get to

Never a dull moment for the local dock workers...

Freedom Hill is to take the Seoul Subway train due west through industrial suburbs and rice fields that sprawl alternately between Seoul and the setting sun. Once you arrive at Inch'on-dong station, take a cab or hike up to Freedom Hill above this town of steep streets and endless ocean terminals. The ocean view from up there is overtly industrial, but sea breezes are crisp, and besides the MacArthur statue, you'll find a whitewashed replica of America's Statue of Liberty and a pavilion from where you can sometimes see a spectacular red fireball sun dropping through container cranes and ships' riggings into an amber ocean. The walk down from Freedom Hill through old Inch'on is a pleasant one down cobble- and flag-stoned byways and stairs past some of Korea's most distinctive veran-dahs and storefronts.

There are three deluxe-priced hotels in Inch'on, the **Olympos**, the **Songdo Beach** and the **New Star** hotels. However, if your budget leans toward a more Korean expe-rience, there are several *yogwan* (inns) among the hills and dales of Inch'on.

Popular nearby diversions include sea-food dining on one of the area's land-linked islands, either **Wolmi-do** (Moon Tail Island) or **Sowolmi-do**. Both sides are famous for their gourmet plates of raw fish and other delicacies from the deep. During the summer, various off-shore islands become favored Korean resort destinations. On these islands, you can tan on the white-sand beaches or wallow in lovely man-made lagoons rimmed by colorful cabanas and bathing beauties. There are several smaller resort hotels in this area, particularly near big **Songdo Beach** south of the city.

You'll also enjoy visiting the big pub-lic seafood market on the southern side of Inch'on's tidal basin. Ask for the *Yonan Pudu O-sijang* (fish market) and any *ajumoni* (housewife) will direct you to this massive covered market next to a small sheltered harbor full of fishing trawlers. Inside three huge huts and under dangling lightbulbs you'll find all sorts of sealife. A local bus service operates from downtown Inch'on near the Olympos Hotel to this marketplace.

.and the shermen Inch'on.

KANGHWA-DO, ISLE OF REFUGE

Mysterious prehistoric men left strange, unexplainable sculpture here. Tan'gun, the founding father of Korea, built an altar on this island's highest peak. The *Tripitaka Koreana* Buddhist sculptures were carved at a temple here. And Koryo and Yi dynasty kings sought refuge on this island from invading Mongol and Manchu armies.

This historic place is **Kanghwa-do**, an island 31 miles (50 kilometers) northwest of Seoul and across the narrow **Yomha Strait**. To visit the rural island, catch an express bus at Seoul's Sinch'on Rotary, and in about 90 minutes you'll be mingling with Kanghwa town's market folk.

Kanghwa town proper is small and easygoing – just the right size for pedestrian tourists who putter around marketplaces and in handicraft shops. Korea's finest rushcraft weaving is meticulously done on Kanghwa-do, so in local shops you'll find numerous baskets, woven into fun shapes, colors and sizes. You'll also discover fine floor mats and doorway hangings which are woven so tightly they let summer breezes in while filtering out pesky warm-weather mosquitos.

Another kind of weaving – silkweaving – is also done in this town. And to that effect you'll hear the sound of machines clacking out reams of silk as you walk along Kanghwa's streets and footpaths.

Take a car ride to the **silk factory** (off the main street on the road opposite the bridge fronting the marketplace). Since visitors aren't allowed inside for tours anymore, take a long look instead at a **bronze bell** hanging idly inside a small slatted pavilion next to the factory. Cast during King Sukchong's reign (1674-1720), this bell used to toll at 4 a.m. to signal the opening of Kanghwa's city gates. When French troops stormed the city in 1866 to seek revenge for the execution of several French Roman Catholic priests, they attempted to haul this 8,520-lb (3,864-kilogram) bell to their ship, but it was so heavy that they gave up the idea.

At the top of this same road is the restored **Koryo palace** where King Kojong lived in retreat during his unsuccessful 39-year-long resistance against invading Mongol hordes during the middle of the 13th century.

From the Koryo palace, catch a taxi up to the neatly restored North Gate, **Pungmun**, for a view of the distant blue mountains of north Korea. On a clear day you can see for several miles across the **Han-Imjin Estuary** and into the forbidden and Communist north.

On the way back to town, ask your driver to stop along the road and send you down a narrow footpath which leads to Korea's oldest and most unique Episcopal Church, **Kam Tok Kyohwe**. This Christian structure, built in 1900 by Bishop Charles Corté about 10 years after his arrival in Korea, harmoniously combines Christian, Taoist and Buddhist elements in its overall design. The front gate of the church is decorated with a large paisleyed Taoist symbol; the church, constructed of wood, is classically Korean in its interior and exterior architecture; a bodhi tree, an old Buddhism-related symbol, was planted in the church's main courtyard at the time of the church's dedication; and atop the roof is a Christian cross trimmed with flourescent light bulbs which show the way at night.

A Prehistoric Dolmen: After seeing this eclectic site, catch a bus at the main terminal and head northwest of Kanghwa town to one of the most mysterious sculptures in Korea. The scenery along this roadway is dominated mostly by fields of ginseng protected by low thatched lean-tos, and typical Kanghwa farmhouses and silos decorated with contemporary folk art. This "art" is in the form of meticulous sheet-metal sculpture attached at the upturns of eaves and along corrugated metal rooflines. Here and there you will see brilliantly painted sheet-metal cranes, lotus blossoms, airplanes, and other such symbolic and surrealistic roofcraft.

About 2 miles (3 kilometers) outside of town, down a dirt path behind a chicken farm, is a primitive stone sculpture constructed of three large, flat boulders. Archaeologists have identified this as a **northern-style dolmen** (in Korean, *chi-song-myo* or *koin-dol*) – a sacred tomb or

land
oplars,
anghwa
land.

altar – which dates back to paleolithic times. Life goes on around it as it stands undisturbed in the midst of peppers, tobacco, and ginseng.

"Flowers of Youth": Further down the bus line, in **Hajonmyon**, there is another old but less-visited stone sculpture. It is a five-story pagoda (*sokt'ap*) that was once a part of a Koryo temple. The temple is gone but the pagoda stands hidden in a pine forest. If you do seek out the pagoda, which is about a mile's walk from the main road past farmhouses, you might also wish to scale **Pongch'on-san**, the high hill behind it. Hikers are promised a panoramic view of the Han-Imjin Estuary and an opportunity to stomp around the ruins of an old stone beacon tower. This tower supported one of 696 beacon fires lit during the Yi dynasty to relay national security messages to Seoul. It was rendered obsolete when the telegraph was introduced in 1894.

Now travel back in time to the Three Kingdoms Period. On the southern end of Kanghwa-do (take a bus to **Onsu-ri** from town), about 10 miles (16 kilometers) south of Kanghwa town, is one of the oldest temples in Korea, **Chondung-sa,** the "**Temple of the Inherited Lamp**." Chondung-sa was named after a jade lamp presented to the temple by a Koryo queen. Formerly called Chinchong-sa, it was built in AD 381 by a famous monk named Ado. Legend has it that the wall surrounding the temple, however, was constructed by three princes to fortify the monastery. Thus the fortress was named **Samnangsong**, or the "Castle of Three Flowers of Youth."

The friendly monks here may invite you to share a vegetarian meal with them or guide you to some of the remaining **Tripitaka Koreana** sculptural woodblocks carved during the 13th century. It took 16 years to carve the Buddhist scriptures on these blocks, a monumental task done in hopes of preventing a consuming Mongol invasion.

On the temple grounds is an **iron bell** about 6 feet (1.8 meters) tall. It was cast in 1097 during the Northern Sung dynasty in a typical Chinese style. Despite its foreign origin, the bell has been desig-

Chondung-sa, one of the oldest temples in Korea.

nated a national treasure. Before departing from Ch'ondung-sa, examine the architecture and unique ornamentation of human images engraved on the eaves of **Taeungjon Hall**. This particular design style was popular during the mid-Yi dynasty and is rarely seen anymore.

About 1½ miles (2½ kilometers southwest of Chondung-sa is the small town of **Sangbang-ni** and the site of **Tan'gun's altar** on nearby **Mani-san**. It is an arduous climb (almost 500 meters up) to the summit where one can get a sweeping view of Kanghwa-do and touch the spot where an important Korean legend was born. Some archaeologists claim Tan'gun's altar is no more than 400 years old, which would date it considerably younger than Tan'gun who, according to popular myths, descended to earth from heaven in 2333 BC.

One last significant excursion that takes the better part of a day is a trip to the "**Eyebrow Rock**" **Buddha** at Pomun-sa on the neighboring island of Songmodo. This pilgrimage starts with a bus ride to **Uip'o**, a fishing village on the west coast.

Foreigners may be asked to show their passports in order to ferry across to the westward island. The ferry ride takes 10 minutes, but the bus ride from the landing on the opposite site to Pomun-sa is about 45 minutes on a bumpy dirt road. The island is serene and carpeted by endless fields of rice, punctuated here and there by pointed church-house steeples.

Pomun-sa is a neatly restored 1,400-year-old temple. It overlooks the light blue Yellow Sea and strangely-shaped islands that dissolve into the horizon. Behind the temple, carved into the mountain, is a stone chamber with **22 small stone Buddhas** enshrined in individual wall niches behind an altar. The Buddha statues are said to have been caught by a fisherman who dreamt he was instructed by a monk to enshrine them here. Steps lead further above this stone chamber through junipers. At the end of a steep, heart-thumping hike is the massive concave "Eyebrow Rock" Buddha sculpted into the granite mountainside. He blissfully overlooks the rice fields, Yellow Sea and setting sun below.

mun-sa's
yebrow
ock"
ıddha.

P'ANMUNJOM, ON THE DMZ

During the economic boom of the past two decades and amidst the apparent tranquillity of life in suburban Seoul and rural Korea, visitors have found it hard to believe that – after 40 years of ceasefire and a Korean War truce agreement – the threat of an all-out war still hangs over this "Land of the Morning Calm."

However, the danger is all too real, and to acquaint overly-optimistic tourists about this potentially volatile situation, the Korean government and United Nations representatives have in recent years sanctioned one of this country's – and indeed one of the world's – most unusual tourist outings. This unique visitor attraction is a day trip to **P'anmunjom**, the site of a small farming village which was obliterated during the Korean War.

Ceasefire truce: P'anmunjom is the historic place at Korea's **38th parallel** where American and South Korean representatives of a special United Nations Military Armistice Commission have been holding periodic talks with North Korean and Chinese negotiators to mutually supervise a ceasefire truce that was signed here on 27 July 1953. That truce agreement formally divided Korea into North and South political sectors and put an uneasy end to the bloody Korean War.

Geographically, P'anmunjom sits in a wide valley just northwest of the broad **Imjin River** and about 35 miles (56 kilometers) due north of Seoul.

Cartographically, and therefore politically, P'anmunjom also straddles land near the western end of Korea's demilitarized zone (**the "DMZ"**), a demarcation line about 2½ miles (4 kilometers) wide which serpentines about 151 miles (243 kilometers) across the waist of Korea between the Yellow and East (or Japan) seas.

This truce camp is the only point of official contact between North Korea **American observer.**

and the free world. This is also a heavily mined, barricaded and patrolled "no-man's land" fit only for well-armed soldiers, a few hundred brave native farmers, and, ironically, several formerly endangered species of birds (such as the spectacular Manchurian crane) which have flourished within the "protected" confines of the DMZ since it was declared off-limits to most humanity in 1953.

"Truce or Consequences": Talks have droned on here ever since the ceasefire with minimal progress toward permanent peace.

The most consistent talks have been the meetings of the Military Armistice Commission (MAC). Called every few months since July 1953, the MAC meetings are a study in failure to communicate. Nevertheless they provide a forum to sound off, defuse potentially dangerous developments and score propaganda points.

The southern sector of P'anmunjom is policed by the American-led United Nations Command (UNC) and not the South Korean army. But the guards are both American and South Korean soldiers attached to the UNC.

Since the mid-1980s there have been many on-off meetings in P'anmunjom between North and South Korean government officials to discuss sports exchanges, family reunions, trade and political matters.

Although there have been no dramatic breakthroughs, talks held here and in the two capitals resulted in the formation of joint North-South table tennis and soccer teams. They also lead to high-level meetings between the two countries' prime ministers and some low-level trade. Despite these developments, the Cold War standoff remains as strong as ever.

Over the past two decades, however, P'anmunjom has encountered a series of dramatic events. For many years the "village" itself was not divided. This changed in 1976 when North Koreans attacked and killed two American officers with axes in a disagreement over the pruning of a tree. Since then the village has been strictly divided between North and South.

In 1984, a Soviet on a northern tour group dashed across to the southern side in a defection which prompted a firefight and left four soldiers dead, three northerners and one southerner. Since then North Korean guards face north instead of south when tour groups come in from the northern side to prevent other would-be defectors.

In 1989, there occurred the most unusual crossing of P'anmunjom in which the receiving side tried to refuse to accept a South Korean student activist, returning from an illegal visit to the north. She came anyway, accompanied by a South Korean Catholic priest. Both received heavy jail sentences.

The negotiating table: The venue for the talks is a simple barracks-like shed which is split exactly in half at the north-south demarcation line. Negotiators sit on either side of a table covered with green felt (which also exactly straddles the DMZ).

On one end of the table is the red, white and blue yin-yanged and

North Korean observer.

trigrammed flag of the south, and at the other is the green and red-starred standard of the communist north.

Visitors are not allowed to visit P'anmunjom during actual negotiations, but on off days, if weather and the political climate permit, you can book a tour to P'anmunjom and the DMZ through the Korea Tourist Bureau (ask at the hotel) or the USO (which is much cheaper). The fee covers the truce village, lunch at a U.S. military base and a hike down a North Korean invasion tunnel (from the southern side, of course).

The tour also includes a military briefing on unexpected hostilities directed at the tour group.

Highway to history: Your P'anmunjom-bound tour bus courses due north of Seoul on national **Highway 1** and follows wartime history through plains and valleys that were the heavily bunkered scenes of massive military advances, retreats and more advances during the Korean War and even during a recent Mongol invasion.

This area is green and lush during the summer, but when winter chill sets in its beauty is bleak and brittle. Or as the late author James Wade described this region in his book *West Meets East:*

"North of Seoul the Korean landscape is austerely beautiful in late winter. A light dusting of snow sets off the dark dots of rice stubble in frozen paddies and the lonely clumps of thatch-roofed farm houses. The steel-gray horizon, rimmed with jagged, ice-streaked mountains, recedes before the jeep as it rumbles past the rail terminal city of **Munsan-ni** and approaches the Imjin River, with its symbolically narrow and precarious **Freedom Bridge**."

Suddenly you realize that the bleak new chain of mountains looming up ahead is North Korea territory.

"Freedom Village": Once past the checkpoints and into the DMZ, you notice an enormous South Korean flag. This marks the village of **T'aesong-dong** (which means "Attaining Success Town"), a community of ex-refugees who have been allowed to resettle in their native habitat.

Called "Freedom Village" by the U.S. military, T'aesong-dong is about a mile from P'anmunjom. Villagers – and soldiers – have to endure propaganda blasted over from the North Korean side by loudspeakers, but for their pains they enjoy certain benefits, among them exemption from military service and from taxation. Otherwise, life generally goes on here in much the same way it does in other parts of the Republic of Korea.

Across the dividing line in the North Korean half of the demilitarized no-man's-land is another village. It boasts bigger houses than T'aesong-dong and a much bigger flag. In fact the village is said to be the biggest in the world. The only difference is that no-one appears to inhabit the village.

While both DMZ villages are propaganda symbols, at least T'aesong-dong has people. American soldiers call the North Korean village "Propaganda Village." However, its real name is Guijong-dong.

View from the Top: Once you reach the exact P'anmunjom talks site, you will be escorted around a heavily-guarded sector formally called the **Joint Security Area**. In the **Conference Room** your American military guide will explain another propaganda "war" involving who had the bigger flag, which ended in a truce when the flags of the two sides were too large to bring into the meeting room. From atop ornate **Freedom House**, you will have a good view of the whole village and from **Guardpost No. 5** you have a panoramic view into North Korea itself.

Since 1987 Western tourists have been able to make the P'anmunjom trip from the northern side. From Seoul this would involve flying to the northern capital, Pyongyang, via Beijing and then a six-hour train journey to Kaesong, a city near P'anmunjom.

As of 1991, South Koreans are still not permitted to travel north as tourists (they are also not permitted by the Seoul government to make the P'anmunjom trip from the south as tourists). And visas are seldom issued by the North Koreans to Americans, unless they are Korean-Americans.

American sentries at the DMZ.

NORTH HAN RIVER LAKE COUNTRY

When a Korean is fraught with wanderlust – when he or she feels like hiking into that beauty which inspired classical brush paintings – he or she dons an alpinist's hat and heads northeast to Korea's finest collection of rivers, lakes and mountains, to the land (as tourist brochures note) "Where Men and Mountains Meet."

This is the great northeast province of **Kangwon-do**, where in a day a happy wanderer can bask on a lake or seaside beach, and hike through crisp mountain mists to a 15th-century Buddhist shrine scooped out of a granite cliff.

For centuries Korea has been referred to as *"sam ch'on li kum su kang san,"* or the land of "3,000 *li* of rivers and mountains embroidered on silk." And in Kangwon-do, for miles in either direction – from the North Han River Valley to the demilitarized zone (DMZ) and the East Sea – this adage rings true. Here you will find a superb tapestry – delicately shaded with silken green rice terraces, swaths of amber grain, and pointilist vegetable patches that wind hither and thither along cold blue rivers and craggy mountain passes.

Probably the most picturesque journey of the above genre is the so-called "road to Sorak-san and the northeast coast" which takes you north of Seoul on a zig-zag course of modern highways, inland waterways and dusty but pleasantly spectacular mountain roads. This adventure – by bus (from Seoul's Chongnyang-ni station), or car – moves in a northeast direction on Highway 46 through mild mountains and along and across the snake-like North Han River and its valleys.

Glassy Lake Country: Several river and lakeside resorts have sprung up here and there along the highway from Seoul to Ch'unch'on. If you see a turn on the river to your hiking, stop and linger a day or two according to whim, but if you'd like a suggestion of where to stay, consider **Nami-som**, an island in the middle of the Han River near a quaint highland town

Boating piers Ch'unch'on Lake.

called **Kapyong**. This journey is about an hour's drive north of Seoul, followed by a 10-minute ferry ride to Nami-som, where you can rent a small house or cabin and become one with splashing rowboats, cooing cuckoos, falling chestnuts and whooshing pines. Wake up early and wait patiently as the rising sun slowly but surely burns morning mists out of the little valleys which surround Kap'yong, lovely Nami-som, and the Han River.

About 12 miles (20 kilometers) further north (a journey you can make by leisurely ferry from Nami-som if you've got the time), you'll round a hill and descend into **Ch'unch'on**, a convenient resort city for Seoulites who like to get away from it all for a day or week to enjoy some of the country's finest, if not the finest, lake country. Freshwater fishing, swimming, sailing and water-skiing are readily available at several colorful resort piers which rim roomy **Ch'unch'on Lake** and other sky blue waterways in the area.

In **Ch'unch'on**, where violet, yellow and green rose cabbages landscape a series of cute mini-parks, you can follow your nose in a number of watery and earthy directions. Pause at **Ethiopia House**, an improbable teahouse which sits above candy-striped boathouses bobbing on glassy Ch'unch'on Lake, and ponder adventurous alternatives over beer.

Some folks ferry-hop around Ch'unch'on through river gorges to riverside villages, sandy beaches, waterfalls (the Kukok Falls near Nami-som are a favorite), and jade green pools that have never been reached by car or train. Others browse through east Ch'unch'on's **Koryo Silk Factory** – the only "handmade silk" factory in Korea – where bright bundles of silk drying in the sun dazzle before you. Still others continue north to **Hwach'on** and the remote **Paro Lake** north of **Samyong Mountains**.

But probably the most popular local tour after a cooling respite along Ch'unch'on's lakebanks is a visit to the nearby **Soyang Dam** and its attendant **Soyang Lake**. On the north side of this concrete monument to engineering and hydroelectricity, you'll find a colorful boat docking area, the **Soyang Pavilion**,

where a road-weary traveler can leave land and embark on a tour of Korea's most splendid inland waterway. Lake Soyang is hyperbolically, but not unbelievably, called by some Korean travel writers "the largest lake in the Orient made by man."

Whatever Soyang's claim to environmental fame, from this pavilion you can proceed for many cool miles on a gliding cruise toward the Sorak Mountains and the northeast coast.

A sidetrip favored by travelers not pressed for time is a brief (15 minutes) diversionary cruise by open-air launch to **Ch'ongp'yong-sa**, an ancient Buddhist temple (about 20 minutes hike and 1½ miles above a sleepy floating dock and restaurant) just north of Soyang Pavilion.

This Buddhist retreat provides deliberate solace seekers with a simple escape from asphalt and beeping buses. A well-kempt trail to Ch'ongp'yong-sa rises easily – but steeply and steadily – along and above a tinkling and rocky stream bed to a waterfall and piney crags which come alive at dawn and at sunset with the amazing harmony of sutras being chanted by resident devotees of the Lord Buddha.

Lakeside residents, plying you with a ready supply of hot toasted cuttlefish, mandarin oranges, O.B. beer and aquamarine bottles of *soju* whisky, are never too many hiking puffs away, but their sale pitches are quiet and unobtrusive – in keeping with the serenity of this lovely hike cum pilgrimage.

It will cost you about 200 won to enter this Buddhist center of desirelessness and non-attachment, and on the back of your ticket, in han'gul, you will be informed:

"This temple originated 1,600 years. A Chinese princess of the Tang period visited here to rid herself of a snake. She brought three bars of gold for the expense of rebuilding this temple, in hopes of losing the snake. At this time the gate of the temple was struck by lightning in the midst of a severe storm. The snake vanished, so the temple was renamed 'Revolving Door' from this incident."

That ticket story is understandably perplexing, but only adds to Ch'ongp'yong-sa's mystique. Art historian Jon Covell

Dragon guardian, Ch'ongp'yong Temple.

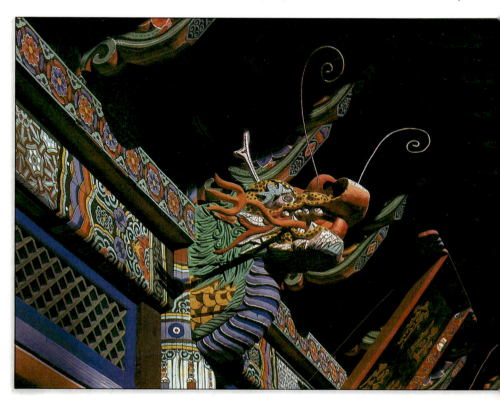

theorizes that this story about the princess and a snake indicates shaman influences creeping into Buddhism. Another theory supposes the temple was the refuge-headquarters of a tantric, or erotic, Buddhist cult. Whatever its origins, you'll find your visit to Ch'ongpy'ong-sa rewarding if only to see its fine outer wall murals – which include, among other themes, an unusual Kwanseum holding a willow branch, a finely executed Oxherding Series and a well-focused tiger panel.

Meanwhile, back on Lake Soyang, you can motor back to Soyang Pavilion near the massive dam, then catch one of many regular commuter specials (these are covered craft with a breezy after-deck) for the hour and 20 minutes glide to a rural docking point just south of isolated **Yanggu** town. The surrounded mountains, which are ablaze with amber and roseate trees in the crisp autumn, are reflected by glassy Lake Soyang, and remind one of similar situations in New Zealand, or the American Northwest. At the Yanggu area dock you can transfer to

a bus or taxi and proceed through hills and exploits to sleepy Yanggu town.

At Yanggu, which lies in a pleasant valley a few miles south of the demilitarized zone between north and south Korea, there are several *yogwan* inns, restaurants and all the other amenities of small town Korea. From here, regular buses race through corn and cabbage country to **Inje**, the "gateway town" to the spectacular Sorak Mountains area.

The 20 miles (32 kilometers) of mostly dirt road between Yanggu and Inje after bracing country airs and quaint rural scenes at every turn: timber and thatch rest pavilions, golden corn clusters drying in the cold glare of a clear autumn day, near shamanist shrines dedicated to good harvesting, and, leaning against haystacks, kerchiefed and pantalooned mountain maidens puffing on long-stemmed pipes. Your bus will proceed in lurches along pleasantly meandering stream beds and through mist-shrouded gullies until it drops down to the wide **Soyang River** bed, **Highway 44**, and Inje town on the river's sandy west of bank.

ake Soyang.

SORAK-SAN NATIONAL PARK

Sorak-san, the "Snow Peak Mountain," is now more formally known as the **Sorak-san National Park**. And as the name hints, this "Snow Peak Mountain" is not just a lone mountaintop. It's actually a series of peaks in the mid-section of the spectacular **Taebaek Sanmaek**, or "Great White Range," Korea's most prominent geographical region.

This panoramic backbone of South Korea's northeast province of **Kangwon-do** is one of those much-publicized "tourist destinations" which live up to the hyperbole and public relations written and spoken on its behalf. The Sorak area is indeed a mountain wonderland, and you'll understand after a visit why early Zen (or *Son*) Buddhist monks chose this region to sit and work at becoming one with the universe.

There are several ways to get to the Sorak area from Seoul. The quickest is by Korean Air Lines domestic aircraft to **Sokch'o** (40 minutes flying time), then by bus or taxi to **Sorak-dong** (another 20 minutes). You can also train to or bus to the terminal fishing town of Sokch'o.

Korea old-timers aren't in such a hurry to get to this place. They prefer, as outlined in the preceding North Han River section, to enter Sorak slowly, from the country's scenic interior, and drift into the area's magic on newly paved, winding roads which meander through the wilds of **Inner Sorak**.

Inje, the renowned "Gateway to Inner Sorak," is as good a place as to begin this exploration. But even in Inje town you'll first have to decide which of two scenic ways you want to take to the Sorak range. One route, the **Southern Route**, goes through the **Han'gye-ryong Pass**; and the other, the **Northern Route**, serpentines through two back mountain passes, the **Cinpur-yong** and **Misillyong** passes, before descending into Sokch'o on the East Sea. However, most first-time and veteran travelers prefer the Southern Route, both for the comfort and scenery.

Preceding pages, the summit of Sorak-san. Left, swaying footbridge to Flying Dragon Waterfall.

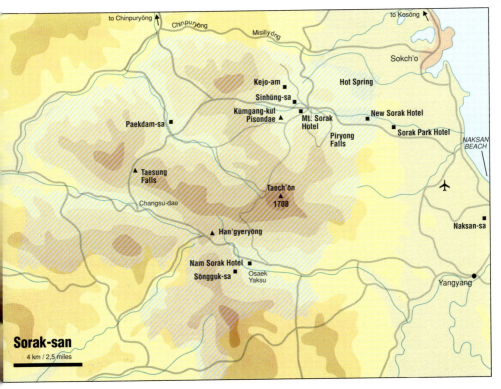

Sorak-san

4 km / 2.5 miles

But if you're up for a bit of "roughing it," head north.

The Southern Route from Inje winds its way through "Inner Sorak," **Naesorak**, through the southern fringes of "Outer Sorak," **Wesorak**, until you emerge at lovely **Yangyang** town on the turquoise blue East Sea. You'll be travelling from Inje to Yangyang on a meandering, newly paved road that enables you to take in the gorgeous sights in expressway comfort.

En route you'll encounter (at **Chang Su Dae**) numerous nature trails (abloom in the spring and ablaze in the fall), veil-like waterfalls, red-bellied frogs, cripple creeks, and (at **Osaek Yaksu**) mineral water springs famed for their therapeutic properties. Some travelers like to pause at **Chang Su Dae** and hike up to the **Taesung waterfalls**, then course onward and up-ward to **Paekdam-sa**, a charming Buddhist temple smack in the interior of Inner Sorak. Both hikes are good for the soul after the traffic of Seoul, but be prepared – with warm clothes, good walking gear, food and drink – if you plan to camp overnight in these desolate parts.

Further east on the Han'gye Pass road, at the very top of this spectacular pass, you can begin yet another trek – this one all the way to the top of Sorak's supreme peak, **Taechon-bong**, the third highest mountain, at 5,604 feet (1,708 meters) in Korea. You can navigate onward and enter the **Sorak-dong resort complex** by its back door. However, again be advised that the 11 hours of steep zig-zagging through beautiful nature can be slippery and dangerous during the winter months.

The Osaek Yaksu medicinal springs at the far east end of the Han'gye Pass road are well worth a stop and the recuperative soak, but if you're feeling fit without the benefit of such therapy, you may want to rush on down to sea-level to a grand seafood meal at **Yangyang**, **Naksan** or **Sokch'o**. Appetite thus satisfied, and mind and body braced by cool breezes off the East Sea, you are now ready to tackle Outer Sorak and her well-equipped bands of happy mountain wanderers.

The 15-minute bus ride from the sandy East Coast into Sorak Village is a grand transition from beach cabana chic to

mountain resort cool. One moment you're sniffing at raw fish and clams arrayed 'neath your beachside umbrella, and the next, you're in a piney lodge considering hot buttered rums and pinenut soup.

Thanks to the Koreans' almost religious dedication to proper hiking, camping and enjoyment of the great outdoors, and the government's far-sighted investment in this wilderness area, the Outer Sorak–Sorak-dong resort complex has become one of the finest woodsy places in Korea, indeed in the world, for leisurely hiking and dining alfresco. Nature strolls here can accommodate everyone – from the most languid non-hiker to an aggressive rock-climbing fanatic. There's even a modern cable car that will carry less aggressive outdoorspersons to a properly catered promontory where they can meditate on **Pison-dae** ("**Flying Fairy Peak**"), a famous rock structure.

When you've settled into one of Sorak-dong's deluxe hotels or simple *yogwan* inns, your next poser will be to decide which of Sorak's many possible mountaineering-excursion themes to pursue.

A large and detailed information sign on the roadside offers a few suggestions, but for openers let us suggest the following Sorak area frolics:

Before you head into the bush, stroll up the main flagstoned and fir-lined path which leads to **Sinhung-sa**, an ancient Son (or Zen) temple originally built near its present location in AD 652. The first Sinhung-sa, then called **Hyungsong-sa**, or the "Temple of Zen Buddhism," was destroyed by a forest fire in 707, rebuilt in 710, burned again in 1645, and rebuilt a third time at its present location in 1648.

"If the signboard date at Sinhung-sa is correct," writes Zen and oriental art authority Dr. Jon Carter Covell, "then Sinhung-sa is the oldest Zen temple in the world. Nothing in China or in Japan is of this age, not by many centuries."

Just before you reach the temple compound proper, you'll pass (on the right side of the cobble path) a neatly kept and fenced-in cemetery full of unusual **bell-shaped tombstones** erected to honor formerly illustrious Zen monks who spent much time meditating in this area.

n the road to
nner Sorak.

In the temple itself, which sits on a pleasant little bluff with a superb view of the surrounding mountains, you'll pass through lattice doors carved and painted in a floral motif and come eye-to-eye with a standard **Amit's Buddha** flanked by **Kwanseum** and **Taiseiji** bodhisattvas. Of a more light-hearted interest, you will also be confronted by "the two crazy idiots of the 7th century" – **Han San and Sup Duk** (known in China as Han Shan and Shih Te) – who grace the temple's northern wall. These absurd, grimacing and "crazy" fellows are often found in such spiritual surroundings, where they temper our overly-serious lives by laughing at the absurdity of existence.

Sinhung-sa offers even more such fantasy, some of it drawing on combinations of shaman, Taoist and Buddhist imagery. Consider the creatures which are half-tiger and half-leopard, and the writhing dragons, cranes and bats – all brilliantly painted on the ceiling. Or the drawing on the main hall's rear wall which shows a Zen patriarch offering his severed arm to a higher-ranking Zen master.

With that Zen mind-full, proceed up this spiritual pass and path to the **Kejo Hermitage** about two miles (three kilometers) upward along a singing stream bed. Kejo Hermitage, a subsidiary of the mother Sinhung Temple, is partially built into a granite cave at the base of **Ulsan-bawi**, a spectacular granite formation that dominates this part of the Sorak area. Like much of Sorak, and like the famous **Diamond Mountains** due north of here, Ulsan-bawi's face is rich with anthropomorphic images. Indeed, about halfway up the Kejo Hermitage, an enterprising fellow with a high-powered telescope sells lingering peeks at one particularly erotic formation at Ulsan-bawi's mid-section.

The hermitage is identified by a bright red Buddhist swastika carved and painted over an entrance arch. A narrow corridor leads to the cave interior where you'll find an altar where candles burn before a small but exquisite golden Buddha.

When monks are inside this ancient niche, chanting sutras and clacking wooden bells by flickering candlelight,

Remote temples are accessible only by foot.

the effect is Zen Buddhism at its most poignant.

Fronting the Kejo Hermitage and Ulsan-bawi is another geologic curiosity which has become a major tourist attraction over the years. This is the famed **Rocking Rock**, a massive boulder which rocks back and forth in its secure place when given a solid nudge. Being photographed in front of this tipsy ball of granite is a touristic must.

If you enjoyed your ramble to the "Rocking Rock," then you're ready for a more challenging trek – this time to the **Kumgang Cave** above the aforementioned Pison-dae (Flying Fairy Peak).

The hike to Pison-dae, a vertical rock that juts heavenward at the entrance to an extremely picturesque gorge, is easy enough, and at every lovely turn you'll find yourself gawking at the beauty of chill pools, small waterfalls, and, in the autumn, fire red maples and golden gingkos. "In Canada you'd have to do a lot of bushwhacking to see country like this," commented a visitor from Vancouver. Another hiker squealed with joy when he rounded a granite boulder and found a smiling grandmother selling cooling bowls of *makkolli* rice wine and *moru-jip*, a beverage made from the berries of a local plant related to the grape.

From this restful camp at the base of Pison-dae, devoted Buddhist pilgrims head up a smaller path to **Kumgang Cave**, which is located near the top of Pison-dae and requires a serious genuflection to exercise. After negotiating 649 stairs to reach this charming cave-shrine, your heart will be pounding in your head, but the extraordinary view from up there – and from a halfway point promontory –will be your earthly reward. Inside the cave is a small Buddha surrounded by burning candles, incense and food offerings.

Meanwhile, back at the Sorak-dong base camp, other hikers have opted to visit the **Flying Dragon Waterfall** (Piryong) at the top of a lovely gorge below 4,412-foot (1,345-meter) high **Hwachae-bong.** A suspension bridge across the narrow gorge and stream leads to the Flying Dragon.

*e famed
Rocking
ock.*"

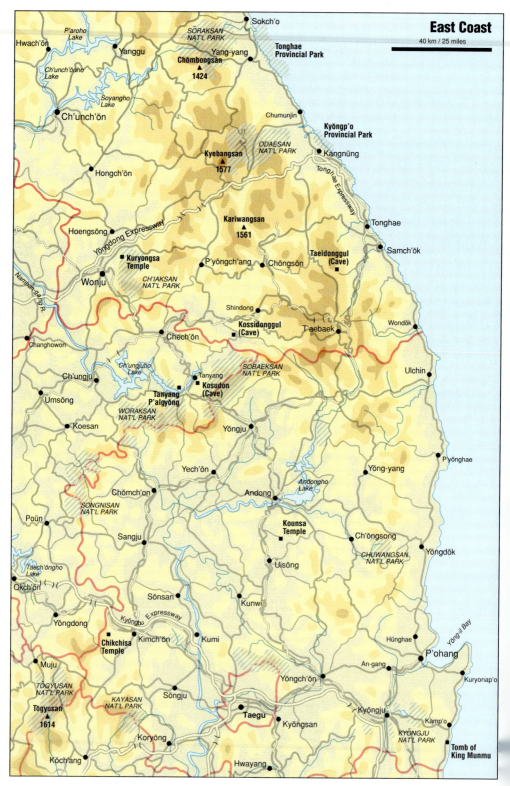

East Coast

40 km / 25 miles

Hwach'ŏn
P'aroho Lake
Yanggu
Ch'unch'ŏnho Lake
Soyangho Lake
Ch'unch'ŏn
Hongch'ŏn
Hoengsŏng
Yŏngdong Expressway
Namhan-gang R.
Kuryongsa Temple
Wonju
CH'IAKSAN NAT'L PARK
Changhowŏn
Ch'ungju
Ch'ungjuho Lake
Ŭmsŏng
Koesan
WORAKSAN NAT'L PARK
Tanyang P'algyŏng
Tanyang
Kosudon (Cave)
SOBAEKSAN NAT'L PARK
Yŏngju
Yech'ŏn
Andongho Lake
Yŏng-yang
P'yŏnghae
Chŏmch'on
Andong
Poŭn
SONGNISAN NAT'L PARK
Sangju
Kounsa Temple
Ch'ŏngsong
CHUWANGSAN NAT'L PARK
Yŏngdŏk
Taech'ŏngho Lake
Okch'ŏn
Ŭisŏng
Sŏnsan
Kunwi
Yŏngdong
Kyŏngbu Expressway
Kimch'ŏn
Kumi
Hünghae
Yŏng-il Bay
P'ohang
Chikchisa Temple
Muju
Koesan
Sŏngju
Yŏngch'ŏn
An-gang
Kuryonap'o
TOGYUSAN NAT'L PARK
KAYASAN NAT'L PARK
Togyusan
1614
Kŏch'ang
Koryŏng
Taegu
Kyŏngsan
Kyŏngju
Kamp'o
KYŎNGJU NAT'L PARK
Hwayang
Tomb of King Munmu

SÖRAKSAN NAT'L PARK
Sokch'o
Yang-yang
Chŏmbongsan
1424
Tonghae Provincial Park
Chumunjin
Kyŏngp'o Provincial Park
Kyebangsan
1577
ODAESAN NAT'L PARK
Kangnŭng
Tonghae Expressway
Kariwangsan
1561
Tonghae
Samch'ŏk
P'yŏngch'ang
Chŏngsŏn
Taeidonggul (Cave)
Shindong
Kossidonggul (Cave)
T'aebaek
Wondŏk
Chech'ŏn
Ulchin

186

THE EAST COAST

Snow country and a ski resort. Highland hot springs overlooking rice terraces and pine forests. The bluest waters and whitest sand beaches in Korea. Stalactite and stalagmite-filled caverns. Even massive, computerized industrial complexes.

Korea's **East Coast**, home of all the above, does indeed live up to travel brochure pronouncements that this is "A Land of Contrasts." As in any country, that promotional cliché is true, but in Korea it is, quite rightly, applicable to this broadly curving coastal region between her 36th and 39th parallels.

At the southern end of this arc are **P'ohang** and **Ulsan**, recently created industrial cities where steel, automobiles and ships are manufactured at astonishing production rates. And to the north, along postcard-perfect pine bluffs, inland lagoons, and cabana-dotted beaches, are seaside retreats which have been favored by hedonistic Koreans since ancient times.

You can begin your tour of the East Coast at several points up and down the East Sea, but probably the most central place to use as pivot point for travel is **Kangnung**, the major city in east **Kangwon Province**. This city of more than 150,000 people is easily reached by train or bus, but the most interesting way to make the 142 miles (228 kilometers) journey from Seoul is by private car.

A motorcar cruise to Kangnung – south on the **Seoul-Pusan Expressway**, then east on the **Yongdong Expressway** – will allow you the time you would need to explore both famous and obscure "tourist attractions" enroute to the East Coast.

This journey along broad expressways cuts a grand swath through cute Saemaul (New Community Movement) villages with turquoise, tangerine and chartreuse rooftops; glassy rice paddies that reflect neatly marching poplars; pine green hillsides that from a distance look like the backs of well-combed sheep; and busy logging camps in the bends of timber-clogged rivers.

If the children are with you, you may want to stop at the **Yong-in Farm Land** and Lion Country at the very early part of the journey; but if they aren't, you may be content to stop and sniff the fragrance of a roadside acacia forest. Koreans like to soak white and pale yellow acacia blossoms in alcoholic spirits (usually in *soju* or *chongjong*), then (after a month or so of soaking) take this spirited essence to a scenic region such as this for a day of sipping and poésie.

Once you get into more mountainous areas, notice the unusual pointy-topped silos of Korean design, bright ears of corn drying along rooftops, and hops plantations which are distinguished by the lacy network of string trellises built to support these twining vines from which *maekju* (beer) evolves. These are subsidiary hops plantations of Korea's old Oriental Brewery.

Land of 10,000 Buddhas: One "road-to-Kangnung" detour you must make is just beyond little **Chinbu** village (about 25 miles or 40 kilometers west of Kangnung). This sidetrip carries you along paved and dirt roads to **Mt. Odae National Park**, a charming mountain area and the location of two of Korea's most well-known temple complexes, **Woljong-sa** and **Sangwon-sa**. The road leading to 5,128-foot (1,563-meter) high **Odae-san** is literally dotted with tiny hermitages, Zen meditation niches, and other impressive remnants of Buddhism which date to the 7th century and Korea's impressive Silla dynasty.

Because cool Mongolian winds and warmer air currents off the East Sea meet in this mountain region, the lush and pine-covered peaks of Odae-san often are wreathed in cool, shifting mists which sometimes give the area an eerie or otherworldly aura when patches of sunshine appear and disappear in improbable shifts and intensities. It is no wonder that early Buddhist masters in Korea chose this place as a prime meditation spot.

Woljong-sa, which sits on the southern fringe of Odae-san about 5 miles (8 kilometers) off the expressway, is a sprawling temple complex distinguished by a superb nine-story **octagonal pagoda** and an unusual **kneeling Buddha** sculpture. The tiered pagoda, which rises 50 feet (15.2 meters), is capped with a sculpted lotus blossom and a bronze finial of intricate design; the kneeling Buddha, meanwhile, has well-weathered features, and (because of an unusual cap he's wearing) looks much like a European tin soldier. Both national cultural treasures are located in front of Woljong-sa's main hall within a grassy plot protected by a low iron fence wrought in a continuous swastika motif.

Along a riverbed road which snakes on up to the higher reaches of Odae-san, you'll see occasional shrines and memorials to monks who've lived and died in this region over the centuries. One forest clearing contains tall stone stupas, most of them notably phallic in design, which are said to contain the cremated remains (*sarira*) of famous Buddhist masters.

Even higher up, just east of Odae-san's main peak, and about 200 meters off the road at the end of a pine-bordered pass, is Sangwon-sa, another temple established by Chajang. According to an information board there, Chajang built this temple in AD 646 during the reign of the Silla Queen Sondok. Zodiacal images adorn its walls, and in a wooden pavilion on the grounds is a large bronze bell said to be the **second largest bell in Korea** (the largest being the Emille Bell at the Kyongju National Museum). This particular Silla bell, also the oldest known bell in Korea, is 5½ feet (1.7 meters) tall and reportedly was cast in AD 725 during the reign of the Silla King Songdok.

Korean-style schussing in the Dragon Valley: Perhaps another 7 miles (12 kilometers) east and just south of the Yongdong Expressway is another highlands area with a decidedly different aura. This is the **Taekwallyong mountain** region where Korea's most modern and well-equipped ski resort is located. Throughout the Taekwallyong area are various ski spots with names such as **Talpanje**, **Chirmae** and **Third Slope**. Most are located in the vicinity of a small town called **Hwoenggye**, but the newest and favorite slopes have been developed in a place called **Yongpyong**, or **Dragon Valley**.

The **Dragon Valley Ski Resort** sprawls over 52 acres and is equipped with chairlift

Village south of Kangnung.

systems, snow-making machines, a ski school, ski rental facilities, and even lighting facilities for night skiing. Chairlifts carry schussers to the top of both intermediate and beginner slopes.

There are longer runs up the sides of the area's **Golden Dragon**, **Silver Dragon** and **Palwang** 4,783-foot (1,458-meter) high mountains, but as of the 1980 season the longest ride, down Taekwallyong's 3,140 feet (957 meters) high **Mt. Twin Dragon**, offered a major headwall drop of about 164 feet (50 meters) that quickly tapered off into a series of cheerful bunny slopes.

Looming over this snow complex are two first rate hotels cum ski lodges, the **Dragon Valley Hotel** and the **Hotel Ju Won**. These lodges offer comfort-seekers both Western and Korean-style accommodation, plus a "Chalet Grill," billiards lounges, discotheque, heated swimming pool, archery range, tennis courts and rifle range for non-skiers and warm weather visitors. But if these places aren't your style, there are also private villas, *yogwan* inns and a large dormitory

facility in the area which can be rented at single, double or group rates.

A few more miles east of the turnoff to the Dragon Valley and ski country the Yongdong Expressway begins to narrow somewhat. Then, after negotiating the **Taekwan Ridge**, you will begin a final, zig-zagging descent to Kangnung town through the famous 99 turns of the **Taekwan Pass**. On a clear day the view from the top of this granite cliff provides a fine first impression of Kangnung and the deep blue **East Sea**.

Kangnung is a sleepy seaside town rich in traditional architecture and hospitable people. It's always been known as the key trading and terminal point in this part of Korea, but has also gained local fame as the site of an annual Tano spring festival (held on the 5th day of the 5th lunar moon, usually in May) that takes place on the banks of a wide river that divides the town's north and south sectors. This Tano celebration is rich in shamanistic dancing, religious rituals and general merrymaking which attract country folk from the seaside and moun-

onks at
angwon-sa,
dae-san.

tains to its colorful tents, sideshows and outrageously colorful carnival atmosphere. It's a true local people's event.

Confucian Reflections on Rising Moons: The Kangnung area abounds with precious distractions worth touring, but perhaps the most prominent are:

• A classical Confucian academy and shrine – **Hyangkyo and Taesungjon** – in the northwest suburbs of Kangnung on the grounds of the **Myungnyun** middle and high schools. This hilltop structure, which was built in 1313, destroyed by fire in 1403, then rebuilt in 1413, has low, brooding rooflines and tapering colonnades typical of Koryo dynasty structures in other parts of Korea. Rooms on either side of this old academy's main hall are filled with boxed spirit tablets that are opened every year when Confucian *chesa* ancestral rites are held here.

• **Kyongp'o-dae Lake** and **Kyongp'o-dae Beach**. This resort just a few miles north of Kangnung has long been a popular Korean recreational spa. Waters off Kyongp'o-dae Beach are often busy with zig-zagging speedboats and sailing craft,

and on shore are numerous tented seafood restaurants where you can choose your lunch swimmingly fresh from gurgling saltwater tanks. Korean tourists like to buy bundles of *miyok* (seaweed for soup-making), dried cuttlefish, and other exotic delicacies from women vendors who ply their trade on this colorful beach.

Just inland of this beach scene – past the clutter of hotels and inns, and rows of shops which sell touristic kitsch souvenirs – is mirror-like Kyongp'o-dae Lake. This fishing lake dotted with islets once had pavilions set like jewels on her shores. This was where local *yangban* aristocrats met with friends to sip wine, compose poems and watch sunsets and moonrises over the nearby T'aebaek mountain range. As an old saying sings, from the old **Kyongp'o Pavilion** on the lake's north shore "you can see the rising moon reflected in the lake, in your bowl of wine, and in your sweetheart's eyes."

If such images keep you in a romantic and classical mood, head back across the lake toward Kangnung, detour northwest a bit, and cross a series of rice paddies by

Sari-ra **(reliquaries)** **Odae-san.**

footpath until you reach the 99 *k'an* living compound, Confucian academy, lotus pond and pavilion built during the 18th and 19th centuries by members of the prominent Yi Ku family clan. This complex is as perfect an example of a *yangban* Yi dynasty living compound as you'll find anywhere in Korea. And what makes it even better is that the Yi family still lives in the main house, just as their ancestors have for the past two centuries.

This compound is picturesque in the white winter – when snow trims its curved roofs, mud and tile walls and cozy thatched servants' quarters – and in the summer – when giant pink Indonesian lotus blossoms rise out of their shallow pond like sleepy dragons.

Black Bamboo Shrine: Another fine Confucian place, this one just a little way north of Kangnung, is **Ojuk-hon** (Black Bamboo Shrine), birthplace of the prominent Confucian scholar-statesman-poet Yi I (1536-1584). Yi I, more popularly known by his pen name Yulgok (Valley of Chestnuts), was one of a select group of Neo-Confucianists who became quite powerful during the 16th century. Among positions he held were royal appointments as Korea's Minister of Personnel and War and Rector of the National Academy.

One biographical sketch notes that Yulgok was an infant prodigy who knew Chinese script at the age of three, "and when he was seven he already composed poems in Chinese. At the age of 19, he entered the Diamond Mountains and was initiated in Buddhism, but soon abandoned it for the study of the philosophy of Chu Hsi."

To honor Yulgok's example and memory, the Korean government has in recent years completely restored and rebuilt his birthplace site. This memorial, on the west side of the road to Yangyang and Sokch'o, is a prim compound rendered in the cheerful yellow favored by the ministry in charge of national parks and memorials.

Ojuk-hon, which has the aura of a shrine (visitors should be properly dressed, and smoking, gum-chewing and photography are not allowed in the vicinity of

Yulgok's memorial tablet house) is a memorial not just to Yulgok, but also to his mother, Sin Saimdang, who was revered during her lifetime as a fine calligrapher and artist. A collection of calligraphic scrolls by Yulgok, his mother, and other members of this Yi family are on display in a small museum at the rear of the Ojuk-hon compound. Also on view are several original paintings by the talented Lady Saimdang. Her precise and flowing studies of flora and fauna are superbly executed.

Before continuing north from this site, marvel for a moment at the fine stand of **black bamboo** which bends in a garden between the museum and Yulgok's house. Then look west toward nearby pine forests and consider these stanzas from Yulgok's famous poem *The Nine Songs of Mt. Ko* (translated by Peter H. Lee):

"Where shall we find the first song?
The sun lances the crown rock, and
Mist clears above the tall grass.
Lo the magic views far and near –
Calling my friends I would wait
With a green goblet in the pine grove."

Proceed north past such sun-lanced rocks, pine groves and the shocking blue East Sea towards **Yangyang**, **Naksan**, **Sokch'o**, **Hwajinp'o**, and, at the northernmost reaches of Highway 7, the sleepy fishing village of **Taejin**.

Just above Yangyang, on the southern skirts of Sokch'o, you'll find what is probably the most charming and impressive religious site in this part of Korea. This is **Naksan-sa**, a Buddhist temple complex originally established at this site by the Silla high priest Uisang in 671 during the 11th year of Silla King Munmu's reign. The main hall and support structures were rebuilt in 858, burned down during the Korean War, then rebuilt again in 1953 by Gen. Hi Hyong-kun and his men.

According to a storyboard, the high priest Uisang prayed here for seven days on a 49-foot (15-meter) high rock by the sea. He wanted to see Avalokitesvara (the God of mercy), the story notes, "but in vain." "In despair he threw himself into the sea and then Avalokitesvara appeared, gave him a rosary made of crystal, and

Ski tot at Dragon Valley.

told him where to worship him. Thus **Wontongp'o-jon**, the main hall of this temple, was built on this spot." Another version of this story notes that Uisang "became a Buddha himself when he saw the image of the Maitreya Buddha rising from the sea in front of him following his seven day prayer toward the sea."

However long Uisang prayed or whatever he saw emerging from the deep, this temple stands in his and Buddha's honor. Several national treasures are housed in Naksan-sa's halls, towers and pavilions. The first item you'll notice is a splendid stone gate, **Honghwa-mun**, built during the reign of King Sejo (r. 1455-1468), who once prayed here. Probably the second most impressive structure is a **seven-story Koryo pagoda** that stands 20 feet (6.2 meters) high in front of the main hall. Its gleaming finial is composed of finely wrought treasure rings, a fortune bowl and a treasure jewel. Third, but certainly not last, is a large bronze bell, called **Pomjong** with four raised bodhisattva images. It was cast in 1496. The bell – 5 feet (1.6 meters) by 3 feet (one meter) in diameter – is inscribed with poetry and calligraphy by the famous poet Kim Su-on and the calligrapher Chong Ran-jong.

A Merciful Apparition: On Wontongp'o-jon's sea side, dominating all natural and man-made items in the area, is a 49-foot (15-meter) high white granite statue of Buddhism's **Bodhisattva of Mercy**, known in Korea as the goddess **Kwanseum-posal**, in China as Kwan Yin, and in India as Avalokitesvara (though Avalokitesvara is an earlier male counterpart). This particular Goddess of Mercy faces the southeast atop a six-foot (two-meter) granite pedestal and open lotus blossom.

The massive statue, the work of Pusan sculptor Kwon Chong-hwan, was dedicated in 1977. According to Ch'oe Won-ch'ol, then chief priest at Naksan-sa, an old priest appeared to him in a 1972 dream and told him where and how to place this statue. Following this apparition, Ch'oe reported his dream to the religious affairs board of the Chogye-jong Order headquarters in Seoul. After considering Ch'oe's vision, the board

wanseum-
ɔsal
Bodhisattva
Mercy),
aksan
emple.

decided to proceed with the project. Some six months of hard labor and 700 tons of granite stone was required to complete his and Kwon's inspired sculpture. "From the day when the granite standing bodhisattva was solemnly dedicated, Naksan Temple went into a thousand-day prayer for national peace and security," reported a Dedication Day story in *The Korean Times.*

From this statue, which stands like an ancient beacon of hope on this quiet and rugged coastline, continue north past **Uisang-dae** and its tiny pink lighthouse to **Sokch'o** town. Sokch'o, an important northeast coast fishing port, has long been a hopping off point for seaside resorts to the north.

Private and government enterprise have developed several sand beach areas north of Sokch'o, but the all-time favorite languishing spot is **Hwajinp'o Beach** about halfway between Sokch'o and the DMZ (demilitarized zone). Korea's presidents have traditionally maintained summer villas here, as have other persons who appreciate comfort and beauty.

Beyond Sokch'o are several quaint fishing villages, exotic inland lagoons quackingly alive with fish and water-fowl, and broad, dune-like beaches as fine as any you'll discover in California. End of the line – and as far north as you can go in southern Korea – is **Taejin**, a friendly town of tiny streets with people who will be pleasantly surprised to see a foreigner this far off the beaten path, and boasting one of the most colorful fish-market docks in Korea.

"Underground Diamond Mountains": With the East Coast Expressway running all the way to P'ohang, traveling in these parts is now smooth and easy.

Mentioned below are some of the sights and sites along the southeast coast the visitor should not miss.

The strangely beautiful **Songnyu Cave**: Just south and then inland from **Uljin** town, **Songnyu-gul**, which is actually a proper limestone cavern adrip with bizarre stalactites and stalagmites, is, as one tour leader describes it, "a spelunker's delight." The easiest way to get there if you don't have a car of your

Cabanas, Hwajinp'o.

own is to catch a local bus from Uljin and travel 5 miles (8 kilometers) south to the Songnyu-gul bus stop. From there the cavern is about a 1.2 mile (2 kilometer) walk west on a dirt path or road across attractive rice paddies and along a curving riverbank.

At the cavern site, even early in the morning, you'll find uniformed guides, a complete curio shop, a lovely pavilion overlooking the chill river, and Korean-style cafes where you can either cool off or warm up, depending on the season.

Inside the 1,542-foot (470-meter) long cavern, which arches in a ragged crescent from a narrow stoop entrance to its final exit, you'll discover red, blue, yellow and white spotlights playing off weird limestone formations. Songnyu-gul's caretakers over the years have given nearly every stalagmite, stalactite, grotto and pool a proper or whimsical name: There's "The Upside-Down Diamond Mountains," "Cloudy Rock," "The Secret Room of a Nymph," statues of "St. Marie," "The Maitreya Buddha," and "Santa Claus." There's even a phallic, fluted, and spot-lit

"Love Ball" that towers over a 90-foot (30-meter) deep "Dragon Pond."

According to brochures about the cavern, it is a quarter of a billion years old. During the Hideyoshi invasions, it is written, sacred Buddha statues from a nearby Songnyu Temple were secreted away in these "Underground Diamond Mountains." However, according to another source, about 500 local residents who hid in the cavern from Hideyoshi's invaders starved to death when they were discovered and the Japanese sadistically blocked Songnyu-kul's narrow entrance.

The Paegam Hot Springs: Approximately 19 miles (30 kilometers) south of Uljin is **P'yonghae**, a quiet farming town where you can book a taxi or chance a bus to Korea's picturesque **Paegam Mountain and Hot Springs**. We say chance a bus, because the irregular buses that crawl up to the Paegam springs on a rocky and dusty road through beautiful highlands country are invariably overcrowded with people, animals and domestic goods. Taxis, though more expensive, are your best ploy. Once there you can rest and

isangdae shermen.

recuperate in some of Korea's most renowned mineral baths.

The Juwang Mountains: Korea hands who like to travel and embark on a getaway-from-it-all journey to the **Mt. Juwang National Park** due west of **Yongdong** and southeast of **Andong** via **Chongsong**. This 2,362-foot (720-meter) high East Coast mountain in north Kyongsang Province can usually be reached only by country bus; but according to visitors who have made the effort to get there, the trip is well worth the bouncing hassle. Consider the following comments made by traveler Cornie Choy:

"Juwang-san, the Mountains of King Ju, stood before me – an Oriental landscape painting on a folding screen. The tiny country inn a friend had told me about is perfectly situated on the grounds of an old Buddhist temple, a clear running stream in front of it. Beyond is a hermitage where only Buddhist nuns live – and all around us are towering granite peaks. My small room in a mud-walled, thatch-roofed hut is rustic, clean and simple . . .

"Eager for a walk, I set out, taking my time, following footpaths thru silent fragrant autumn woods whose leaves display their bright farewell, and along the sides of deep gorges with dragon waterfalls and fairy bathing pools the color of jade. . . By noon, I am deep in the mountains making my way up a rocky path which leads thru a narrow gorge where the sun never shines. As I come out of the gorge, I find myself in a quiet sunlit valley. There, hidden away from the rest of the world, is a lone Buddhist hermitage. Looming all around it, like fearless guardians, are the peaks of **Nahan-bong**, **Miruk-bong**, **Kwanseum-bong**, **Chichang-bong**, **Piru-bong** and **Pirot-bong** – all named after loyal disciples of Buddha.

"Approaching the hermitage, I notice the hermit monk – young, handsome and proud – chanting sutras to the rhythm of the wooden *mokt'ak* which he strikes . . . He invokes in me the following beautiful poem written by a Buddhist monk:

"Reach out your hands to me, Oh Buddha./With your mother-gentle hands of skyblue celadon, embrace this break- **Uisangdae**.

196

ing and falling reed./Lower a thick warm rope to this soul sinking into the darkness./I am longing for your Lord./Like the white foam which rises to the brim of the seas./Distill my longing into a single ruby bead. . ."

Pogyong-sa: In the foothills of **Naeyon-san**, just about 9 miles (15 kilometers) north of Pohang, is Pogyong-sa, a temple that offers a long history and a hike to a nearby pool and waterfall. A Western-style *yogwan* down the road to the right is a good spot to stay overnight. It offers a picturesque view of the mountains and is within drumbeat range of the Buddhist temple. If you can sleep with one ear alert for the early morning drum-call to prayer, you might want to repair outside for the sight of a sunrise and birds leaving nocturnal perches. The only human sounds you may hear will be your own stirring about and distant sutras being chanted by monks celebrating all life on earth.

Chinese Mirrors of Madung and Pumran: Once sleep is washed from your eyes, stroll over to Pogyong temple.

Just before reaching the temple proper, you will see a walled-in hermitage. Next to it is Pogyong-san where monks hold retreats for lay Buddhists. According to the sign posted at Pogyong-sa, this temple was built during the Silla dynasty when Buddhism was first introduced to Korea. At that time, priests Madung and Pumran returned from China with the new religion and two mirrors. One mirror had 12 facets and the other had eight. The eight-faceted mirror was given to Priest Ilcho, one of their disciples, who was told that if he went eastward, he would find a deep pond in Chongnamsan on the east coast of the Silla kingdom. If he threw the mirror into the water and filled the pond with earth and built a temple there, Buddhism would flourish.

The eight-faceted mirror is said to be buried under Pogyong-sa's **Choggwang Hall**. Fine Buddhist paintings are hung in Choggwang-jon and Taeung-jon, but what distinguishes this temple from most others is its backdrop of numerous waterfalls that streak the mountains which form this lush valley. There is a rather easy

hike along the trail beside the temple to a clear pool, and further to 11 other waterfalls where you can – if you will – enjoy a cool summer splash.

P'ohang: At the southern end of your East Coast adventure looms P'ohang, a seaport and resort area that since 1968 has been the apple of Korea's industrial eye. This is because P'ohang is the location of the model **P'ohang Iron and Steel Company Ltd (POSCO)**, Korea's successful producer of industrial steel and its by-products. This monument to Korean industry rises like a fiery sculpture along the rim of **Yongil Bay** and the East Sea.

POSCO is one of the world's biggest steel producers. P'ohang itself is not just dominated by POSCO. It *is* POSCO. Just as Ulsan is "Hyundai Town" where every major firm is part of the Hyundai group, so P'ohang appears a one-company town. Schools, gymnasiums, housing complexes are all part of POSCO. Were it not for the fact that this is capitalist South Korea, one might say the firm has achieved the socialist ideal in which everything is run for and provided by the state, or in this case, the company. POSCO is also an environment-conscious company and the town is remarkably clean considering it is based on steel.

If you're further interested in the fire and drama of ore-melting, blast furnaces, and bloom, slab, ingot and coil casting, tours can be arranged by contacting the Korea National Tourism Corporation of the POSCO public relations office.

Ullung-do: Few foreigners venture out to this island 166 miles (268 kilometers) northeast of P'ohang. Indeed, because of its location Ullung-do is one of Korea's best-kept secrets. But, look out – the word is getting around as tourism to this island is now being promoted by the government.

Some of the best sights and travel experiences in Korea are on this island, which is about halfway between Korea and Japan (and is the farthest east one can go and still be in Korea). Embark on the *Han Il Ho* speedboat ferry in P'ohang, and six hours later you'll be strolling into **To-dong** town on Ullung-do's southeast coast. (Another proposed ferry from **Imwon** in Kangwon province may be in operation.)

A diverging footpath into town takes you past children and adults sitting and lying outside their homes on straw mats. On warm summer nights they relax on these mats while chit-chatting with neighbors. Clapboard walls without windowpanes flimsily divide the outside from the indoors during the warm season. Until the late 1970s there were no roads nor cars on the island. The noises were the same sounds of animal and man as they had been for centuries. Now there is a round-island road and, of course, cars and trucks. However, the air is still sea-fresh and the stars shine in the clear night skies.

There are many *yogwan* in town – almost all of them without locks on the doors; Ullung-do, in fact, has long had a reputation for being theft-free. A few of the *yogwan* fronting To-dong Harbor have rooftop decks where one can sip a sunset beer and watch fishermen dock their boats. Meals, which include freshly caught seafood, can be ordered at most *yogwan* or cafes.

Behind the town and up a path towards the rugged mountains and forest is a mineral water fountain that spews out of a stone-carved turtle's mouth set in the mountainside. Foreign visitors like to splash a bit of Johnny Walker "on the rocks" and mix it with the fresh mineral water. The island's freshwater is very soft (as you'll find out when you bathe), and it's also pure enough to drink straight from waterpumps.

Bat caves, **Chuk-do-beef** and **Night squidfishing**: To get a 360-degree view of Ullung-do, hike up 3,228-foot (984-meter) high **Songin-bong**, the island's highest peak. Set off at daybreak and you'll be high among the clouds by mid-morning and back down just as the sun's heat becomes oppressive.

To circle the island, you can either hike 25 miles (40 kilometers) across valleys and along the coast (which takes three days) or hire a boat. Either way, you'll find coves with bat caves (in Korean, *pakkwi-kul*) and sun-toasted beaches with warm clear water.

The beach at **Wata-ri** on the east coast features a freshwater falls that rushes into a saltwater pool. Stop for a morning swim at this beach, shower under the falls, and boat across to **Chuk-do**, a flat-topped islet jutting out across the water.

Approach this island from the south side, then scale its deep hillside. The hike up the steps to the top may seem arduous, but the men on this island actually carry calves on their backs all the way up to this island's highland farm. The fattened, corn-fed cattle are then lifted off the island by rope onto barges and sent to Ullung-do to be eaten. Chuk-do beef is renowned as the tastiest and tenderest in Korea. Four families who live on this small island mountaintop also raise watermelon (which some say is the sweetest in Korea), and the young, thin bamboo growing here is used for stretching out and drying squid in Ullung-do. Large mulberry leaves are grown here, too, for silkworm production on the mainland. Indeed, though the island is small, there is even room for a camelia forest which blooms in early to late February. Next to the camelia forest are palownia trees – the only tree, according to Korean mythology, on which a phoenix will land.

All along Ullung-do's coast, steep mountainsides drop straight down to a sea which is a most unusual, clear shade of blue – like liquid blue laundry bleach. Women divers with heavy lead weights tied to their waists bring up catches of seacucumbers, lobsters, crabs, abalones, prawns, and other shellfish.

Off the northeast coast is a sea grotto of unique, craggy candlestick rock formations with nesting sea birds. The northernmost rock, **Kongam**, has a hole through which you can boat.

On the southwest side of the island, just north of **Namyang**, is **T'aeha-dong**, the landing site of the first Koreans to migrate to this island 1,000 years ago. A children's shrine, which may be locked, is maintained in this town. Nearby is **Sat'ekam beach**, a cove with warm, calm waters ideal for swimming.

Climax your Ullung-do experience with a squid-fishing expedition. Squid fishermen set off at night, and once at sea they light up a string of bright lights across their boats to attract the squid. The brightly-lit squid boats bobbing in the dark are a memorable-sight.

West Coast

32 km / 20 miles

Pŏngt'aek

Kyŏngbu Expressway

Chungbu Expressway

Umsŏng

Manghyang Garden

Chinch'ŏn

Koesan

Haptŏk

Sapkyoho Lake

Ch'ŏnan

Onyang

Independence Hall of Korea

Chŭngp'yŏng

Sŏsan

Kaeshimsa

T'aean

Yesan

Hyangch'ŏnsa

Ch'ŏngju

T'AEAN HAEAN NAT'L PARK

Hongsŏng

Choch'iwon

Poŭn

Anmyŏn

Kwangch'ŏng

Kongju

Ch'ŏng-yang

Taech'ongho Lake

Taech'ŏn

KYERYONGSAN NAT'L PARK

Taejŏn

Okch'ŏn

Puyŏ

Kanggyŏng

Nonsan

Kŭmsan

Yŏngdong

Sŏch'ŏn

Kŭmgang R.

Hamyŏl

Muju

Yellow Sea

Kunsan

Okku

Pongdong

Samnye

Wibongsansŏng Fortress

TOGYUSAN NAT'L PARK

Kimje

Chŏnju

Chinan

Puan

Horam Expressway

Shint'aein

Imshil

Changsu

PYŎNSANBANDO NAT'L PARK

WIDO I.

Chŏngju

Kaltam Res.

NAEJANGSAN NAT'L PARK

Olympic Expressway

Hamyang

Hongnong

Koch'ang

Sunch'ang

Namwon

Hwangsan Victory Monument

Chirisan
1915

Changsŏng

Tamyang

Koksŏng

Yŏnggwang

Kurye

Pulgapsa

Somjin-gang R.

IMJADO I.

Chido

Kwangju

Hwasun

Sŭngju

Hadong

Hamp'yŏng

Naju

Muan

Sŭngjuho Lake

Sunch'ŏn

Kwang-yang

CHAŬNDO I.

AP'AEDO I.

Yŏngsanho Lake

Pŏlgyo

PIGŬMDO I.

Mokp'o

Yŏng-am

Posŏng

Yŏch'ŏn

WOLCH'ULSAN NAT'L PARK

Yŏsu

Haenam Bay

Changhŭng

Chindo Bridge

Kangjin

Taegu Ceramic Kilns

Kohŭng

Tolsan

HAT'AEDO I.

Haenam

Toyang

Chindo

Yongjangsansŏng Fortress

Taedŏk

KOGŬMDO I.

CHINDO I.

KOGŬMDO I.

THE WEST COAST

A journey down Korea's West Coast – with occasional side trips island – provides fascinating nature sights and cultural insights into the southwest provinces of **Kyonggi-do**, the **Ch'ungch'ong-dos**, and the **Cholla-dos**.

Korea's jagged West Coast, cut by the whimsical Yellow Sea, is dotted with myriad peninsula islets floating offshore, and bordered by sandy beaches overlooking quiet pine glens. Along this coast village fishermen and seasonal beachgoers regulate their activities according to tidal changes, because the tide differential is so extreme. In certain areas at low tide, the **Yellow Sea** exposes vast mud flats 17 feet (5.2 meters) to 25 feet (7.6 meters) offshore – a distance second in tide extremes only to the Bay of Fundy in Nova Scotia.

To reach the West Coast, head south from Seoul on the **Seoul-Pusan Expressway**, otherwise known as the **Kyongbu Expressway**, then veer west and southwest on Highway 21 into the lush, terraced valleys and rolling hills of Ch'ungch'ongnam-do.

Onyang Stopover: Travelers enroute to the coast may find **Onyang**, about 11 miles (18 kilometers) west of **Ch'on-an** on Highway 21, to be a refreshing stop along the way. A hot spring and **Hyonch'ungsa Shrine**, which is dedicated to Korea's great 16th-century naval hero, Admiral Yi Sun-sin, have long attracted visitors. But since the **Onyang Folk Museum** in **Kongok-ni** opened in 1978, tourist traffic to Onyang has increased. Touted as having the best all-around collection of Korean folk art in the world, the privately-owned Onyang Folk Museum boasts over 7,000 traditional Korean folk articles – only a portion of the vast collection Kim Wondae has accumulated over the past two decades. Three diorama display halls depict the life and traditions of Koreans with authentic household articles, work utensils, and religious, recreational and scholastic items.

Primed after a stimulating hot bath, a pilgrimage to Admiral Yi's shrine, and insights into Korean culture, you head westward to **Mallip'o Beach** and Korea's largest arboretum.

Flora Koreana: Nature lovers may flee to popular Mallip'o Beach on the western tip of a peninsula which flares into the Yellow Sea like a snarling dragon. Just north of Mallip'o Beach lies **Ch'ollip'o,** another kind of haven for flora and folks fond of flora. On a 200-acre sanctuary, more than 7,000 varieties of plants, almost exclusively of temperate climates, thrive on a stable climate, the longer springs and autumns in this region, and on the fog and mist which provide a natural water-sprinkling system. The **Ch'ollip'o Arboretum** is nurtured and owned by Ferris Miller, a naturalized Korean originally from Wilkes-Barre, Pennsylvania, who has lived in Korea for over four decades.

Some of the plants in Miller's arboretum are indigenous. Others were imported from around the world. There are, for example, two varieties of magnolia indigenous to Korea at Ch'ollip'o, and 180 pax variety from elsewhere. The entire magnolia family, however, accounts for 800 members. Hollies have been hybridized at the arboretum; there are presently 450 hollies. Among the many botanical wonders flourishing in Miller's arboretum are such rare species as the *glyptostrobus lineatus*, a conifer from southern China, and *magnolia biondii* from north central China.

Although Ch'ollip'o is a private arboretum, Miller welcomes people who are genuinely interested in plants, who have a respect for nature, and who can resist picking flowers without permission.

"The Beach": Veteran westerners in Korea have long favored the West Coast's Taech'on Beach, or **Taech'on-dae**, as a spring through fall resort haven. This fun spot, about 9 miles (14 kilometers) from the town of Taech'on, can be reached by bus or train and car from Seoul.

As you near **Taech'on** town, fields of yellow barley – the staple added to rice or boiled into drinking tea – cut bright yellow swaths across the summer rice terraces. Taech'on is a lush agricultural

Preceding pages, autumn is a great spectacle, particularly along Korea's western coast.

area, but it's also well-known in Korea for its coal mines in surrounding hills which contribute the base fuel from which *yont'an*, or charcoal heating briquettes, are made. Other industries are salt-making and cuttle-fishing.

"The Beach" (Taech'on to locals) is actually unofficially divided into two sectors – a northern stretch called "KB," or the **"Korean Beach,"** and a southern stretch called the **"Foreigners' Beach."** This was originally a Christian missionaries' resort, and many Taech'on homes are still occupied by missionaries or their descendants, by members of Seoul's diplomatic and banking corps, and by a more *nouveau corps* of wealthy Korean business and government leaders.

The Korean Beach – where discos and wine houses co-exist with sleepy fishermen's huts – is a non-stop boogie scene during the peak summer season. But the well-manicured foreigners' beach maintains a residential dignity.

During spring through fall the foreigners' sector of Taech'on is reminiscent of northern California's coastline, what with its piney bluffs, rocky back bays, and offshore isles. On a clear day, you can see for nearly 40 miles (64 kilometers) across the Yellow Sea in the direction of China and toward the island of **Wonsan-do.**

Paekche Capitals: Further inland from Taech'on, away from frolicking surf and missionary resorts, lie the ancient towns of **Kongju** and **Puyo.** To get to these towns, it is necessary to return to the Seoul-Pusan Expressway.

Kongju is about 22 miles (35 kilometers) southwest of the expressway on Highway 36. It was once the capital of the Paekche Kingdom until the capital was moved south to Puyo. Both Kongju and Puyo have retained the limelight in the 20th century because of Paekche relics which have recently been excavated in the central and south-eastern provinces of Korea.

In Kongju, a **national museum** was dedicated in 1972 to house relics found around town. Almost half of the 6,800 display items were excavated from **King Muyong** (r. 501-523) **tomb.** As you browse past Muyong's gold crown ornaments, his exquisitely engraved bronze mirror, and other Paekche articles, remember that it was this same craftsmanship which was taught to the Japanese by emigrant Paekche artisans.

From Kongju, head further southwest 31 miles (50 kilometers) and deeper into Paekche history and legacy to Puyo on the curving Highway 23. Along the way, pause at **Kap-sa** temple on the outskirts of **Kyeryong-san National Park.**

Paekche historical remains abound in Puyo. For openers, there is in a park near the entrance to town a seated stone Buddha and a five-story stone pagoda – one of three left from the Three Kingdoms Period. Other relics are displayed in the **Puyo National Museum.** Prehistoric stoneware vessels, shamanistic instruments, gilt-bronze and stone Buddhist statues, gold and jade ornaments and other treasures attest to the development and excellence of Paekche craftsmen, who were influenced by central Asian and North and South China artists. Much of the stonework is damaged due to the Silla and T'ang China attacks that brought this dynasty to its end.

The Puyo museum building is a curiosity that was designed by a Korean architect according to traditional Paekche lines, which were adapted by the Japanese. Indeed, the modern rendition looked so Paekche in style that it was criticized for its Japanese resemblance.

Paekche legacy extends itself beyond the museum. Along the serene **Kum River** at **Paengma-gang (White Horse River),** remnants of the grandeur and the fateful fall of the Paekche kingdom of some 1,300 years ago are preserved. Picnic on the flat rock (**Nan-sok, Warm Rock**) on the riverbank at **Saja,** just as the Paekche kings used to. On the opposite side of the river is the picturesque **Nakhwa-am (Rock of the Falling Flowers)** bluff with a pavilion on its brow. Tradition says that the T'ang dynasty general Su Ting-fang lured a protective dragon out of the river with a white horse's head, and thus was able to cross the river and conquer Puyo. Out of loyalty to their king and to preserve their dignity, court women jumped to their deaths from Nakhwa-am into the river. As recorded in some Korean epics, they looked like falling blossoms as their colorful *ch'ima-chogori* dresses billowed in their deadly flight.

From these Paekche visions, head southeast along Highway 23 to Kwanch'ok Temple outside of **Nonsan** and to one of the most impressive Buddhas in Korea (Kwanch'ok-sa is also accessible from Seoul via the Seoul-Pusan and Honam Expressways).

The Unjin Miruk: As you scale up the stone steps on the P'anya hillside to **Kwanch'ok-sa (Temple of the Candlelights)**, all the superlative descriptions you've ever heard regarding the **Unjin Miruk** – the 1,000-year-old, largest standing stone Buddha in Korea – stir you with anticipation. Your curiosity is piqued when, at the top of a flight of stairs, your first glance at the Unjin Miruk is through the clear, horizontal window of the temple (if the temple doors are open). All you can see of the "Buddha of the Future" is its face – its eyes peering back at you through the holy sanctum.

The "Standing Stone Kwansaeum Maitreya" in its totality is awesome. Its disproportionate massiveness, extended earlobes, crown, and large hands formed in a mudra all suggest a higher evolved spiritual being. Its face, however, which is scrubbed clean occasionally, has flat features and exotic, almond eyes, not unlike the Koreans, and sculpted toes – all of which give it human qualities. Situated in the rear of the temple courtyard, the Unjin Miruk stands sedately at the foot of a stand of dwarf maple and scrub pine.

Also included at Kwanch'ok-sa are a five-story stone pagoda, lantern, and altar which were constructed while the Unjin Miruk was being sculpted.

From Nonsan, as you head along the old road to **Chonju**, you will pass the **Nonsan Army Basic Training Camp** near **Yonmu**. This camp is the largest in Korea, and almost every young male in the country has been trained here at one time or another.

Continuing southward on Highway 23, your vehicle passes through several

The Beach," which locals refer to as aech'on.

small villages and various monuments to the past. In **Kum-ma (Gold Horse)** village, just past an open-air granite carving shop, there is a gracious poplar carriage road and rivulet that cuts through a field. About 300 feet (100 meters) down the right side of this road, one of two pairs of banner stone posts which once belonged to a temple entranceway remains. Across the road from these stone posts is the oldest stone pagoda in Korea, **Miruk-sa** (originally named **Wanghung-sa**). This granite tower was built during the Paekche period around AD 600-610 by King Pop and his successor-son, King Mu. It stands 44 feet (13.5 meters) high, and is large enough for the curious to walk through. Formerly either seven or nine stories, it was partially destroyed by lightning during the reign of Silla King Songdok (r. 702-737). The pagoda was reinforced in 1915 during the Japanese occupation, but today the six remaining stories of the pagoda are surrounded by rubble. Workmen reconstructing Miruk-sa in 1965 discovered a unique gold plate with Buddhist scriptures and other treasures.

Two more sculptures lie along the country road south toward Chonju. The first outside Kum-ma village are a pair of stone Miruk standing on grass mounds facing each other some 600 feet (200 meters) apart across a rice field. They are said to be about 120 years old, but their purpose remains a mystery. Between them the Honam Plain stretches without a mountain in close proximity. The second sculpture is **Wanggung Tower** which is in the middle of a field. Some say it was once in the palace of the Mahan dynasty, but most historians claim it was originally placed at this site as part of the remains of **Ch'esuk** temple which was built during the end of the Unified Silla period. This five-story granite tower is 29 feet (9 meters) high and 10 feet (3 meters) wide, and its grounds are still tended to by a gardener despite its seclusion.

Along the Honam Expressway to Chonju, mountains and hills roll endlessly in every direction. Considered

Burial mounds, Chonju.

the "rice bowl of Korea," Chollapuk-do is a veritable cornucopia of food. In the late spring, rains water the fields, and the farmers can be seen bent over, planting rice together in even rows. The Korean curve motif is everywhere in this pastoral scene – in subtle curves of terraced rice paddies, the rolling curves of mountains, hills and burial mounds, and the upcurved roofs of traditional farmhouses.

Chonju City, Papar and Pi Pim Pap: Chonju, which is 58 miles (93 kilometers) south of Seoul, is the provincial capital of Chollapuk-do. It is the ancestral home of the descendants of Yi Song-gye, founder of the Yi dynasty, and is famous for paper products (fans, umbrellas and proper papers), *pi pim pap*, and food in general.

Papermaking was introduced to Korea by the Chinese about 1,000 years ago. The Koreans, however, became so adept at this fine craft that both Chinese and Japanese calligraphers came to favor Korean papers over their own.

Technology has encroached on the handmade papermaking industry, but in Chonju villagers still actively perpetuate this tradition in their homes and in makeshift factories. The sound of new paper pulps swishing in water rises out of windows, and in backyards white sheets of paper hang like drying laundry.

Despite modernization, papermaking is still best done by hand. Fibers of the *ttang* tree, mulberry stems, bamboo (all brought from other areas in Korea) and other flora are stripped and cooked into a soft pulp and then bleached in a soda solution. They are then transferred to a large wooden and cement vat. Rectangular bamboo mat screens suspended from resilient bamboo poles are dipped in and out of these pulp-filled vats, and – with a rhythmic finesse that has made this process a fascinating sight – a sheet of sopping wet paper is eventually sieved onto the bamboo screens. The entire process may be observed at **Oh Dong-ho's factory** at the end of Chonju's main street – just before a small bridge and to the left along a red brick wall.

A variety of paper in various textures

and colors is available in Oh's paper and antique shop in town called **Koryo Tang**, "**The House of Meaning Taste**." In Oh's paper stocks are *unhyang-ji* of course mulberry, a basic wrapping paper; *wha-son-ji* for brush painting; *chang-ji* ("paper of 1,000 years") from the *ttang* tree for calligraphy; *chang p'an-ji* for *ondol* floors; *ttae ju-ji*, algae paper; *chuk-ji*, bamboo paper; *p'i-ji*, bark chip paper; and recycled paper made from various secondary papers. If you have trouble finding Oh's paper place, ask a local to direct you to **Pungnam-mun**, Chonju's ancient south gate. "The House of Meaning Taste" is near this entrance.

Ah, but ask any Korean what Chonju is *really* famous for and the answer will be "*Pi pim pap!*" Don't leave Chonju without tasting the state-of-the-art in this food form. At the famous, long-established **Han Il Kwan Restaurant** (progenitor of the two Han Il Kwan branches in Seoul), the *pi pim pap* comes with the rice deliciously mixed with soy sprouts and topped with broiled and sliced meat, fern bracken, strips of boiled squid, bluebell roots, toasted sesame seeds, pine nuts and a sunny-side-up egg. This savory dish is further accompanied by a bowl of beef broth and side dishes of cool seaweed and onion soap further spiced by at least five kinds of *kimch'i*.

Indeed, even at the simplest Chonju restaurant expect to see amazing foods piled up at your table, in some cases *at least* as many as 20 different side dishes. When in Chonju, don't be shy – eat!

Before leaving town, however, be sure to visit the private antique shop-museum **Chon Bok T'uk San P'um Ch'on** run by Chon Jin-han and located near the **T'o Chong (Provincial Central Headquarters)**. Chon's family collection is one of the best in Korea. It includes traditional Korean masks, Silla ceramic pieces, woven goods, and fine antique jewelry.

A Chonju city bus or taxi will get you out to **Songgwang-sa**, a fine Buddhist temple between Chongju and **Mai-san**. Located in a corner of a quaint village

Admiral Yi duplicates and friend, Chonju.

that produces *onp'an-ji* paper for *ondol* floors, Songgwang-sa offers the jaded temple seeker some of the finest mineral color murals in Korea. Flying fairies and *mudang* (sorceresses) are painted directly on the walls and ceiling of this temple. These 150- to 200-year-old artworks were rendered in earthy and warm greens, orange, blues and yellow. Its characters posture and prance as if they were part of a modern animated film. Carved wooden fairies, wispy as clouds are suspended from the ceiling above three enormous gilded maitreyas. Even the main altar is splendidly wood-carved.

Horse Ears and Frozen Fairies: The winding road on to **Mai-san**, **Horse Ears Mountain**, is a joyful cruise in its newly paved condition. There are charming and classical sights at nearly every highway turn. Just five minutes outside of Chonju, for example, you will see on your left a series of hills covered with hundreds of traditional Korean grave mounds. This is an unusually crowded pre-Christian-style cemetery.

A few miles further, a splendid Buddha can be seen enshrined in a large granite bluff. All along this 21-mile (34-kilometer) haul eastward and up and over the **Chinan Plateau** to **Chinan**, farmers are out planting rice in the late spring, and, at other times, tending plots of hay, tobacco, onions and ginseng.

The famous Mai-san "Horse Ears" are not visible until you get quite close to Chinan town. There, over to the right yonder, they spring up from behind a large knoll above a meandering riverbed. From Chinan, lovely Mai-san is but a two-mile (three-kilometer) cruise southward through an oak forest where mushrooms are cultivated under clusters of short logs leaning against trees.

As everything in Korea has its divine or mythical reason for existence, the two Mai-san peaks are no exception. Legend notes that before Mai-san was created, two fairies – one male, the other female – once lived there. They were enjoying their respite on earth when one day their heavenly creator called for them to make their ascent back home.

He warned them to let no mortal eye witness their flight, so they carefully planned their departure for the next full moon night. This was so the moon could light their path to heaven.

The chosen night was overcast, so they decided to wait until dawn, an escape deadline decreed by their creator. As the two fairies were ascending to heaven, however, they were spotted by an early-rising housewife. They looked back at this eagle-eyed mortal, and were transformed into stones and fell back to earth as the two curious peaks of Mai-san. Moral: Don't procrastinate. If you are curious as to which frozen-in-place fairy is which, the peak to the left is called **Sut Mai** (Male Horse Ear) and the one to the right is **Am Mai** (Female Horse Ear).

A Hermit's Stone Vision: Once you reach Mai-san, your expedition has just begun. The hike through narrow **Chong-hwang Pass** between the two horse ears is a stair-climbing, heart-thumping rise up 132 steps. Up there, near **Hwaom Cave**, you can rest a while and enjoy a panoramic view of Chinan and environs. Continue into a small valley on the south side of the ears, veer to your right (while negotiating another 181 steps in segments) and you will come to one of the most bizarre Buddhist temples in Korea. Built by the hermit monk Yi Kap-yong, this **T'ap-sa (Pagoda Temple)** religious site is a collection of stone pagodas, some of them 30 feet (9 meters) high. All were built without mortar and have stood in surrealistic splendor in this narrow valley since the early part of this century. The Spanish architect Gaudi would weep with joy if he could return to life and study hermit Yi's architectural fantasy. The path past these "Shaking Pagodas" continues through the steep mountains to temples such as **Unsu-sa**, **Kundang-sa** and **Isan-myo Shrine**, all just about a half-mile walk away.

A white statue of the Hermit monk Yi sits comfortably at the foot of his Maisan temple complex. Yi holds on to a wooden walking staff and stares west toward the rising sun that bathes him, his narrow

Rice-planting, Chollanam-d area.

valley home and his zany pagodas with amber light of morn.

A *yogwan* at T'ap-sa's base offers accommodations to the weary body and soul not keen to rush back to civilization. **Kumsan-sa** (Gold Mountain Temple) on the western slope of **Moak-san**, is reputedly the most beautiful temple in **Chollapuk-do**. It is about 21 miles (34 kilometers) southwest of Chonju. Take the old Highway 1 heading southwest from Chonju toward Kwangju, and some 16 miles (26 kilometers) later, just north of **Wonp'yong-ni**, veer eastward along a side road that will lead up to Kumsan-sa.

The pathway to the temple entrance is adorned with a line of cherry trees and Himalayan pine (*Nakyop song* "Falling Needle Pine") and a pool off to the right side of the path. This short walkway induces a meditative calm which prepares the traveler for Kumsan-sa itself.

First built in 599, Kumsan-sa was rebuilt in 766 by High Priest Chinp'yo Yulsa during the Silla dynasty and enlarged in 1079 (during the Koryo period) by High Priest Hyedok Wangsa. The complex was burned during the 1592 Hideyoshi invasion, then finally rebuilt in 1626. Today, its main hall, **Miruk-jon**, stands three stories high, making Kumsan-sa the tallest temple in Korea. This spaciousness is devoted to housing 10 designated cultural assets from Silla, Paekche, and Koryo periods. Miruk-jon, a worship hall for the god Avalokiteswara, is one of these 10 treasures.

Inside Miruk-jon, a huge golden Maitreya (Buddha of the Future) stands 39 feet (12 meters) tall, holding a red lotus blossom in its left palm. It is flanked by two crowned bodhisattvas, Taemyosang and Pophwarim. Below the statues, behind the wooden grill, a stairway leads down to the Maitreya's feet. One may walk down the steps to kiss the candlelit Maitreya's feet and make an offering.

Next to Miruk-jon, above the left slope of the hill, is a stupa made of stone and a six-story granite pagoda where a monk's body minerals are enshrined after cremation. The pagoda's roofs are flat and subtly curved at the corners, in traditional Paekche style. The roofs to all of the temple structures, in fact, were never measured with anything but the eye.

In Taejung-jon worship hall behind wood-carved doors which survived the 1592 Hideyoshi invasion, a gold-gilt Sakyamuni Buddha sits with a mandala around it – a rare embellishment.

In the second largest hall, the Nahan-jon Buddha sits with 500 sculptured disciples, each exhibiting different facial expressions. On the way back down the path, there is a Zelkova elm tree. Large and branching, it is renowned as a fertility tree. If one throws a stone up the tree trunk and the stone doesn't drop, legend says that person will soon have a child.

"Inner Sanctum" Mountain: From Kumsan-sa, traverse tobacco fields along the main tributary road here and rejoin the world's mainstream and traffic on the Honam Expressway bound southwest for **Naejang-san National Park**. In this national park an entry tunnel of red maple trees paints fiery fall colors on the reflective faces of visitors.

The journey up to Naejang (Inner Sanctum) Mountain National Park near **Chong-up** is a peaceful prelude to a pilgrimage to **Paegyang Temple**. Up here, in maples and mist and steep mountain passes, you will find a pleasure pavilion placed aesthetically onto a massive and living scroll.

Upon reaching the Paegyang (White Sheep) Temple you will already be properly inspired and in the mood to consider this place and its Son, or Zen, Buddhist origins. Originally built in AD 632, Paegyang-sa was then called **Paegam-sa** after Mt. Paegam. Son master Hwangyang Suro Sa renamed it Paegyang-sa in 1574. Despite its reclusiveness this temple befell malevolent forces four times – twice it was destroyed by invaders. It was rebuilt a fifth time by Son master Sangmanam Taejongsa in 1917. In its present form it sits like a jewel in the midst of mountain foliage that seems to be afire during late autumn. An aged and lonely bodhi tree broods in the temple's main courtyard.

Just outside of Paegyang-sa enroute to the city of Kwangju, the **Changsong Lake and Reservoir** seems to stretch endlessly through the mountains like a wide river. From here it is about an hour's drive to Kwangju via Honam Expressway. The landscape is a continuum of hills and mountains – here and there a burial mound cut and manicured into a piney slope.

Tamyang Bamboo: One of the most revered plants in Korea is bamboo, called *tae-namu* (or great tree) in Korean. It is splintered into chopsticks, carved into spoons, harvested for its delicious tender shoots, and immortalized in paintings and poetry.

The center of bamboo growing and craftsmanship in Korea is **Tamyang**, north of Kwangju on the main highway. The best time to visit Tamyang is on market day, which falls on days which end with the number 2 or 7. The market is held along the **Paekchin River**. Across the river is a bright chartreuse bamboo forest. The bamboo is usually not cultivated longer than three years, as its purposes are not for construction, but specifically for basket weaving. Villagers bring these utilitarian objects down from their nearby village homes on market day, which starts around 9 a.m. and peters out by 3 p.m. Straw and bamboo mats are sold near the market above the riverbank.

Tea For You: **Kwangju**, the ancient provincial capital of **Chollanam-do**, is a low-key city where at night, in many areas of the central city, vehicular traffic ceases and streets become pedestrian malls busy with strolling townfolk.

Kwangju competes with Chonju for honors such as "best food in Korea" and "the most food served in Korea." This is because in the past wealthy landlords established gracious food standards, and also because the lush Honam Plain in Chollanam-do has agriculturally helped supply that gourmet reputation. Also, the country's best *ch'ungchong* (barley and rice wine) and *makkolli* (a simpler form of rice wine) are served here with an array of *anju* (drinking snacks) which make a veritable dinner out of a drink.

Mudung (Peerless) Mountain hovers like a guardian over Kwangju City. A resort area has been created at its base among acacia trees and beside a whis-pering stream. Along Mudung's right flank are two factory buildings which are used for tea production during spring and autumn tea-harvesting seasons. A tea plantation previously owned by the famous turn-of-the-century Yi dynasty artist Ho Paek-nyon (now cared for by Buddhist monks) sprawls next to Mudung's **Chung Sim (Pure Mind) Temple**.

Perhaps tea has helped purify the minds of local monks. A monk at Chung Sim-sa explained that in Korea green leaf tea was traditionally the preferred brew of only monks and scholars. They believed this tea purified their blood and stimulated them so that they could resist sleep, and study until dawn. It must work, because even today Mudung-sa monks cultivate *chon sol* – "Spring Snow" tea – on slopes adjacent to their temple.

The small *chon-sol* leaves must be cut at a very early growth stage and then steamed and dried nine times in the early morning dew and mist (intense heat or cold spoils the delicate leaves). This is a very tedious tea-cultivation process which apparently only Buddhist monks can patiently manage. The tea, which smells of aromatic persimmons, is said to aid digestion and whet the appetite.

The two-story **Kwangju Museum** was built to house Yuan dynasty booty that was discovered in a sunken 600-year-old Chinese ship in the Yellow Sea in 1976. This archaeological find is exhibited on the ground floor gallery. A map there illustrates the spread of Yuan dynasty kilns throughout Eastern China down to Hong Kong, across to Korea's west coast, and on to Japan, Tenega Island and Okinawa. Among the finds are early 14th-century Luang-Ch'uan wares – including celadon vases with two rings and a peony design in relief, cups shaped like flowers, and a celadon druggist's mortar and pestle.

Upstairs on the second floor is a gallery of Cholla Province treasures which includes Neolithic Korean relics from Taehuksan-do, 11th- to 14th-century bronze Buddha bells, Yi dynasty scroll paintings, and white porcelain.

The golden Miruk-bul (Buddha of the Future) Kumsan-sa, Moak-san.

ANDONG, HAHOE AND PUSOK-SA

Take a side trip inland from the East Coast's pleasurable beaches, ski resort, phenomenal caves and hot springs to Andong, where Yi dynasty *yangban* (aristocrats) still walk down the streets. Andong has become synonymous with *yangban* since the Andong Kwon clan served in high government positions during Korea's last dynasty.

Stately Haraboji: The hour-long ride on Highway 34 westward from **Yongdog** to Andong – or the 6-hour-long, roundabout train ride from Seoul – begins to get interesting as your bus or train enters the outskirts of Andong town. The monotony of hills and grain fields and modern Saemaul cement villages is broken by several sturdy, warm, wooden houses with white rubber *komusin* (Korean shoes with upturned toes) lined up outside lattice doors on the *maru* (wooden porch).

Andong is full of small surprises and ironies. Expect to see stately *haraboji* (grandfathers) dressed in *hanbok* (traditional Korean clothes) and sporting horse-hair hats, top-knots, horn-rimmed glasses, and wispy beards, strolling around town. Although the 20th century has encroached on this provincial town with a multi-purpose dam and concrete architecture, a few *yangban* manors have managed to survive through the ages with a traditional graciousness and charm. These houses are easily recognized by their roofs of charcoal-colored tile which curve upward over thick wooden beams, white and cement-covered mud walls, windows and doors of paper and wood, a hard wooden *maru,* and weathered wood railings that surround the house. Above the front entrance, a signboard in an ancestor's finest calligraphic script proclaims the dignity of the dwelling. These old houses preserved to this day are not without modern trappings. You can easily spot electrical wiring and an ubiquitous television antennae.

An ironic juxtaposition of buildings in the heart of town has placed the **Andong**

Taewon Buddhist temple at the foot of a knoll which supports the classical Catholic cathedral, built of red brick with a white cross atop its spire.

Outside of the town is a seven-story brick pagoda, **Ch'il Ch'un Chon T'ap**, with Unified Silla era relief engravings of god-generals and devas. This pagoda is thought to be the oldest, biggest pagoda in the country. You'll find both in **Sinsedong** along the railroad tracks.

Tosan Sowon, Thousand Won Academy: An epitome of Confucianism that shouldn't be missed while in the Andong area is **Tosan Sowon Confucian Academy**. The academy is a 17-mile (28-kilometer) inter-city bus ride north of Andong, and a one-mile walk down a winding paved road that overlooks a peaceful blue lake and green rice paddies.

Tosan Sowon was initiated by Yi Whang (also known as T'oegye, Tong, T'oedo and Ch'ongnyangsanin; 1501-70), one of the foremost Confucian scholars of Korea and once Chief of Confucian Studies and Affairs. The name Tosan Sowon was given to the academy in 1575 by King Sonjo. The government also later acknowledged Yi Whang and his academy by depicting both on the commonly circulated 1,000 won note.

Confucianism is no longer instructed at Tosan Sowon, but one can stroll through the hallowed **Tosan Sodang lecture hall** at the main entranceway, see the wooden plates that were used for printing lessons in the **Kyongchanggak archive**, and study some of Yi Whang's relics – his gnarly walking cane and books of his teachings rendered in his personal calligraphy. The wooden, tiled Yi dynasty house behind the academy and over the ridge has been the abode of Yi Whang's descendants for the past 16 generations.

An older institution, and one which is still very much alive with followers, is the **Pongjong-sa Buddhist temple**, 10 miles (16 kilometers) northwest of Andong city. But perhaps a more awesome sight is the 40-foot (12.4-meter) high **Amit'aba Buddha** carved on a mammoth boulder on the mountain at **Chebiwon**, 3 miles (5 kilometers) from Andong enroute to **Yongju** on Highway 5. This Buddha,

which dates back to the Koryo dynasty, stands on single lotus petals. Its robe and hands are carved into a massive granite boulder, and its head and hair are carved of two separate pieces of rock set into holy place. A stone pagoda sits higher on the slope among gnarled pines.

Charming Hahoe: A purer essence of Yi dynasty architecture and rural life has been maintained for the past 500 years in a hamlet called **Hahoe**. This village is a half-hour ride southwest of Andong. During the Yi dynasty Hahoe was celebrated for its literati, military leaders, and for a form of mask dance drama that evolved there. Today, it is appreciated for its rustic, traditional aesthetics.

Hahoe is certainly off the beaten track, which has helped to keep it traditional. The Andong inter-city bus makes infrequent round-trips as far as **Chungni** (about 2½ miles or 4 kilometers north of Hahoe). Be advised to take a taxi or wait at a bus stop at the western fringe of town for a privately-run bus to **P'ungsan**, which is 10 miles (16 kilometers) west of Andong. P'ungsan is your last glimpse of paved Korea; the zigzagging 5-mile (8-kilometer) dirt road to Hahoe passes Chungni, cutting through grain and vegetable fields, and, finally, the bus deposits you in 16th-century Korea. Earthen thatched huts, larger *yangban* manors of wood and tile, the surrounding T'aebaek Mountains, and the serpentine Naktong River which bends around Hahoe, speak of a Korea that is warm, hearty and strongly rooted in tradition.

The dirt path that wends around the hamlet is inlaid with chips of ceramic and tile. Cows are tethered in the front yard, chewing on hay. Under the tiled and thatched cave of each home is a row of fermented soybean (*twoenjang*) patties drying in the sun. *Chige,* or A-frames used for carrying heavy loads, lean against mud walls. In all its natural, raw beauty, Hahoe is perhaps the most picturesque village in Korea.

Admittedly, there are a few modern obstructions; even the oldest house, said to be around 550 years old by the local museum curator, is equipped with a large refrigerator on its hard wooden *maru.* Also, television antennae sprout on its lichen-covered tile roof, and electrical wiring creeps along its walls.

Across the path from the *yangban* manor is a museum which imitates Yi architectural lines and is painted in bold Saemaul colors. This museum honors an educated 16th-century aristocrat from Hahoe, Yu Song-yong. Yu competed with the famous Admiral Yi Sun-sin for court favors during the Japanese Hideyoshi invasions of the 1590s, and eventually became the king's prime minister. Yu's voluminous books of genealogy, various personal articles and government documents are displayed in the museum. The Yu clan remains the most influential in Hahoe.

Probably the most glaring visual obstruction in Hahoe is an off-white school building. It stands out most noticeably when seen from the hill top across the river. The school was a Saemaul Undong (New Community Movement) project. The Hahoe villagers vetoed future Saemaul developments, and with the blessing of government officials, managed to keep their hometown in thatch. The

The "Floating Rock," Pusok-sa environs.

hamlet is far from the eyes of most foreigners. In fact, seldom do foreigners ever come to Hahoe, so don't be surprised to find the local folk returning your stares.

The "Floating Rock": Another place that is not too accessible but really shouldn't be passed up while in the Andong area is Pusok Temple 37 miles (60 kilometers) due north of Andong along Highway 5 and a long, bumpy road. Pusok-sa (Floating Rock Temple) was established in 676 by High Priest Uisang, who returned to Korea from China with teachings of Hwaom Buddhism. It is said that Uisang's former lover reunited with him in the form of a huge granite "floating rock." She later transformed herself under the main hall – her head beneath the gilded-clay Buddha and her tail 60 feet (18 meters) away under a stone lantern – so she could help protect Uisang's temple. That same legendary "floating rock" still hangs protectively – and precariously – outside Pusok-sa's main hall.

Despite the dragon-in-residence and floating rock protectors, the temple was burned down by invaders in the early 14th century. It was reconstructed in 1358. Fortunately, however, it was just beyond Hideyoshi's destructive reach in the 1590s, so the famed Muryangsu-jon (Eternal Life Hall) main hall has been preserved to this day. This hall is considered to be the oldest and most classical wooden structure in Korea. Its Koryo architectural style is said to have been influenced by Greek artisans through India, and this structural theory is evidenced by the way the hall's main support pillars gradually taper off at the ends.

Predating the temple by at least 50 years and complementing its Koryo architecture is a 9-foot (2.7-meter) tall gilded-clay sitting Buddha, the only one of its kind in Korea. Also, Pusok-sa's interior Koryo paintings of Buddha and the Four Kings are considered to be the oldest wall paintings in Korea outside of ancient tomb art. The temple is one of the most inaccessible in Korea. However, for the serious traveler and student of ancient culture, Pusok-sa is one of the more rewarding detours he or she can make while in this country.

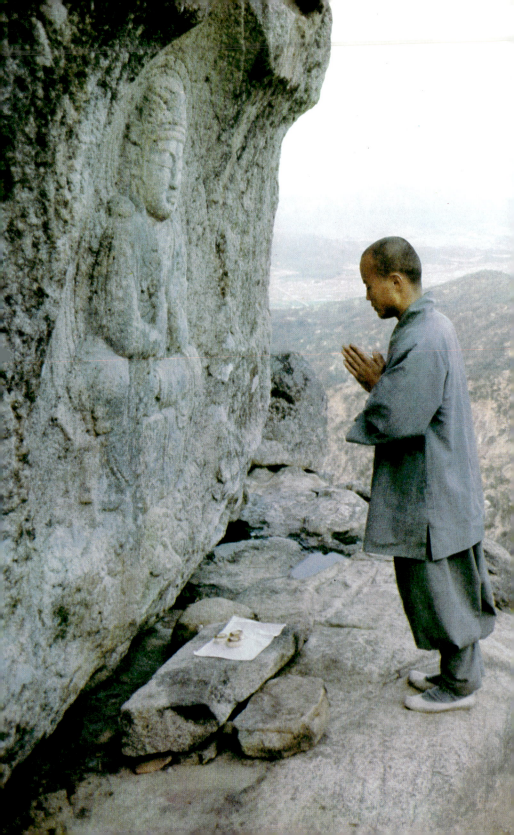

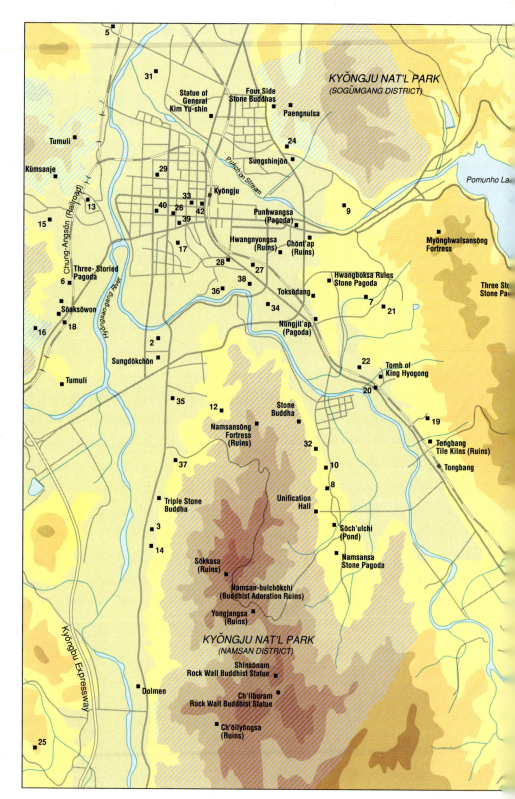

KYŎNGJU NAT'L PARK
(SOGŬMGANG DISTRICT)

5

31

Statue of
General
Kim Yu-shin

Four Side
Stone Buddhas

Paengnulsa

Tumuli

24

Kŭmsanje

29

Pukch'ŏn Stream

Sungshinjŏn

Pomunho La

13

33

Kyŏngju

9

Myŏnghwalsansŏng
Fortress

15

40   26   42
       39

Punhwangsa
(Pagoda)

Three- Storied
Pagoda

6

17

Hwangnyongsa
(Ruins)

Chŏnt'ap
(Ruins)

Hwangboksa Ruins
Stone Pagoda

Three Sto
Stone Pa

28

27

Sŏaksŏwon

18

38

Toksŏdang

7

21

36

34

16

Nŭngjit'ap
(Pagoda)

2

22

Tomb of
King Hyogong

Sungdŏkchŏn

20

Tumuli

35

12

Stone
Buddha

19

Namsansŏng
Fortress
(Ruins)

32

Tongbang
Tile Kilns (Ruins)

37

10

Tongbang

Triple Stone
Buddha

8

3

Unification
Hall

Sŏch'ulchi
(Pond)

14

Sŏkkasa
(Ruins)

Namsansa
Stone Pagoda

Namsan-bulchŏkchi
(Buddhist Adoration Ruins)

Yongjangsa
(Ruins)

KYŎNGJU NAT'L PARK
(NAMSAN DISTRICT)

Shinsŏnam
Rock Wall Buddhist Statue

Dolmen

Ch'ilburam
Rock Wall Buddhist Statue

Ch'ŏllyŏngsa
(Ruins)

25

Tombs

1 Kwaerüng (Royal Tomb)
2 O-nüng: Tombs of Silla Kings Hyökköse, Namhae, Norye and Pasa
3 Samnüng (Royal Tomb)
4 Tomb of Kim Tae-sŏng
5 Tomb of Queen Chindŏk
6 Tomb of King Chinhüng
7 Tomb of King Chinp'yŏng
8 Tomb of King Chŏnggang
9 Tomb of King Hŏndŏk
10 Tomb of King Hongang
11 Tomb of King Hyoso
12 Tomb of King Ilsŏng
13 Tomb of Kim Yu-sin, Silla General
14 Tomb of King Kyŏngae
15 Tomb of King Munsŏng
16 Tomb of King Muyŏl
17 Tomb of King Naemul
18 Tomb of Kim Inmun & Kim Yang
19 Tomb of King Sinmu
20 Tomb of King Shinmun
21 Tomb of King Sŏl Ch'ong
22 Tomb of Queen Sŏndŏk
23 Tomb of King Sŏndŏk
24 Tomb of King T'alhae
25 Tomb of King Kyŏngdŏk
26 Tumuli Park

General Points of Interest

27 Anapchi (Duck and Geese Pond)
28 Ch'ŏmsŏng-dae Astronomical Observatory
29 Folk Museum
30 Golf Course
31 HwangsŏngPark
32 Hwarang (Flower Youth) House
33 Küm Ho Kak Kisaeng House
34 Kyŏngju Nat'l Museum
35 Najŏng
36 Panwŏl Fortress Site
37 Pŏsŏk-chŏng (Abalone Stone Pavilion)
38 Sŏkbinggo
39 Sunghye-jŏn

Tourist Stops

40 Bus Terminal
41 Kyŏngju Tourism Agency
42 Post Office
43 Tourist Information Center

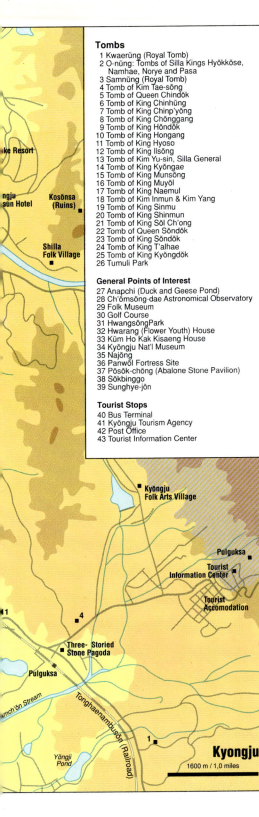

Kyŏngju Folk Arts Village

Pulguksa

Tourist Information Center

Tourist Accomodation

Three- Storied Stone Pagoda

Pulguksa

mch'ŏn Stream

Tonghaenambusŏn (Railroad)

Yŏngji Pond

Kyongju

1600 m / 1,0 miles

KYONGJU

It's the massive burial mounds – brown and dusted by frost in the winter, and carpeted with a dark-green nap in the summer – which punctuate any visit to **Kyongju**. Like so many camel humps rising here and there in populated and rural areas, they dominate all other physical realities in this riverine valley between Taegu and Pusan. Even the sweeping **T'oham Mountain Range** that hovers west of here is temporarily forgotten as one motors through this busy town. The mounds, memorial tombs known as *nung* to Koreans, represent for now and all time the glory that was Silla, and the wonders one can behold – and which wait to be unearthed for our amazement – in the Kyongju area.

Opulent Shaman Kings: Kyongju was well known to Asia's ancients as Kumsong, the home of powerful and opulent shaman kings. Today, it's an easygoing resort town where rice cultivation and tourism are more important than wars of conquest. Its distinction as a one-time seat of power, however, cannot ever be forgotten. This 83-sq. mile (214-sq. kilometer) valley is literally dotted with 1st to 8th century and later burial tombs, tired pagodas, fortress ruins, granite standing and relief sculptures, palace grounds and other remnants of the rich Three Kingdoms Period. The particulars of ancient Silla's history are discussed in earlier sections of this book, but even if you haven't bothered to brief yourself, a short tour of the Kyongju sites will prove to be a very knowledgeable and an inspirational one.

Art historians and archaeologists indulge in superlatives when writing of Kyongju's man-made treasures:

"The monuments of Silla's greatness preserved in the Kyongju Branch Museum and scattered in the vicinity of the town provide material for the study of the art and the whole civilization of two epochs of great importance in Far Eastern history. Together with other objects of artistic and historical interest to be found here and there over the peninsula, they deserve thorough study and a prominent place in the art history of the world," wrote archaeologist-historian Helen B. Chapin in 1948. Chapin was supremely impressed, but she was writing nearly 30 years before the most amazing of Kyongju's treasures had even been excavated.

A commentator, Evelyn B. McCune, author of *The Arts of Korea, An Illustrated History*, noted 31 years later that ceramics, precious wrought metals, paintings and stone sculptures unearthed in the Kyongju region have introduced the world "to the sophisticated art of refined shamanism." Modern Korea is experiencing a growing awareness of its cultural heritage that is emerging, ghost-like, from these recent finds.

The enthusiasm of both art historians was unanimously underscored by international art critics who had never even been to Korea when several exquisite, but never before publicized, Silla pieces were shown in a spectacular exhibit, "5,000 Years of Korean Art," which began touring the United States in 1979. Dominated by the porcelain, granite, gold and jade works of ancient Kyongju-Silla, it catapulted Korea into Asian art chronicles. Listed here are some of the major sites.

The Sillan Tombs at Tumuli Park: In this unique "park" of 182,000 sq. yards (152,000 sq. meters) on the southeast side of Kyongju are located some 20 tombs of varying sizes which were originally heaped into place as early as the mid-1st century. Until quite recently, this restored, landscaped and lamplit complex of mounded graves was just another neighborhood in Kyongju, but when private individuals and government archaeological teams began to find literally thousands of important items here, the area was cleared of homesites and designated a national museum and park-site of major historical importance. The restoration of Tumuli Park was begun in 1973, and the complex was officially dedicated and opened to the public for viewing in 1975.

Jade Tiger Claws and a "Heavenly Horse": The largest of the tombs, that of King Mich'u (r. 262-285), has been identified in ancient chronicles as the "**Great Tomb**." However, a secondary tomb, the so-called **Ch'onma-ch'ong**, or "Heavenly Horse" or "Flying Horse" tomb, is probably the most well-known gravesite in Tumuli Park (sometimes called the Tomb Park). This tomb, about 88 feet (27 meters) in diameter and 42 feet (12.7 meters) high, was excavated in 1973, and in its collapsed wood and stone burial chambers were found numerous important treasures – including sets of gold and jade tiger claw earrings, a solid gold, 40-inch (125-centimeter) long belt-girdle with dangling gold and jade ornaments, a 12-inch (32-centimeter) high gold foil crown embellished with 58 carved jade pieces, and an unglazed stoneware pot ornamented with a dragon's head and turtle's body.

More than 10,000 objects were discovered in this unknown king's tomb, but the most celebrated find was a painting of a galloping, winged horse. This flying horse study, the first early Silla painting ever discovered, was painted onto a birchbark saddle flap in white and vermillion and bordered by a rococo frame. Visitors to

Preceding pages, devotional session ami the stillness on a hilltop. Below, Kyongju's Tumuli Park moundscape

224

this tombsite can now literally walk into the tomb, which has been scooped out and converted into a domed glass, metal and concrete gallery. On display here are a detailed diorama-model of the tomb's burial chamber, photographs of the actual excavation in progress, and more than 100 excavated Silla pieces. Many of the most important treasures are safely displayed in larger national museum structures at Seoul and at the nearby Kyongju Museum.

The Kyongju National Museum: As the editors of the informative book *Korean Art Seen Through Museums* have written, "The National Museum in Kyongju is, so to speak, actually a museum within a museum." The phrase is apt, because so many of Kyongju's treasures are in the open air where they can be seen, touched, experienced. But in this vast and modern compound on the eastern skirts of Kyongju you can see some of the finest of more than 80,000 items unearthed during recent and old-time digs in this area: metal work, paintings, earthenware, calligraphic scrolls, folk art objects, weapons, porcelains, carved jades, and gold, granite and bronze sculptures wrought in shamanist, Buddhist, Taoist and Confucian motifs.

Among important pieces here is the huge bronze **Emille** (pronounced "Em-ee-leh") **Bell**, The Divine Bell for the Great King Song which is one of the world's oldest, having been cast in AD 771. It is also one of the largest, weighing 20 tons and measuring 10 feet (3 meters) in height and 7½ feet (2.3 meters) in diameter. This Buddhist bell, which originally hung in a pavilion at nearby **Pongdok Temple**, is embellished with four relief devas who kneel facing each other on lotus blossom cushions. It is said that the bell's sonorous tones can be heard 40 miles (64 kilometers) away on a clear day. The bell's name, it has been written, comes from an ancient Silla term which literally means "mommy". The bell was given this name because its sound resembles the voice of a lost child crying for its mother.

Pulguk-sa: This sprawling temple complex about 10 miles (16 kilometers)

Pulguk-sa

A typical Korean Buddhist temple is made up of many shrines which are often housed in several special halls. In the layout of its compound, Pulguk-sa, like many things Korean, is both typical and unique. The arrangement of halls and courtyards, the selection of icons, the emphasis placed on particular architectural details — all reflect the varied beliefs and styles of the temple's original builders and many renovators. However, most temples of comparable size will include the fundamental shrines found here. Among important structures at Pulguk-sa are:

1 *Yoňhwa-kyo* and *Ch'ilbo-kyo* entry bridges

2 *Ch'ŏngun-kyo* and *Paegun-kyo* entry bridges

3 *Anyang-mun* gate

4 *Chaha-mun* gate

5 *Chong-ru* passageway

6 *Kuknak-jŏn* hall with its *Amit'a Buddha.*

7 *Sŏkka-t'ap* pagoda

8 *Tabo-t'ap* pagoda

9 *Taeung-jŏn* hall which houses a *Sŏkka Buddha*

10 *Musol-jŏn,* or old meeting hall

11 *Viro-jŏn* (Viroch'ana hall)

12 *Kwanŭm-jŏn* (Kwanseŭm-posal hall)

For more detailed information please see the feature section article on Korean Buddhist iconography.

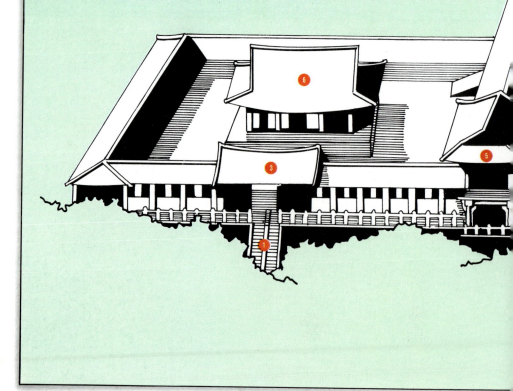

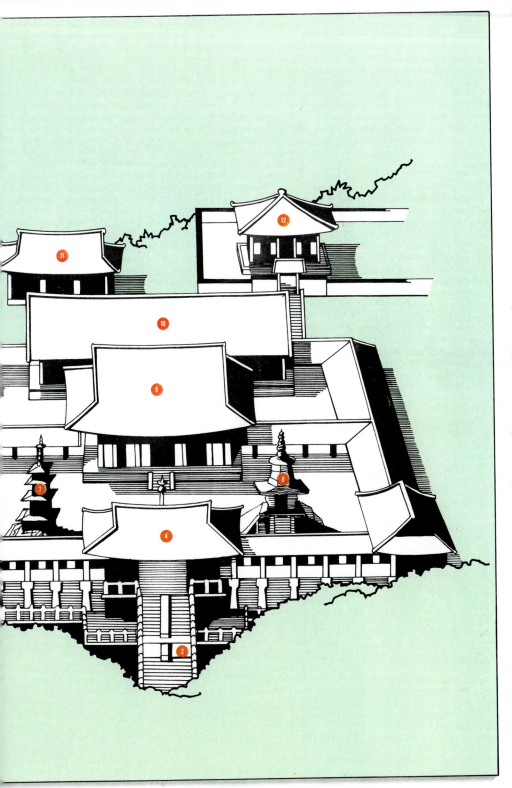

due east of Kyongju on the western slopes of Mt. T'oham is one of the oldest surviving Buddhist monasteries in Korea. First built during the reign of Silla King Pophung (r. 514-539), Pulguk-sa, "Temple of the Buddha-land," is also Korea's most famous temple. Its renown comes not from its age or size but probably because it stands, flawlessly restored, as a splendid example of Silla-era architecture in a spectacular hillside setting lush with manicured stands of pine, plum, peach, pear, cherry and cryptomeria trees. It also enshrines some of the country's and Korean Buddhism's most important national treasures.

Wonderfully stone-crafted steps and bridges carry the visitor on an uphill stroll to the broad granite block terraces on which this pristine temple compound stands. Almost all of the hand-painted wood structures on these terraces are of recent Yi dynasty construction, but most of the stone structures, pieced together of large granite blocks fitted without mortar are original. The architect credited for this stone masterwork, Kim Taesong,

also supervised the construction of the nearby Sokkuram Grotto, an annex to Pulguk-sa and one of Buddhism's most-celebrated shrines. Architect Kim directed his design and structural skills during the reign of King Kyong-dok, the 35th Silla king (r. 742-765), when Pulguk-sa underwent several major modifications and restorations

Blue and White Clouds: Two double-tiered stone staircases, the **Sokkye-mun**, used to lead pilgrims and tourists up to Pulguk-sa proper. The larger, 33-stepped staircase to the right has been given two names, one for its lower flight (called **Chongun-kyo**, the Blue Cloud Bridge), and the other for its upper flight (**Paegun-kyo**, the White Cloud Bridge). The smaller, left staircase, meanwhile, was similarly named. Its lower flight is called **Yonhwakyo** (Lotus Flower Bridge), and the upper flight is **Ch'ilbo-kyo** (the Seven-Treasure Bridge). The Blue Cloud and White Cloud bridges terminate at an entrance gate called **Chala-mun**, while the Lotus Flower and Seven-Treasure bridges climb up to a secondary entrance

Mask dance images by a Kyongju maskmaker.

gate known as **Anyang-mum**. Both are grand entry-ways, but these days tourists and devotees alike have to enter the temple via new stairways and gates on the left and right sides of the temple.

On the interior side of Anyang-mum, is the **Kuknak-jon** hall where you'll find a bronze **Amit'a-bul**, or Buddha of the Western Paradise and Boundless Light. This delicately sculpted Buddha's features have been gilded in recent years by Pulguk-sa's tidy monks.

Through the small **Chong-ru** entry pavilion, is Pulguk-sa's main worship hall, **Taeungjon**, and an expensive courtyard dominated by two unusual and impressive multi-tiered Silla pagodas.

The smaller of the two pagodas, called **Sokka-t'ap**, is 27 feet (8.2 meters) high and the larger **Tabo-t'ap** is 34 feet (10.4 meters) high. Legend says these neighboring pagodas were built by Asa-dal, an esteemed artisan who came to Silla from Paekche.

Both stone pagodas (which have been considerably restored in recent years) are considered premier examples of such Silla pagoda construction. Inside a niche on the left side of the Tabo-t'ap you'll spot a small growling lion sitting on a neat lotus pedestal. He's Tabo-t'ap's (the Many-Treasured Buddha's) guardian.

The Sokka-t'ap structure appears less amusing, but a reliquary time capsule of great historical and artistic value was found inside this pagoda in 1959. As a government survey notes, "The relics included *asarira* box containing gold images of Buddha and a scroll of Dharari sutras, the oldest Buddhist literature of its kind remaining in the world today. The inscriptions engraved on the cover of the relic box says that in AD 706. King Sondok placed within the pagoda four *sarira* (remains of Buddha or high priests), a gold Amit'a figure, and a volume of sutras in memory of three deceased royal family members – King Sinmun, Queen Mother Simok T'achu and King Hyoso."

In this courtyard's Taeung-jon hall is an image of Sakyamuni, the Historic Buddha, who is flanked by appropriately subservient bodhisattvas and other disciples of the Lord Buddha.

ontemporary eo-Sillan ancers at a urist revue.

Other Pulguk-sa structures and objects deserving meditative attention are the nine-pillared **Musol-jon** hall, the compound's oldest and largest structure; the **Viro-jon**, which houses a **Virochana Buddha** found clutching his right forefinger in an overtly sexual Diamond First mudra; and **Kwanum-jon**, a hall which is home to a 10th-century wooden image of **Kwanseum-posal**, the popular Bodhisattva of Mercy known to Chinese Buddhists as Kwan Yin. Nearly all of the halls are painted in the gay, day-glow colors and designs popular in contemporary Yi Dynasty *nouveau* building circles.

Sokkuram, The Stone Cave Hermitage: This Pulguk-sa annex, several winding miles northeast of Pulguk-sa proper, has become a major pilgrimage site for practitioners and students of Buddhism and Buddhist art. Sokkuram is a grotto temple, set among pines and maples, which enshrines a white granite Sakyamuni Buddha image considered by some art historians to be the most perfect Buddha image of its kind anywhere. Unlike grotto temples in other parts of Asia, Sokkuram was not carved out of a granite hillside or built inside an existing cave. Rather it's an artificial chapel built of large stone granite blocks placed on a summit. After a pleasant hike through a lower woods and an ascent up a flight of stairs, you will enter as classical a Buddhist shrine as you would ever expect to see in the Far East.

The base Sokkuram structure consists of a square antechamber and a round interior chamber with a dome-shaped ceiling. As you enter the chapel you will first pass stone images of the **Eight Generals**, each representative of one of the Eight Classes of Beings. Then comes a pair of wild-eyed gate guardians in typical *t'aekwon-do* fighting postures. Specifically, they are set in a *sipsu*, or "10 hands" posture, and a *palsae*, or "picking fortress out" posture.

Next are the **Four Deva Kings**, Guardians of the Four Quarters. A pair of these directional deities cavort on either side of the main passageway. All are framed in the radiant aura of haloes, but they also are depicted in the act of stomping on little threatening demons.

These devas are usually found in a painted or wood-carved form at the main entrance to Korean Buddhist temples.

Inside the main chamber is **Sakyamuni**, sitting in repose on a lotus dais. At his forehead is a typical protuberance, and atop his head are neatly cropped spirals of curly hair. Facing the grotto's entrance and the East Sea, the Buddha Sakyamuni sits with his right hand palm downward over his right leg. This is the mudra position referred to as "Calling of the Earth to Witness." The left palm, meanwhile, faces up in a meditation pose.

Cavorting on walls of the inner chamber are relief sculptures of the **Ten Great Disciples** and **Eight Great Bodhisattvas**. The most curious of these is an 11-headed Avalokitesvara, or **Kwanseum-posal**, who has been placed on the back wall of the Sokkuram rotunda directly behind the Sakyamuni Buddha. This Goddess of Mercy is unusual because 10 of her heads have been placed into a crown atop her head. Art historian Chapin explains this multiplicity:

"An old legend explains the eleven heads: formerly endowed with only one, the Compassionate Lord grieved so deeply over the sufferings of creatures that his one head split into eleven fragments, whereupon his spiritual father, the Buddha Amitabha, picked up the shards and placed them on his son's head where they grew each into a separate head. Thus, the Bodhisattva's power to see and relieve suffering was multiplied eleven times."

While the individual sculptures may be matched by some of those in the cave temples of China, nevertheless the chapel as a whole is unequalled in the art of the Far East.

Ch'omsong-da: This astronomical observatory tower, one of the oldest structures in Korea, was built during the reign of Queen Sondok (r. 632-647), Silla's 27th ruler. Astronomers question just how the tower was used, but they point with intrigue at the following coincidences: 365 stones, the number of days in a calendar year, were used in its construction; and there are 12 rectangular basestones, plus 12 separate levels of stones above and below a central window. Could this constructional recurrence **Pulguk-sa.**

of the number 12 imply the zodiac, or the number of months in a year? This telescope-shaped tower probably served several generations of Silla geomancers who attempted to foretell astrological fates in this historic region.

P'osok-chong (The Abalone Stone Pavilion): The world's hedonists have a particular fondness for this site just east of the old road to Pusan. This place received its name from the shape of a curving, stone-rimmed ditch which was cut in the ground next to a pleasure pavilion used by Hon-gang, the 49th Silla king. This serpentining ditch was a large board game of sorts which involved the drinking of wine and the impromptu composition of poetry. Nearby stream water was channeled in and onto its waters were set afloat cups of wine. A guest was challenged to compose a proper poem before his cup made a floating round of the channel. If he didn't compose a satisfactory poem, he had to chug-a-lug his entire bowlful of wine and try again, and again, and … according to ancient chronicles, it was great royal parlor fun.

The Pomun Lake Resort Complex: The Korean Government says in its promotional brochures: "If the tourist has time or inclination for only one sidetrip outside of Seoul, Kyongju should be the choice." With that thought in mind, the government has created what is probably the most complete resort complex in Korea – the Pomun Lake Resort, a sprawling playland about 4 miles (6 kilometers) east of Kyongju proper. Three deluxe class hotels had sprung up on sprawling Pomun Lake's shores. A 900-seat convention hall, an 18-hole golf course, a folk arts amphitheater and a lakeside marina with a posh clubhouse are just a few of the amenities which await Kyongju tourists who stay at Pomun Lake. The Korea National Tourism Corporation's master plan for this area sees an eventual hotel capacity of 3,000-plus rooms. All new structures are being built "Silla-style" in keeping with this grandiose KNTC master plan.

The Pomun resort of Kyongju continues to spearhead the energetic growth of tourism in the area. The Kyongju Chosun

In ancient times, men would try to compose a poem before their teacup floated this waterway.

and the Kyongju Concorde hotels have been joined by the new Kyongju Hilton, with 324 rooms, has further raised the level of the hotel services and facilities to international standards. Further hotel development in the area will include a 400-room Kyongju Hyundai, a luxury hotel due to open in 1992. In 1993, a gigantic folk village, called Sillachon, will open to the public. The village will reconstruct all aspects of the Silla history and culture.

If time is still on your side, consider hiking to the top of Nam-san, South Mountain, above the valley's **Nam-san Village**. There, perhaps an hour of huffing and puffing away, you'll find amazing Buddhas and attendant bodhisattvas etched into sheer granite boulders and cliffs. All look east, like the Sokkuram Buddha, toward the rising sun.

Kyongjuophiles also strongly suggest that visitors do not miss a visit to **Kum Ho Kat**, Kyongju's most opulent and traditional *kisaeng* house; or a respite at **Anapji**, a beautifully landscaped duck and geese pond-park which was a favorite idyll of Unified Silla kings.

Also high on the Kyongju must-do list is the impressive **tomb of General Kim, Su-yin**, which is rimmed by carved stone zodiac figures; the **Punhang (Famous Emperor) Temple** with the oldest datable pagoda in Korea; and perhaps first before all, **O-nung**, the five mounds memorial park on the south side of Kyongju where, tradition says, Silla's first, second, third and fifth kings, and first queen, are buried. At this site is a fine memorial hall, **Sungjong-jon**, dedicated to Silla's first ruler, Pak Hyokkose (57 BC-AD 3). The memorial hall was erected by Kim Yong-jo, the 21st Yi king, in 1759.

Still haven't seen enough Silla-era Buddha images? Then head for **Pagoda Valley** on the eastern slopes of Nam-san, or the **Buddha Valley** just north of T'ap Valley, or the **Kuksa Valley** east of Nam-san, or the more remote **Sungbang Valley**. This litany of place names and their resident treasures grows longer and more awesome with every passing lunar year – and every new discovery – in Kyongju.

THE HISTORIC
SOUTH CRESCENT

In 1592, the Japanese warlord, Toyotomi Hideyoshi, dispatched 150,000 troops to begin an ambitious assault on the Chinese Empire. Korea had the bad fortune of being in the way and of being loyal to China. When the Korean government refused to grant Japan free access across its frontiers, the Japanese disposed with courtly etiquette and proceeded to fight their way through. After six years of war, they finally retreated, failing to conquer China, but thoroughly devastating Korea. Thousands of Koreans were either killed or taken to Japan as slaves, vast tracts of crucial farmland had been razed, the country's social order was in shambles, and much of Korea's great cultural legacy was destroyed or stolen. Nearly four centuries have passed since this tragedy, yet all along Korea's southern coast monuments and memorials remain to keep alive memories of this Imjin War. The dominant theme in this region, despite more recent wars and wrenching transitions, is still the Japanese invasions.

Taegu: The logical starting point for a swing through Korea's southern crescent area is **Taegu**, capital of **North Kyongsang Province**. Taegu serves as a clearing house for a variety of produce harvested in this agriculturally rich province and it is an industrial center as well. The definitive product of this city, however, is apples. This may seem an odd claim to fame, but the Taegu apple is a state-of-the-art fruit, renowned throughout Asia.

Though at first glance Taegu may appear to be at best a half-hearted attempt at a city or an overgrown village, a closer inspection reveals it to be a uniquely Korean compromise between urban and rural extremes: It is big enough to offer good hotels, restaurants and 20th century entertainment, yet small enough to retain a relaxed ambiance that is all but lost in Seoul or Pusan. Few of Taegu's buildings are so imposing as to obstruct the view of the surrounding mountains. Streets are dominated by pedestrians rather than ma-

Preceding pages, autumn around Soraksan.

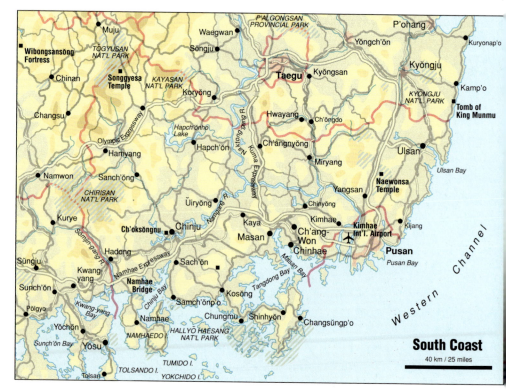

South Coast

40 km / 25 miles

chinery. And traditionally styled clothing is still very much in evidence, especially (for no apparent reason) in the environs of **Talsong**, an earthwork fortress dating back to the prehistoric Sam-Han era.

Talsong was originally constructed of several artificial hills in the middle of the broad plain that is now largely filled by Taegu. Presumably these hills supported a Korean variant of the motte-and-bailey forts once common in Europe. Late in the 14th century, at the end of the Mongol occupation and the beginning of the Yi dynasty, the fort was enlarged and stones were added to its existing earthworks. In 1596, during the Imjin War, the fort was again enlarged – to its present circumference of 4,265 feet (1,300 meters) and height of 13 feet (4 meters). The fort is now a popular park, complete with a small zoo that includes several claustrophobic lions donated by the local Lions Club. The entrance to Talsong is a favorite meeting place for the city's senior citizens, who lounge amicably along its cobblestone walkway, traditionally sartorial in pastel silks and cotton voile.

West Gate Market, one of the largest and oldest in the country, is just a short walk away, across **Tongsan Hospital.** The narrow alleys of the market are lined with cauldrons of noodle soup billowing steam, mobile vendors with carts devoted exclusively to such specialized merchandise as sewing needles and arcane mousetraps, and clustered networks of permanent stalls dealing in even more mundane necessities.

Redolent Pharmacopoeia: Yak-chong Kol-mok, "medicine alley," is the site of one of Taegu's more notable sensory delights. The street is a center for wholesale purveyors of traditional medicines. A stimulating barrage of scents ooze out of buckets and boxes of prepared pharmacopoeia and wafts up from exotic herbs drying on woven mats set out in the sun. The precise blend of aromas shifts gradually as one meanders down this pungent street. Indeed, mere pedestrian inhalations will probably relieve you of any afflictions of the nasal passages – or soul. Should simple breathing prove ineffective, there are several licensed herbalists

Many of the original city gates still remain.

who are able and willing to prescribe healing brews.

Taegu also has its own brand of nightlife which, if lacking the polish of posher establishments in Seoul, is well-endowed with enthusiasm. Most after-hours partying in Taegu is centralized in several blocks near the "**old station**" at the center of town. Standing with your back to the station, expensive "businessmen's entertainments" are to your right; on your left are rock-and-roll clubs and wine stalls. Adjacent to the latter is one of the city's larger markets. At night the two merge in a spirited confusion of side alley vendors, eclectic shopfronts, blasting nightclub bands, band throngs intent on entertaining themselves.

Start your Taegu evening with a sidewalk snack of steamed crab, or, if you dare, raw sea cucumbers. Continue with dinner in a smoke-billowing *bulgogi* house or in an inexpensive but elegant Western-styled restaurant, then move out to explore such tantalizers as the **Theatrical Beer Hall** or one of many ubiquitous and raucous *makkolli* bars.

For tamer daylight diversions there is **Su-song Reservoir** on the southern outskirts of the city. In winter the reservoir's ice is crowded with skaters, most of whom seem to be primarily engaged in falling down, though some soar by with regal grace on racer skates.

Rented rowboats replace skates in summer, whereupon suitors display their naval aptitude by dodging excursion boats which are busy transporting less athlete adventurers to a small island in the middle of the reservoir. The umbrella tables of outdoor restaurants contribute to a carnival atmosphere, as do mechanical swings and miniature ferries wheels.

Taegu has several other recreational areas: **Tong Chon Resort** and **Mangwuli Park** are out past the new train station, on the Naktong River where the Communist attack that began the Korean War was finally halted. **Apsan Park** includes a cable car ride up to the summit of **Ap Mountain** for a panoramic view of the Taegu plain. Near the old train station is Taegu's small reconstructions of old government buildings. The original

Icecapades at Su-song Reservoir.

structures were built in 1601 as part of a complex of administrative buildings which remained in use until 1965.

In addition to the train station and the highway bus terminal adjacent to it, Taegu has four depots for back-road buses, one for each of the cardinal directions.

These buses serve remote villages and mountain hamlets out of range of highway express buses or trains, and in many of these places foreign visitors are still a considerable surprise. Goats, chickens, and pigs on their way to market are often included among the passengers. Disembark with them and their owners and you'll be rewarded with a rare glimpse of a genuine village market day. Transistor radios and plastic serving trays may now be bartered for livestock and vegetables, but such rural events have yet to lose their timeless appeal.

The annual cycle of village life fluctuates between intense periods of field labor and long stretches of off-season leisure. Rise at dawn and follow the *makkolli* merchant on his delivery rounds to village taverns. A cluster of children outfitted in their school uniforms hurry through the morning fog to schoolyard chores. Farmers lash wooden plows to the backs of bullocks and lead them out to rice fields. Women gather at the village well to pound laundry with wooden bats. And the resounding toll of a brass gong announces a funeral. Join the stragglers in the procession led by a bier laden with paper flowers and you will witness a remarkable blend of solemn ritual, mourning, and carefree frivolity as the deceased is escorted to the netherworld. On festive days, such as Ch'usok and Lunar New Year's Day, everyone gathers to dance to the pulsing rhythms of hourglass drums and clanging gongs. There are no strangers on a country festival day: exhibit the slightest touch of whimsey and you will be accosted, festooned with ribbons, plied with liquor, and dragged into a frenzied dance.

Back-road buses are cheap, crowded, and not especially comfortable; but, except for a possible stiff back, they offer a low-risk gamble for anyone inclined to exploration. Pick a destination at random

cal folks
n the road
Haein-sa.

(place names ending in "sa" are safest, as they promise a temple at the very least), stock up on emergency provisions and try your luck.

Temple-hopping in Taegu: The **So-bu-ju-c'ha-jang** (West Depot) will get you to **Yong-yon-sa**, a tiny temple perched high in the mountains with an exquisite set of guardian deva paintings, miles of hiking trails, cordial inns, and an invigorating stream for bathing.

The bus to **Unumn-sa** from **Nambu-ju-ch'a-jang** (South Depot) is a challenging, but rewarding, test of stamina. After enduring several hours of some of Korea's most jarring dirt roads, you will be left at a dead end town consisting of a gas station, a single inn and restaurant, and a few dozen farmhouses, including some handsome examples of traditional folk architecture. The path to the temple follows a meandering stream through a spacious pine forest. The surrounding mountains harbor several small hermitages. Set in an open field, Unmun-sa is a restful sanctuary for a community of Buddhist nuns, who go about their work and worship unperturbed by occasional visitors who drift through to enjoy the scenery or to study the many fine paintings adorning her temple walls.

Chikji-sa, easily reached from Taegu via **Kimch'on**, is a gem of a temple, recently repainted in an entrancing blend of blue, magenta and gold. Exquisite figures and landscapes embellish virtually every available external wall space and Chikji-sa's shrines are populated with a bewildering array of finely carved statues. A quick stroll through the temple grounds is likely to induce a giddy overload of visual stimulation, but taken slowly Chikji-sa is a rare pleasure. The beauty of the temple, and of the forested mountains rising above it, has not escaped general notice. It is one of several temples associated with Samyong Taesa, who was both a Buddhist saint and a military hero.

Samyong was born in the town of Milyang in 1544. His family was of the *yangban* class and he was well-educated in the Confucian Classics. After losing both his parents, Samyong left his home **Chikji-sa.**

to wander in the mountains. He eventually made his way to Chikji-sa where his study of Zen led to his attainment of enlightenment. He became chief priest of Chikji-sa in 1574.

Needles and Noodles: Soon after, he set out wandering again and met Sosan, the most prominent Korean Buddhist master of the period. According to an apocryphal legend, they engaged in a contest of magic. Samyong began by arduously transforming a bowl of needles into noodles. Sosan received the bowl, promptly turned it upside down, and needles crashed to the floor. Samyong's next feat was to stack eggs end-to-end vertically, several feet into the air. Sosan followed suit, but started from the top. Samyong responded by turning a clear blue sky to a thunder storm and challenged Sosan to return the torrential rain to the sky. Sosan calmly met the challenge and added his own flourish by transforming the ascending droplets into a flock of birds. Duly humbled, Samyong asked to become a disciple of the greater master.

Several years later, the Japanese inva-sion began and Sosan emerged as the leader of a voluntary militia of monks, which eventually grew to a force of 5,000. Sosan was too old for battle, so he appointed Samyong as field commander for his militia. Under Samyong's command, Korea's warrior monks earned a reputation for their fierce courage and played a major role in repulsing the Japanese.

Samyong is particularly admired for his courage in venturing into the Japanese headquarters camp to attempt a peaceful solution to the deadlocked war. Although this first attempt proved a failure, he later traveled to Japan, secured the release of 3,000 Korean hostages, concluded active hostilities, and opened the way for a resumption of peaceful relations between the two countries. After the war, Samyong retired to nearby **Haein-sa**, where he died in 1610, at the age of 66.

Haein-sa's Ancient Library: Ritual drums thunder down through the mist-wreathed **Kaya Mountain**, temporarily silencing the clack of prayer knockers and the hum of chants. The smoke of cooking fires mingles with the delicate aroma of in-

Entrance to Haein-sa's library.

cense as the monks of **Haein Temple** prepare a meal of unpolished rice, mushrooms and mountain herbs.

Undoubtedly the most rewarding of Korea's more accessible temples, Haein-sa is still isolated enough to be a meditative haven; yet it is only an hour from Taegu by bus, and accommodations are available within easy walking distance of the temple grounds. The scenery of **Kaya-san National Park**, beautiful in any season, is stunning in autumn, with craggy peaks and languid streams surrounded by fiery maples and oak.

Haein-sa houses the **Tripitaka Koreana**, a collection of more than 80,000 woodblocks engraved with Buddhist scriptures. This vast library was completed in 1251, during the Koryo dynasty, after nearly two decades of labor. It was a mammoth task undertaken twice. A first set, carved as a plea to the Buddha for aid against invading Khitan tribes, was destroyed by Mongols when they took their turn at invasion. Retreating to virtually impotent exile on Kanghwa Island, King Kojong ordered the creation of a second set in hopes of inducing an avataristic intervention against the Mongols. It is difficult to assess whether the King's hopes were justified or not: the Mongols finally departed in 1382 due to the collapse of their dynasty in China.

The Tripitaka library was moved from Kanghwa-do, which was too near the capital for safety, to Haein-sa early in the Yi dynasty. The building which now protects the wood blocks was constructed in 1488. It was designed with an adjustable ventilation system to prevent deterioration of the precious blocks. A much more recent concrete structure utilizing an array of modern devices to ensure a controlled environment was intended as a new and improved replacement tests and now sits neglected within smirking distance of the more efficacious old library.

One of the first statues you are likely to encounter in the temple complex is not a gilt deity, but a curious self-portrait of a monk carved in wood and painted true to life. The figure sits in apparent rigor mortis in a glass case in Haein-sa's small museum, surrounded by displays of

Aerial view of Ch'ungmu Harbor, Kyungsang-nam-do.

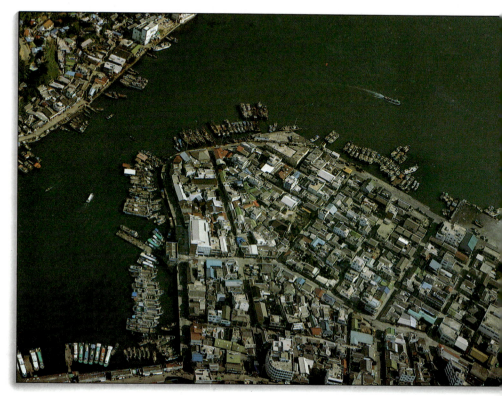

elaborate embroidery and remnants of the temple's past. More typical statues are to be found in the compound's numerous shrines, including an imposing 18th-century trinity (with Virochana at altar center) in the main hall. Outstanding among the paintings along the inside walls of this hall is a mural depicting scenes from the life of Buddha.

In common with most of Korea's major temples, Haein-sa has a flock of hermitages scattered through the surrounding mountains. All are a meditative lure to exploration.

Sacks of dried wild mushrooms spill out into the streets of the local "resort" town and in several restaurants you may indulge in a fungi eating spree in a semi-private *ondol* (heated room). While most of the town's inns are adequate, albeit a bit mundane, there is a virtual palace located on a low hill at the western edge of town traditionally styled with massive pine timber construction and wood-floored hallways.

Huffing Tankers and Fish Mongers: Wedged between a range of mountains and the sea, the big port city of **Pusan** is a raucous melange of masts, loading cranes and buildings; honking cabs, train whistles, and the throbbing air horns of passing ferries; suited businessmen, deck hands, navy cadets and fish mongers. Tiny punts propelled by the sweep of a single sculling oar slide through the shadows of huffing tankers. Urban gentlemen in angler outfits toy with their delicate bamboo poles, waiting patiently for nibbling minnows, and scruffy trawler crews unload the day's catch of squid and dog sharks. Dockside fish market matrons hawk 12-inch (305-centimeter) abalones, brilliant orange sea apples, deep sea clams, and fishes of all sizes, shapes and colors.

For those willing to dare the murky water of Pusan harbor, **Songdo Beach** is just a stone's throw southwest of **City Hall**. Even if you prudently abstain from swimming, it offers an interesting alternative to staying in town, as there are several inns and hotels with a uniquely Pusan flavor. Somewhat cleaner waters are available at three sandy beaches to the east of the city. The most popular is

partment
omplexes
Pusan.

Haeun-dae, which has good hotels and a properly bustling resort town.

A few small Buddhist temples are scattered around town and two large, important ones are within easy reach by bus or taxi, **Pomo-sa**, the closer of the two and the headquarters of the Dyana sect, is a mountain temple a few miles from **Tongnae Hot Springs**. The courtyards of the temple are well-landscaped and in traditional Korean style – with trees, stone lanterns, relics and a pagoda dating back to the Silla dynasty.

Korea's Largest Temple: T'ongdo-sa is half an hour to the north along the highway to Taegu. The road leading to the temple is a long, slow incline snaking alongside a boulder-strewn stream, sheltered by a forest whose name means "pine trees dancing in the winter wind."

With a total of 65 buildings, T'ongdo-sa is Korea's largest temple. Many of the buildings are dispersed throughout the surrounding mountainside, so the temple does not appear especially expansive on first encounter. However, virtually every major Buddhist deity is honored in a separate shrine in the central cluster of buildings, an unusual largesse even for so large a temple compound. The buildings themselves comprise an unusual variety of exceptional architecture, some left pleasantly unpainted or faded to the muted brown of weathered pine. Clustered around several courtyards, T'ongdo-sa is guarded by a massive quartet of wooden devas, each towering figure rendered in vivid and intimidating detail. Inside, one fine mural depicts Chi-jang's boat which escorts the deceased to paradise.

In addition to the many fine statues housed in the shrines, an excellent collection of artwork is on display in the temple museum. Woodblock prints are available for purchase.

According to legend, T'ongdo-sa was founded in 646 by a Korean religious leader named Cha-jang who traveled to China in search of a truth capable of saving his nation. There he experienced a miraculous visitation by a holy being who presented him with relics of the Buddha, including his yellow robe. Cha-jang returned to Korea to create his temple, naming it "T'ong-do," which means

"salvation of the world through mastery of truth." The gifts received in his vision are preserved in a stone monument in the temple.

Due east of T'ongdo-sa, on a highway running north from Pusan to Kyongju, is the urban antithesis of these two vestiges of Korea's heritage: **Ulsan**, an exemplar of the "economic miracle" of modern Korea. One of the centers of Korea's industrial network, Ulsan is a concrete and steel concentration of petroleum refineries, heavy industry, shipyards, power plants and automobiles.

The first South Coast city to fall during the Hideyoshi invasion was Pusan, but throughout the war sea battles were waged all along this jagged coast. Near the main nightlife district of Pusan there is a small park, made conspicuous by an imposing tower which dominates the city's skyline. The park contains two statues; one is a high-kitsch representation of a dragon, the legendary king of the sea; the other is of the patron hero of the south coast: **Admiral Yi Sun-sin**. It was largely his staunch patriotism and military skills that

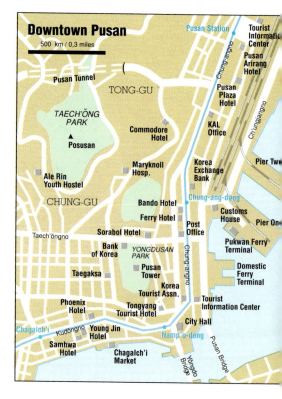

244

prevented the Imjin War from becoming a total disaster for Korea.

Admiral Yi Country: Admiral Yi was born in Seoul in 1545. Eight years later, his father, a Neo-Confucian scholar who preferred poverty to politics, moved the family to Asan, a remote town near Onyang, to escape the high cost of living and political intrigues of the capital. Though he disappointed his father by choosing a military career, Yi is credited with a thorough knowledge of the Classics and a legendary adherence to the stern tenets of Confucian rectitude. Twice stripped of all titles and rank as the target of factional conniving, he reputedly endured humiliation and accepted reinstatement with genteel grace.

In 1592, four years after the first of these incidents, Yi was appointed fleet commander for the eastern coast of Cholla Province. A year later the Japanese invaded. In less than a month they had overrun the country, routed the untrained and ill-equipped Korean army, and occupied the capital. Only the ingenuity and prowess of the Korean navy and, later, the assistance of China prevented Korea from becoming the first acquisition of a Japanese Empire.

Admiral Yi quickly became the bane of the Japanese navy, which gradually disintegrated in a series of Korean victories, climaxing in a naval rout at **Hansando**, near **Ch'ungmu**. During these battles Yi introduced his famous "turtle-ships." Generally regarded as the first iron-clad warships in the world, the heavily armed and highly maneuverable turtle-ships were virtually impervious to the limited firepower of the Japanese navy, whose ships carried only token cannon.

Later in the war, Yi suffered his second demotion, and the Korean navy was turned over to a rival, Won Kyun. Under Won's command the Navy was promptly decimated. Yi was hastily pardoned and asked to resume command of the admiralty, but his once powerful navy now consisted of only 12 ships. Exhibiting a remarkable blend of strategic genius and gall, he led his paltry fleet in an assault of 133 Japanese ships and won. This astonishing victory revived the dwindling Korean

he port of usan is busy ear-round.

resistance, marking the turning point of the war. Less than a year later, as the Japanese were attempting to retreat from their debacle without further loss, Yi was mortally wounded by a stray bullet in the last battle of the war (fought in the narrow strait of Noryangjin).

Noryangjin cuts between the mainland and the island of **Namhae**, at the western end of the scenic **Hallyo Waterway**. To the south is **Yosu**, the site of one of Admiral Yi's major naval bases and now an industrial and resort town. To the east are **Ch'ungmu** and **Hansae-do**.

An "Uncommon" Voyage: Regular ferries run from a terminal behind Pusan's City Hall throughout the Hallyo Waterway to Ch'ungmu and Yosu, to the port cities of **Masan** and Chinhae, and to the island of **Koje-do**. The terminal has two entrances, one marked "Tourist," the other "Common." Unless circumstances permit or require only a hasty trip, free of surprises, join the commoners. In the tourist section you may book passage on a sleek hydrofoil which will get you to your destination promptly, in a seat, and dry, but salt spray fogs the windows, the ride is reminiscent of a plane in heavy turbulence, and, well, why bother?

The common boats are slow, noisy, lacking in seats and other amenities, and inclined to lurch a bit in high seas. But they are also a lot of fun. Libations are liberally dispersed and everyone has a grand time singing, gambling, cajoling passing fishermen to toss up a portion of their loot, supervising the chaotic loading and unloading of passengers and protesting livestock, or enjoying the scenery, which slides by slowly enough for each subtle nuance to be fully absorbed.

The waterway is sheltered from the open sea by hundreds of islands which are the ancient peaks of an inundated mountain range. Submerged valleys have become countless secluded harbors, many of them now crowded with the vibrantly painted boats of fishermen and divers, and to the north of the waterway are **Masan** and **Chinhae**, the two urban ports of the area. Masan is a gritty industrial city, struggling to catch up with its new status as a Free Port. Chinhae, smaller

Many Koreans still live in traditional homes.

and more spacious, is a naval station famous for the cherry trees that swath the city with blossoms each spring.

Charming Ch'ungmu: Ch'ungmu is deservedly the most popular local destination out of Pusan. The dock of this still rustic resort town is small, but always busy with ferries returning from neighboring islands, small private fishing trawlers, tourist excursion boats, and all manner of hired craft which take watersportsmen out for an afternoon of fishing or skindiving. Ch'ungmu's marketplace begins on the dock, where catches are sold directly from piers, and continues a considerable distance into town, where local specialties such as traditional horse-hair hats, reed baskets and, of course, all kinds of fishes are available.

The many tidy restaurants in town serve a variety of seafood. Clams, oysters, soft-shelled crabs and unidentifiable mollusks are thrown into everything, to the delight of those who have an appetite for submarine curiosities and to the horror of those who don't.

There are plenty of inexpensive inns and on **Miruk Island** to the south there is a modern tourist hotel. Near the hotel, on the north slope of a mountain which dominates the island, is **Yonghwa-sa**, a tiny temple with an unusual set of appropriately diminutive altar paintings. **Kwanum Hermitage**, a short walk away, has a lawn instead of a courtyard, a handsome stone gate, and careful landscaping which manages to convey a sense of serenity, despite the incongruity of stone lanterns wired with electric lightbulbs.

Ch'ungmu was directly named for Admiral Yi; *Ch'ung* ("loyalty") and *mu* ("military valor") were borrowed from a title conferred on the Admiral posthumously. There are several memorials to him in the area, including a concrete scale model of his base on **Hansan-do**. The largest of the mainland memorials is at **Ch'ungyol-sa**, a shrine where Yi's sword and other weapons and gifts he received from the emperor of China are on display.

On the way to Ch'ungmu, you will pass between the mainland, to the north, and the island of Koje, to the south. **Koje-do** is Korea's second largest island (after

h'ungmu
Harbor.

Cheju) and one of the most beautiful areas of the country. The ferries to Ch'ungmu stop at several of the larger towns on the northwest coast of Koje-do. With careful scheduling it is possible to spend much of a day exploring the beaches, hillsides, and pastoral towns of the island, catch a ferry (or bus) and arrive at the more accommodating Ch'ungmu by evening. The harbor town of **Changsungp'o**, serviced by its own ferry from Pusan, is the island's main eastern port, but it's hardly more than a village if compared to Ch'ungmu or other area "cities." This is a good place to get the feel of a tiny Korean coastal town, and is also a good point of departure for a hiking and camping outing. Excursion boats may be hired to **Haekumgang**, a striking camelia-covered rock outcropping off the island's southern tip. Haekumgang, undercut with anemone-infested caves, may also be reached from Ch'ungmu by hired boat. Ferry service continues west from Ch'ungmu to **Samch'onp'o** and Yosu and shuttles run from Yosu to the islands of **Namhae** and **Odong**, both of historic and scenic interest. Odong is covered with camelia and bamboo and was the place where bamboo arrows were made for Admiral Yi's fighting men. Namhae is connected to the mainland by a red suspension bridge that crosses the strait of Noryangjin where Yi was killed.

Buses connect Namhae, Yosu and Samch'onp'o to Chinju, one of Korea's most enchanting and least visited small cities. The **Nam River** runs through the center of this city. In early morning mists, ghostly anglers squat along the shore with the patience of statues, and elderly gentlemen in traditional dress stroll along the winding walls of **Chinju Castle**, bringing the distant past breathtakingly close. Even the perfectly mundane concrete traffic bridge that crosses the river takes on an air of timelessness.

Patriotic Chu Non-gae: Chinju Castle was attacked in one of the first battles of the Imjin War. After an heroic defense by the Korean army assisted by a civilian militia, the attack was repulsed, and a planned drive into Cholla Province was thwarted. Less than a year later, the castle was the

Fishing vessel, Koje Island.

site of an equally heroic defeat after 10 days of fierce fighting. The Japanese celebrated their victory with a banquet in **Ch'oksongnu**, a spacious pavilion within the castle. One of the Korean women brought in to provide entertainment was Chu Non-gae, a *kisaeng* hostess whose patron, a Korean military official, had died in the battle for Chinju. During the banquet Non-gae lured one of the Japanese generals to the edge of the cliff between the pavilion and the Nam River. There she threw her arms around his neck and dived into the river, dragging him down with her to a patriotic and much-celebrated suicide-assassination.

Non-gae's selfless courage is commemorated now, four centuries later, in a special ritual held on the last day of lunar June at a small shrine built in her honor above the rock from which she jumped.

The walls of **Chinju Castle** and **Ch'oksongnu** have been tastefully reconstructed and several shrines, temples and pavilions are preserved within the castle grounds. The most imposing structure is Ch'oksongnu, which is raised on stone pillars to provide a pleasant view of the Nam River below. A small gate leads to the cliff where Non-gae lured the general to his (and her) death. Evidently the river was either considerably deeper then or the general a remarkably poor swimmer, or they were killed by hitting the rocks along the shore and not by drowning. A peculiarly Korean form of graffiti embellishes the cliff – names (presumably of Non-gae's posthumous admirers) carved into the rock-face. Off to one side of Ch'oksongnu is the shrine in Non-gae's honor. In it is her portrait.

Chinju is one of few Korean cities that has developed into small urban centers without losing their individual identity or rural ambiance. Wander through the narrow streets, browse in the tiny shops, visit one of the several small temples scattered around town, or spend the day simply – rowing a rented boat around Ch'inyang Lake or enjoying the amusement of an ancient lakeside resort town.

Fifty miles southwest of Chinju, the town of **Hadong** sprawls alongside the **Somjin River** running down from **Chiri**

Koje-do fishtraps.

Mountain. Regular buses follow the river upstream to **Kurye**, a small city on the southern edge of **Mt. Chiri National Park**. The highest mountain of the **Sobaek Range**, Chiri-san is a stark jumble of snow-covered peaks in winter, cool and lush in summer, and brilliant with turning foliage in autumn. There are many small temples tucked in the valleys of the mountain and two major ones – **Hwaom-sa** and **Sanggye-sa** – are both easily reached from Kurye.

Hwaom-sa was founded in the Silla dynasty. A 15-foot (4.5-meter) stone lantern, the largest in Korea is preserved from that period on the temple grounds. The dominant structure of the temple is the imposing, two-story **Kakhwangjon** ("Awakening Emperor Hall"), built in the 18th century and named in honor of the Chinese Emperor whom legend credits with funding its construction.

A Sacred Skull: According to legend, Sanggye-sa was founded by Priest Sambop in 723 during the Silla dynasty. Sambop dreamed of becoming a disciple of the great Buddhist master of the time,

Hui-neng, a patriarch of the Tsaochi sect of Chinese Son Buddhism. Hui-neng, however, died before this dream could be realized. Sambop found some consolation in studying transcriptions of Hui-neng's discourses which were brought to Korea. This motivated him to visit Kaiyum Temple in China, where Hui-neng's skull had been preserved. While there, Sambop bribed a priest at the temple into giving him the revered skull. Returning to Korea, Sambop made his way to Chiri Mountain where he built a shrine for his pilfered relic. This shrine gradually developed into Sanggye Temple.

Tea was introduced to Korea from China during the Silla dynasty and cultivated in plantations on the slopes of Chiri-san. An ancient tea ceremony ritual has virtually disappeared in recent years, but some attempts are now being made to revive it. All that remains of the plantations of Chiri-san, however, are wild tea plants that may still be found growing on the mountain's slopes.

K'ogusu is a week-long spring festival, generally celebrated in mid-April,

Monks heading for the temple.

peculiar to this area of the country. No one now seems to be quite sure what the festival signifies, but it is resolutely celebrated anyway. Hordes of celebrants, predominantly women, descend on the temple nearest their village fully armed with instruments of revelry. Rising sap is gateherd from the forests and brought to the temples to be drunk as a guarantee of continued good health. Sustained by this and other elixirs, villagers sing and dance in the temple grounds.

For Love of Ch'unhyang: After continuing north from Kurye around the base of Chiri-san, you will come to the ancient city of **Namwon**, which is the birthplace of Ch'unhyang, the favorite heroine of Korean literature. It is not known whether her birth was more than a literary event, as no proof of Ch'unhyang's actuality exists. However, the story of her life is set in Namwon and has had sufficient effect on Korean life and thought for quibbles to be immaterial.

"Ch'unhyang-chon" ("The Story of Ch'unhyang") is a simple, romantic tale. Mong-nyong, the son of an aristocrat,

falls in love with Ch'unhyang, the daughter of a *kisaeng*. The two are secretly married. Soon after, Mong-nyong's father is transferred to a government post in the capital and the two lovers are separated. A lecherous governor is appointed in Namwon who is determined to add Ch'unhyang to his roster of lovers. Remaining faithful to Mong-nyong, she flatly refuses to comply with the governor's wishes. She is promptly imprisoned and beaten under the personal supervision of the enraged governor. Meanwhile, Mong-nyong is appointed Royal Inspector of Cholla Province. He soon hears of Ch'unhyang's maltreatment and comes to rescue her and punish the governor. The two lovers return to Seoul where they of course live happily and prosperously to a grand old age.

Ch'unhyang's staunch fidelity is still revered and her story is an essential part of Korea's literary legacy. She is honored in Namwon with a shrine and an annual festival held on the 8th day of the 4th lunar month, roughly mid-March by Western reckoning.

Cherry blossoms brighten the early spring.

Confucian Chunghak-dong: Hidden in a high valley on the eastern face of Mt. Chiri is **Chunghak-dong**, one of a few villages which have been granted permission to abstain from Saemaul Undong, the "New Community Movement." The colorful concrete rooftiles, ersatz chalets, paved roads, electricity and plumbing that have redefined most Korean villages have not affected Chunghak-dong – though "monoleum," a soft, flexible linoleum in vogue in Korea, has infiltrated onto some porches and living room floors. The formal courtesy of Confucianism is meticulously observed in Chunghak-dong. Unmarried men still wear their hair in single long braids, and education is still conducted in the old Yi dynasty style – the teacher wearing his horse-hair hat while lecturing on the Confucian Classics to his students (who sit cross-legged on the *ondol* floor dressed in traditional white *hanbok*). Visitors are obliged to impose on the hospitality of village residents, as no inns or restaurants are available, and the trip to Chunghak-dong is difficult enough that so far protective isolation is still possible in this timeless place. It is reached only after two jostling hours by bus from Hadong and an arduous three-hour hike.

So-so Mokp'o: To the south of Kurye is the city of **Sunch'on**, with regular bus service to **Songgwang Temple**. One of the three largest temples in Korea, Songgwang-sa is a sprawling complex of buildings and courtyards. It is the center of Son Buddhism, the Korean version of Zen, and is the only temple in Korea with Western monks and nuns in permanent residence.

Originally a small hermitage built during the Silla dynasty, Songgwang-sa was expanded in the 12th century after Pojo, a Son Master, settled there with his followers. A tiny, intricately carved, wooden statue of Buddha, believed to have been carried by Pojo in his travels, is preserved in the temple. The temple includes a number of architectural treasures. The oldest is the 400-year-old **Kuksajon**. One unique feature of Songgwang-sa is the pair of arched, covered bridges spanning a shallow stream at the temple entrance.

At the southeastern extreme of the Korean peninsula is the port city of **Mokp'o**, a drab shipping town with few indulgences for the frivolous visitor.

Mokp'o's docks abound in coarse vignettes: six-foot (two-meter) sharks for sale in a fishmonger's shop, a trawler festooned with gaudy banners, sulking ponies hitched to cartloads of produce, blubberous hogs screeching in protest as they are hauled ashore.

The major pastime distraction of this city is the interesting view from **Yudalsan**, a craggy twin-peaked mountain which cuts into the center of the city. Several miles of winding pathways allow visitors to earn a vista in corresponding proportion to his or her particular degree of health or ambition.

Mokp'o is chiefly of interest as a point of departure. A variety of more or less seaworthy craft access to a significant number of Korea's 3,000 islands. A poor man's cruise to **Cheju-do** is available, taking seven hours to reach its destination. And eight hours to the west of Mokp'o is **Hong-do**, the "Red Island," named for the pink hues of its rock and famous for the imposing, contorted rock formations that line its coast. Food and lodging are available on **Huksan Island**, from which a private boat may be hired to Hong-do.

Canines and Spirits: Considerably less demanding is a trip south of **Chin-do**, a large island only two hours from Mokp'o by ferry. Chin-do is famous for its rare breed of dog and a unique style of shamanism. A pedigreed Chin-do-*kae* has a short, nearly white coat of fur with a touch of ochre along the inner curve of its characteristic arched tail. An annual Chin-do dog show is held in the autumn, billed in the English-language press as a "beauty contest." In one show, 90 pedigreed Chin-do dogs competed for the grand prize: a refrigerator.

Among the rituals peculiar to the shamanism of Chin-do is the *Sik-in kut,* or literally, a "ceremony to wash out the soul of the dead." Participants dress entirely on white *hanbok* and gather at the shore to cleanse the soul of a departed relative. Free of worldly taint, the soul is placed in a miniature boat and sent off to heaven.

Refuge of solace up in the hills.

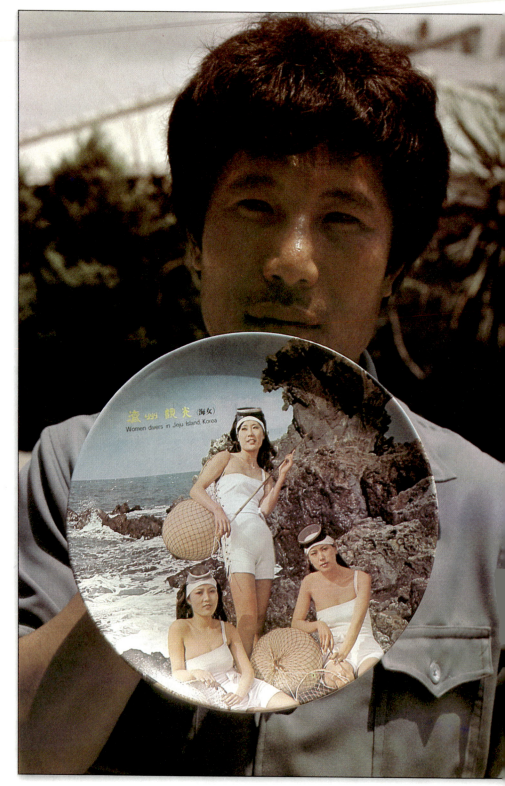

漁업 韻味 (海女)
Women divers in Jeju Island, Korea

CHEJU-DO, "OVER THERE"

receding
ages,
e village
f Mosulp'o,
heju-do.
eft,
aenyo on
hoto-plate.

In a 1975 jet-set travel article about "undiscovered worldwide tourist destinations," *Newsweek* magazine nicknamed **Cheju-do** the "Island of the Gods" and raved about its people, culture, seafoods, climate, beaches, golf courses, horseback riding, challenging hiking trails, sportsfishing grounds and volcanic peaks and craters. Later, *The Asian Wall Street Journal* headlined a story about Cheju-do with: "Korean Hopes to Transform Tranquil Cheju Island Into Bali of North Asia." The Korean Government, however, has long preferred to call Cheju-do "Korea's Hawaii" and "The Hawaii of the Orient."

Whichever sobriquet you choose for Korea's biggest and most famous island, such descriptions completely debunk stereotypical visions of this country as a land of frozen mountain passes and howling Siberian winds.

Though logic would argue the contrary, there are indeed uncanny geographical similarities between Cheju-do and the Hawaiian isles. On this egg-shaped island, which lies about 93 miles (150 kilometers) south of Pusan in the channel between Korea and Japan, offshore waters are of the same aqua-turquoise color as Hawaii's. These colors in turn lap against the same type of black lava shelves, jagged outcroppings and steep cliffs which rim Oahu, Maui, Kauai and the Big Island of Hawaii. Also, cloud-wreathed **Halla-san (Mt. Halla)** at 6,400 feet (1,950 meters) is the highest mountain peak in Korea and a dead ringer for either famous Haleakala Crater on Maui or the active volcanic peaks Mauna Kea and Mauna Loa on the Big Island.

Unlike Hawaii, Cheju can't advertise that its deep fissures and frozen lava swirls are the products of still active volcanoes, but it can boast to be home of the world's longest known lava tubes – **the Snake and Manjang canverns** located at **Kim Nyong** between **Cheju City** and **Songsanp'o.** The Manjang cavern,

Chejudo

16 km / 10 miles

the longer of the two tubes, is 7,629 yards (6,976 meters) long with a diameter that ranges from 10 feet to 66 feet (3 meters to 20 meters). During the summer tourists can join local guides on lamplight tours of these caverns filled with bats, spiders, centipedes and unusual lava formations; but you are advised to wear warm clothes because temperatures drop to a soggy 48°F (9°C) and cooler inside.

Probably Cheju-do's most distinctly Hawaiian-like phenomena are man-made structures. Particularly similar is a network of low walls of lava rock construction which lace the Cheju countryside. These walls, which from the sky look like irregular, wind-torn spider webs, border pastures and garden plots throughout the island, and many are almost exact replicas of lava rock walls which flow hither and thither in rural Hawaiian areas.

However, due to Cheju temperate locale – at north latitude 33° 20' and east longitude 126° 30' – and the absence of coconut palms (though there are pineapple fields) – these romantic comparisons to Hawaii and Bali must end. Once winter sets in, icy off-shore winds knife across Cheju-do and shatter all Polynesian allusions. Though the average monthly temperature from June through September is a balmy, semi-tropical 71°F to 80°F (22°C to 27°C), this pleasant level dives to an average of 44°F to 50°F (7°C to 10°C) from mid-November through March.

Yes, "The Hawaii of the Orient" gets cold, but despite occasional temperature changes and sometimes fierce winds, this splendid island – which since ancient times has been renowned for its winds, women and stones – is worth any traveler's detour. When weather gods are cooperating, Cheju-do is one of Asia's great vacation idylls.

She can be easily reached – either by ferry from Pusan or Mokp'o or the island of Wan-do, or by regular Korean Air and Asiana flights from the major mainland airports and from the Japanese cities of Tokyo, Osaka, Nagoya and Fukuoka.

Yang, Ko and Pu: According to Cheju myths, the original inhabitants of this island were three male demigods – **Yang, Ko** and **Pu** – who emerged from three

Rape (mustard) blossoms at Sogwip'o.

holes in the ground (called **Samsong Hyol**) located at **Cheju-si** (*si* means city), about 300 yards from the **KAL Hotel**. These male progenitors were hunters and fishermen who had the good fortune to later meet three princesses who brought with them grains, livestock and other forms of agriculture. Yang, Ko and Pu married these princesses and thus was Cheju society born. The births and meetings of these original Cheju ancestors are celebrated on special feast days every April, October and December by natives.

Until about AD 1000, however, Cheju, like many other detached island places in Asia, survived in relative isolation. Frederic H. Dustin, a longtime Chejudo resident who in 1975 authored *An Introduction to Cheju-do*, a booklet on Chejudo's history, geography and mythology, writes that it wasn't until about the end of Korea's Koryo Dynasty (918-1392) that Cheju was influenced by off-island events.

Tambulla, Do-i, T'amlla: It was during the reign of Koryo King Kojong (1214-1260), Dustin notes, that Cheju received its present name. *Che* means simply "across" or "over there," he writes. And *ju* in earlier times referred to an administrative district. Therefore, Cheju is the *do*, island, in the district over there. Previously the island was variously known as Tamlla, Tambulla, Do-i, Tanna and T'amlla, the latter appearing to be the most common in historical references.

In the 13th century, after the Koryo kingdom of mainland Korea had been subjugated by Mongol invaders, Cheju-do became a Mongol possession for about 100 years (from 1276 to 1375). Professor Sang Yong-ick of the Cheju National University reports that during this time the armies of Kublai and Genghis Khan "used Cheju-do as a bridge to invade Japan." One Japan invasion by Kublai Khan, according to Professor Sang, involved 33,000 men and 900 vessels, many of which were constructed of wood milled from trees on Halla-san.

These Mongol conquerors permanently altered Cheju ways. As Professor Sang notes, "Language and habits were greatly changed. The present day dialect (unlike the languages spoken on the Korean

ongsanp'o.

mainland) is a direct result of influence by the Mongols (and) until very recently, it was still possible to find leather hats, fur clothing and fur stockings of Mongol style in use in mountain areas. Through the Mongols Cheju (also) became a stock-raising area. Cheju became a famous breeding area for horses . . . (and) Buddhist was brought to Cheju by the Mongols along with temples and statues."

"Abounds in Horses and Cattle": The first Westerners to visit and tell the outside world about Cheju-do (and Korea proper) were Dutch sailors who shipwrecked at **Mosulp'o** on Cheju's south shore on August 16, 1653. These men – of the Dutch ship *Sparrow Hawk* enroute from Batavia to Taiwan and then Nagasaki – had ventured into fierce Cheju-area winds, which, according to survivor-author Henrik Hamel, "blew so boisterously, that we could not hear on another speak, nor durst we let fly an inch of sail. . ."

In a later account of the shipwreck off Cheju (which the Dutch named Quelpaert, after a type of Dutch sailing vessel), Hamel said of this place:

"This Island which the natives call Sehesure, lies 12 or 13 Leagues South of the Coast of Corea, and is about 14 or 15 leagues in Compass. On the North side of it is a Bay, where several Barques lye, and whence they sail for the Continent, which is of very dangerous Access to those that are unacquainted with it, because of several hidden rocks, and that there is but one place where Ships can Anchor and Ride under Shelter for in all other places they are often drove over to the Coast of Japan. The Island is all encompass'd with Rocks, but abounds in Horses and Cattle, which pay great Duties to the King; so that notwithstanding their Breeds of Horses and Herds of Cattle, the Islanders are very poor, and despis'd by the Inhabitants of the Continent. In this Island there is a Mountain of a vast Height, all cover'd with woods and several small Hills which are naked, and enclose many Vales abounding in Rice . . ."

Hamel's is a 330-year-old description which, except for the occasional streetlamp, automobile or bus, endures to this day in Cheju-do's rural areas. It's a

Fisherman, P'yong-dae-

very early description of a North Asia Eden, but despite such good publicity, Cheju-do didn't become known as a premier Asia tourist destination until just over three decades ago.

Author Dustin recalls that it wasn't until 1958 – an incredibly late exploratory date by contemporary tourism standards – that the first "really significant" group of tourists descended on Cheju-do. Dustin was a member of that initial tour, which was led by long-time resident (and now naturalized citizen) Ferris Miller. Dustin quotes Miller as saying of the 1958 visitation:

"Over 100 people went, by boat of course since there were no commercial planes then, and the occasion was considered so important that the governor and the major of Cheju City met the ship. There were no hotels so we rented all of the seven or eight inns in town, staying three nights. We also took over two bath houses, one for men and one for women, with runners to guide visitors to them through the unpaved, unlighted streets."

That idyllic Cheju-do situation has changed considerably. The island is now criss-crossed with paved streets and highways and dotted by hotels and *yogwan* (inns). Six major hotels on the island even have casinos, a rarity in Korea, where you can enjoy high-stakes games of chance

A US$700 million development project at Chungmun, on the south side of the island, reached first-stage completion in 1991, with two major international **hotels**, the **Hyatt** and the **Shilla**, and other facilities including a golf course and botanical gardens.

A simple drive around Cheju-do, or a cruise along one of the two crosscut highways which skirt Halla-san's west or east slopes, are both worthwhile. But whichever course you choose, you'll soon find yourself driving past pine forests, tangerine orchards, pineapples fields, mushroom caves, dancing waterfalls, bizarre rock formations, and rural charms that will draw you yet deeper into Cheju-do's calm and beauty.

Among the island attractions one shouldn't miss are:

• Cheju-do's superb **beaches**. Favorite

crescents of sand are located at **Hyopje**, **Kwakji**, **Hamdok** and **Songsan** along Cheju's upper half, and at **Hwasun**, the aforementioned **Chungmun** and **P'yoson** in the south sector. Most of these spots feature superb seafood restaurants, gaily-painted tent cafes, and rentable recreational facilities.

• The **Hallim weavers village** on the northwest short. At this quiet spot, where you'll see sheep grazing on rolling hills, you'll find the **Hallim Handweavers** complex where Koreans trained by Columbian Roman Catholic priests and nuns are creating some of the finest Irish woolens outside of Ireland.

This village's unusual cottage industry was begun in the early 1960s by Father Patrick J. McGlinchey, who imported 500 sheep and the proper grass to grow for grazing. The colorful priest first arrived on the island in 1954 and has since become something of a legend for his contribution to Cheju's development.

At the Hallim Handweavers factory you can watch Koreans shear sheep, then wash, card, spin, warp, thread, weave, check, tenter and steam raw wool into a weavable product. And following the clacking of looms, you can buy superb woolen sweaters, ponchos, caps, mittens, skirts, scarves, blankets and berets (also sold at their Seoul shop in the Chosun Hotel). Only traditional Irish patterns are created by Hallim's industrious "Irish of the Orient."

• The series of **waterfalls** on both the east and west sides of lovely **Sogwip'o Town**. The strong **Chongbang Falls** right in Sogwip'o town is often referred to as "the only waterfall in Asia that plunges directly into the sea."

• The **tol-harubang**, or grandfather stones. These carved lava rock statues, 52 in all, are seen on all parts of Cheju-do. However, nobody's quite sure what to make of these phallic fellows with funny smiles. Anthropologists say they probably represent legendary guardians who once flanked the entrances to Cheju's largest townships. Other scholars compare them to mysterious statuary found in some parts of the southern Korean peninsula, Tahiti, Okinawa, Fiji and even

The other side of Songsanp'o.

Easter Island. Suitable places to study these images up close are at the entrance to the **Samsonghyol Museum** in Cheju City or in front of **Kwandok-jok-jong** (a 15th-century pavilion), and the oldest standing building on Cheju-do, which faces Cheju City's main square). If you find these tol-harubang fellows charming, miniature lava rock reproductions are for sale at souvenir shops scattered throughout the island.

• Koreans suggest that you also see the curious **Yongdu-am**, or "**Dragon's Head Rock**," on the sea in Cheju City's western suburbs near Cheju's main airport. According to Cheju legends, this dragon descended from Halla-san and, upon reaching the sea, was petrified in place.

Probably the most dominant memories one will have of this island after a proper tour will be pictures of its famous diving women, awesome Halla-san, and if you visit in the springtime, brilliant fields of rape that paint broad yellow splotches across Cheju-do's pastureland.

Cheju-do's diving women, called *haenyo*, have been a symbol of this island and its purported matriarchal culture. They are immortalized in folk songs, contemporary promotional brochures, as plaster-of-Paris sculptures, and on postcards, souvenir pennants, cups, plates and *ad trinketum*. Indeed, these hardy and amphibious females, whose free-diving exhalations pierce the air with oxygen-releasing shrieks and whistles, have been celebrated for centuries by Chejudoites and Korean mainlanders alike.

When sea and weather conditions are favorable, scores of the *haenyo*, who range from teenagers to wrinkled grandmothers, can be seen bobbing offshore between free dives for seaweed, shellfish and sea urchins. In their slick and black ankle-to-neck wetsuits, face masks and snorkels, they look more like members of a navy demolition team than the sexy sirens they are supposed to be, but they are still the favorite target of every camera-bearing tourist who visits Cheju-do. But remember to ask for permission before photographing the *haenyo*, since they are often shy or might want to be reimbursed for their bathing beauty modeling.

*Left,
woman picks
seafood.
Right,
Cheju City
tol-harubang.*

TRAVEL TIPS

GETTING THERE

BY AIR

Kimp'o International Airport, 16 miles (24 kilometers) west of Seoul, receives over 400 flights weekly from most world destinations. Two international terminals and a domestic terminal in the same complex are connected by a regular bus service. Through the 1980s and into the 1990s, every year saw additional carriers coming on line. Among the most recent additions are Aeroflot and Qantas. Seoul can often be added as a stopover on northeast Asia air tickets at no extra cost. It is less than 13 hours from the U.S. West Coast, 2½ hours from Tokyo and 3½ hours from Hong Kong.

BY SEA

The overnight *Pukwan* ferry to Pusan departs from Shimonoseki, Japan, at 5 p.m. every day except Saturday. First and second class "western style" berths are available on this 952-passenger ferry. The adaptable traveler, however, may want to try the economy Japanese-style "suite" – a communal cabin with a mat-padded floor (blankets and straw pillows are provided). One-way tickets range from US$55 to US$90 with discounts for round trips (5 percent), students (25 percent), children between 6 and 12 (50 percent). Infants under 6 are free.

The top deck of the *Pukwan* is a pleasant, vantage point for a first hour sail before dusk, as the ferry chugs past islets that trail into the East Sea. At 6 p.m. the ship's *mogyokt'ang* (Korean-style bathroom) opens until 8 p.m. and features a hot tub for passengers' leisure and soaking pleasure. Dinner is pricey and travelers are advised to pack *kim-pap* (laver-wrapped rice and vegetable rolls) and snacks. The *Pukwan* pulls into the "Land of the Morning Calm" at 8.30 a.m. the next day.

Note: The outgoing *Kampu* ferry runs from Pusan to Shimonoseki at the same time the *Pukwan* ferry sets out. For more information, contact:

Tokyo Office	(03) 567-0971
Osaka Office	(06) 345-2245
Shimonoseki Office	(0832) 24-3000
Seoul Office	(02) 738-0055
Pusan Office	(051) 463-3161
Cheju Office	(064) 23-6927

TRAVEL ESSENTIALS

VISAS & PASSPORTS

Visitors are required to have a valid passport. Exception are holders of: United Nations passport (visa still required); U.S. military ID card, provided travel order bears "Korea" on travel point; one-entry travel certificate issued to Korean residents of Japan; certificate of identity issued to residents of Hong Kong (holders need prior permission from Ministry of Justice); seaman book (except U.S. seamen); *Kinderausweis* issued to nationals of Germany.

The following may enter Korea without a visa: Korean nationals, diplomatic of official passport holders of Iran, the Philippines and Paraguay; holders of re-entry permit; United Nations military personnel; nationals of Greece, Liechtenstein, Mexico, Switzerland, Austria, Bangladesh, Belgium, Chile, Colombia, Costa Rica, Denmark, Dominican Republic, France, Finland, Germany, Iceland, Italy, Lesotho, Liberia, Luxembourg, Malaysia, the Netherlands, Norway, Peru, Portugal, Singapore, Spain, Surinam, Sweden, Thailand, Tunisia, Turkey and United Kingdom.

There is a W6,000 airport tax.

CUSTOMS

Non-Korean nationals may bring in 400 cigarettes, 50 cigars or 250 grams of pipe and 100 grams of powdered tabacco (total quantity not to exceed 500 grams). Korean nationals may bring in one bottle (not ex-

The Bank Who Cares for your business.

BANK DAGANG NEGARA
(STATE COMMERCIAL BANK)

HEAD OFFICE : Jl. M.H. Thamrin No. 5, Jakarta   Phone : 321707, 3800800,
P.O. Box : 338/JKT Jakarta 10002, INDONESIA
Telex : 61628 BDNULN IA, 61649 BDNULN IA, 61621 BDNLN JKT, 61640 BDN FX IA.

OVERSEAS OFFICES :

NEW YORK (AGENCY) &
CAYMAN ISLANDS (BRANCH)
45 Broadway Atrium 30th floor
New York, N.Y. 10006,
U S A
Telex :   226698 BDN NYUR
226690 BDN NYUR

LOS ANGELES (AGENCY)
3457 Wilshire Boulevard
Los Angeles, C.A. 90010
U S A
Telex :   3716724 BDN LA USAG
3716705 BDN LA USAG

HONG KONG (REPRESENTATIVE) &
STACO INTERNATIONAL FINANCE LTD
6/F Admiralty Centre Tower II
Queensway, Victoria
Hong Kong
Telex :   60322 BDN – HX
60323 BDN FX – HX

SINGAPORE (REPRESENTATIVE)
50 Raffles Place 13-05
Shell Tower, Singapore 0104
Telex : DAGANG RS 24939

THE PROBLEMS OF A

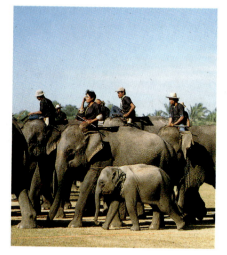

HEAVY TRAFFIC.

You'll come across massive Thai jumbos at work and play in their natural habitat. In Thailand, elephants are part of everyday rural life.

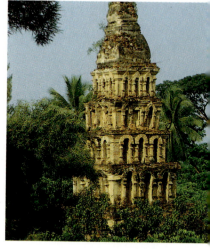

FALLING MASONRY.

A visit to the ruined cities of Sukhothai o Ayutthaya will remind you of the country's long and event-filled history.

EYESTRAIN.

A problem everyone seems to enjoy. The beauty of our exotic land is only matched by the beauty and gentle nature of the Thai people.

GETTING LOST.

From the palm-fringed beaches of Phuket to the highlands of Chiang Mai there are numerous places to get away from it all.

OLIDAY IN THAILAND.

GETTING TRAPPED.

bunkers mostly. The fairways, superb club
ouses and helpful caddies make a golf trap for
layers of all standards.

HIGH DRAMA.

A performance of the 'Khon' drama, with gods
and demons acting out a never-ending battle
between good and evil, should not be missed.

EXCESS BAGGAGE.

Thai food is so delicious you'll want to eat more
and more of it. Of course, on Thai there's
no charge for extra kilos in this area.

MISSING YOUR FLIGHT.

In Thailand, this isn't a problem. Talk to us or your
local travel agent about Royal
Orchid Holidays in Thailand.

Thai
We reach for the sky.

Ask for it every day, everywhere you go.

Wherever you're going in the world, a copy of the International Herald Tribune is waiting for you. Circulated in 164 countries, on 70 airlines and in hundreds of quality hotels worldwide, the IHT brings you a view of the world that is concise, balanced and distinctly multinational in flavor. And you can get it six days a week, even when you're traveling.

Herald INTERNATIONAL Tribune

Published With The New York Times and The Washington Post

7th Floor, Malaysia Building, 50 Gloucester Road, Hong Kong.
Tel: (852) 861 0616. Fax: (852) 861 3073. Telex: 61170 IHT HX.

138 Cecil Street, #07-02 Cecil Court, Singapore 0106.
Tel: (65) 2236478. Fax: (65) 2241566. Telex: RS 28749 IHT SIN.

A region of endless variety. **Insight Guide: China** *acquaints you with the Land of Extremes. Rediscover China from Beijing to the Yellow River; the exotic Silk Road; Yunnan's diverse communities.*

Cityguide Beijing *provides fascinating insights into the Forbidden City, residence of the Chinese emperors for many centuries. Or plunge into the hustle and bustle of colourful Hong Kong. Taiwan allows you to enjoy both Chinese culture and aggressive consumerism. Korea presents an unexpected potpourri of seasons, scenery, traditional religions and dress. And Tokyo is one of the most fast-paced and interesting cities in the world.*

펼만났오!

Beijing
China
East Asia
Hong Kong
Korea
Taiwan
Tokyo

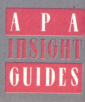

A P A
INSIGHT
GUIDES

ceeding 760 cc) of alcohol. Foreign nationals may bring in two bottles (not exceeding 1520 cc). Other limited items are perfume (two ounces) and gifts up to value of 100,000 won. Narcotics, obscene publications and literature deemed "subversive" are banned. Permission must be obtained to bring in firearms and explosives.

Cats, dogs and birds must be accompanied by a vet health certificate issued at point of origin. Quarantine is 10 days. Cats and dogs require a rabies vaccination certificate.

Korean antiques dating earlier than 1910 should be checked and appraised by the Cultural Property Preservation Bureau near the Capitol Building (Tel: 720-2122) and a permit should be secured. A limit of three kilograms of red ginseng with a sales receipt is acceptable.

For more information, contact Seoul Immigration Office, 39-1 Seosomundong Chung-gu, Tel: 776-8858, or Kimp'o Customs Office, Tel: 636-7070.

MONEY MATTERS

Currency: Procuring won, Korean currency, outside Korea is virtually impossible. In country, however, there are forign exchange bill or traveler's check), major banks (some with branches in large hotels) and a few major department stores (e.g. Midopa and Lotte) in Seoul. The most viable currencies are difficult to exchange. Remember to retain all exchange receipts for reconversion on departure. Up to $500 may be reconverted without a receipt. As of mid-1991, the exchange rate per US$ is W726.

Won (W) comes in 1,000, 5,000 and 10,000 denomination notes and 1, 5, 10, 50, 100, and 500 *Won* coins. Bank drafts for large amounts (normally drafts of W100,000) are available.

Credit Cards: American Express, VISA, MasterCard and Diners Club cards are readily accepted in major hotels, department stores and restaurants.

Banking: Banking hours are 9:30 a.m. to 4:30 p.m. Monday through Friday, 9:30 a.m. to 1:30 p.m. on Saturdays. Contact any of the following banks for further information.

HEALTH

Except for those whose itineraries include cholera-infected areas, no certificate of vaccination is required.

If immunizations are needed, they are administered at the International Clinic at Severance Hospital which uses disposable needles for preventive measures, and at the Seoul Quarantine Office at Kimp'o Airport.

WHAT TO WEAR

Influenced by climate and occasion, clothing in Korea follows function rather than style. Business suits are the proper mode, even in the summer, for metropolitan business activities. Otherwise, dress is casual. Backless or mini-dress and shorts, though appropriate for muggy weather, are not acceptable wear in the public. An umbrella, sunglasses and rainy-day footwear are practical accessories to pack.

GETTING ACQUAINTED

GEOGRAPHY

Land Divisions: Land is defined from province to the block and street. In the city, land is bound by *si*, city; *iku*, ward; and *dong*, precinct. In rural areas, the land divisions are: *do*, province; *si*, city or large town; *up*, town; *kun*, district; *myon*, township; and *ri*, residential area. Other commonly used Korean words in addresses are *no*, *ro* or *lo* for road or street and *ka* for block.

CLIMATE

Korea's location in the mid-latitudes and East Asian Monsoon Belt means four distinct seasons with varying moods. A spring thaw comes in mid-April and lasts little more than two months. Early spring northwesterly gusts bring swirls of golden dust from the Gobi

Desert and a light rain. As summer approaches, humid southerlies vie for control and the spring drizzle becomes an occasional downpour by summer (June-October).

July and August are the hottest, most humid months, especially in the inland basin around Taegu; the temperature there climbs to over 85°F (30°C). Autumn, by far the most splendid time to be in the country, comes in late October when the air currents shift back to the crisp northerlies. This climatic ideal intensifies by the end of November when the Siberian freeze whips down the peninsula for six months in a cycle of three consecutive cold days followed by four milder days. The northern inland region of the peninsula has a winter temperature mean of –4°F (–20°C) (Chungkangjin, north Korea, the peninsula's coldest spot, has a temperature mean in January of –6°F (–21°C) while the southern provinces, in contrast, winter in less severe temperature (Cheju-do's temperature mean for January is 39 °F (4°C). The coldest months are January and February when the temperature drops to – 10°F to 35°F (–12 °C to 1.5 °C).

The favorable months in Korea are April (10°C or 50°F in Seoul), May (16°C or 60°F), June and September just before and after the summer rains (19°C or 66°F) and in October (12°C or 54°F). Call 735-0365 in Korea for more information on the weather.

TIME ZONES

International time differences are staggered as follows:

Seoul	12 p.m. today
Japan	12 p.m. today
Hawaii	5 p.m. yesterday
San Francisco	7 p.m. yesterday
New York	10 p.m. yesterday
London	3 a.m. today
Paris	4 a.m. today
Bonn	4 a.m. today
Bangkok	10 a.m. today

For the local time, call 116.

CULTURE & CUSTOMS

National Anthem: "Aeguk Ka" ("Love of Country"), the Korean national anthem, was written during the Japanese occupation (composer unknown) and set to music later by Ahn Eak Tai. The national anthem is played throughout the Republic every workday evening over the radio in Korean government offices and in main thoroughfares as the flag is lowered. Proper public protocol – silence and standing at attention – is requested.

NATIONAL FLAG

The Korean flag, *t'aekuk ki,* was adopted as the national flag in August, 1882, not long after the "Hermit Kingdom" opened its front and back doors to foreign powers.

Appropriately, the flag symbolizes the oriental *yin-yang* (in Korean, *um-yang*) philosophy of the balance and harmony in nature of opposite forces and elements which are in perpetual motion. The colors of the flag are red, black, and blue against white. The red and blue circle in the center of the flag symbolizes the dualism of the universe. The upper red paisley represents *yang* nature: positive, masculine, active, constructive, light, heat, dignity, etc.; complemented by the lower blue paisley, *um* nature: negative, feminine, passive, destructive, dark, cold, hope, etc. The black trigrams in each corner are also of Chinese origin (from the Tao Te Ch'ing). They basically symbolize the four seasons and cardinal directions. In clockwise starting with the upper left corner, the three solid bars (*K'un*) represent heaven, spring, east, and benevolence; the upper right bars (*Kam*): moon, winter, north, and wisdom; lower right bars (*K'on*): earth, summer, west, and righteousness; and lower left bars (*I*): sun, autumn, south, and etiquette.

CIVIL DEFENSE

Held usually on the 15th of each month around 2 p.m., the 15-minute civil defense alert drill brings city traffic to a grinding halt. Everyone takes cover in buildings or underground arcades, temporarily abandoning their vehicles. Every few months, a 15-minute blackout drill is held around 9 p.m. Advance notice is given in the local media.

KOREAN NAMES

Korean surnames, most of which are but one syllable, are easy to learn as they are to forget. The problem is that many Koreans share the same romanized surname (although some of the Chinese characters may be written differently). Referring to someone by his surname can only become confusing and futile after meeting many Koreans. To compound the problem, Korean wives retain their maiden names (but they usually will make allowances for foreigners who mistakenly call them by their husband's name). Thus, it is ideal to learn the entire Korean name.

Korean surnames were derived from the Chinese during the early Three Kingdoms Period. The most common surnames in order of the most numerous are Kim, Yi (Lee I, Rhee), and Pak (Park), followed by Choi, Chung, and Cho. Throughout the ages, surnames have dictated one's social position, a tradition still honored only in reclusive villages. Whether *yangban* (aristocrat) or *pyongmin* (commoner), one's name would be recorded in a family tree book, *chokbo*, which traced one's lineage back to the origin of the clan. The *chokbo* is a kind of heirloom still updated and passed on these days.

Given names are usually two syllables and of Chinese origin. Either the first or second character is predetermined and is related to the "theory of the five elements." It is given to all family members of the same generation. The other character is freely selected.

TOJANG (NAME SEALS)

Seals, engraved by professional artisans, are as important as personal signatures, especially on legal documents. It, too, was originally a borrowed custom from China, initially a status symbol used by royalty. During the Three Kingdoms Period (57 BC-AD 918), a dethroned king had to symbolically transfer power by handing over his imperial seals.

Seals today are more popular than ever as they are used by government offices, companies, and organizations, and for personal flourishes on stationery. The seals are carved of ivory, stone, marble, plastic, wood, smokey topaz, jade and other materials. The ink is made of sticky scarlet vegetable dye which is permanent.

TIPPING

This western custom is expected only in businesses which cater primarily to westerners. A 10-15 percent service charge is automatically added to major hotel room and restaurant tabs (read the bill to make sure before tipping). Airport baggage porters are tipped generously at the exit door according to a set standard. Taxi drivers do not expect a tip unless they perform extra service. Unless requested for, they may not return the change if it is small. Anything from W500 is acceptable.

ELECTRICITY

The 100 volt current is sufficient and safe for 110 volt electrical devices. It is slowly being converted to 220 volt power.

BUSINESS HOURS

Mondays to Fridays

Banks	9:30 a.m.– 4:30 p.m.
Embassies	9:00 a.m.– 5:00 p.m.
Department Stores*	10:30 a.m.– 7:30 p.m.
Private Companies	9:00 a.m.– 6:00 p.m.
Govt/Post Offices**	9:00 a.m.– 6:00 p.m.

(* Closed once a week on a weekday, but open also on Sundays and Holidays;
** Closed at 5:00 p.m. during winter)

Saturdays

Banks	9:30 a.m.– 1:30 p.m.
Department Stores	10:30 a.m.– 7:30 p.m.
Private Companies	9:00 a.m.– 1:00 p.m.
Post Offices	9:00 a.m.– 1:00 p.m.

HOLIDAYS

1 January, **New Year's Day** – The first three days of January are recognized by the government as the beginning of a new year according to the lunar calendar. It is celebrated by exchanging greetings, worshipping at family ancestral shrines and eating rice cake soup.

Lunar New Year – The beginning of the lunar year has recently been added to the holiday list. In 1991, Koreans had two days followed by a two-day weekend in February in which to enjoy this traditional period.

1 March, Samiljol (Independence Day)– Observance of the 1 March, 1919 independence movement against colonial Japanese rule which features an annual reading of the Korean Proclamation of Independence at Pagoda Park in Seoul.

5 April, Arbor Day – Attention is given to Korea's reforestation program.

Han-sik-il (Cold Food Day, mid-April) – On the 105th day of the lunar calendar, Koreans visit their ancestors' graves with offerings of fruit, rice cakes, meat, wine and other dishes. Traditionally, fires were not lit on this day for reasons long since forgotten.

5 May, Children's Day – This successor to a former "Boy's Day" was proclaimed a national holiday in 1975 to honor Korea's youth and to focus attention on the importance of the family institution in Korea. On this day, children are dolled up, usually in traditional clothes, and taken on holiday excursions to parks and children's centers.

Buddha's Birthday (mid-May) – This "Feast of the Lanterns" day is celebrated on the 8th day of the 4th lunar month in honor of the birth of Buddha. Buddha's Birthday was also designated a national holiday in 1975. It is colorfully commemorated with temple rituals and parades throughout predominantly Buddhist Korea.

Tano (early June) – This summer festival day on the 5th day of the 5th lunar month is one of Korea's most important celebrations. On this day, new summer food is offered at family ancestral shrines in traditional homes. It has customarily been a day when girls dressed in *hanbok* dresses gather in parks and compete in stand-up swinging matches – thus the name "Swing Day".

6 June, Memorial Day – On this solemn holiday, the nation remembers and honors war heroes. Memorial services are conducted throughout the nation, but perhaps the biggest tribute is paid at the National Cemetery in Seoul.

15 June, Farmer's Day – A day to honor the nation's agricultural workers. Farmer's Day is a day of feasting and celebrating with ancient "farmer" folk music and dance.

17 July, Constitution Day – A legal national holiday to commemorate the proclamation of the Constitution of the Republic of Korea on 17 July, 1948. Patriotic gatherings are held in town squares and other such public places throughout the country.

15 August, Liberation Day – A national holiday commemorating Japanese acceptance of Allied surrender terms in 1945 and thereby releasing Korea from some 36 years of Japanese colonial domination. This day also marks the formal proclamation of the Republic of Korea in 1948. This is a day of speeches, parades and other such activities by Korean patriots.

Ch'usok (September or October) – Ch'usok – which occurs on the 15th day of the 8th lunar month – is the Korean counterpart to America's Thanksgiving. On this day, people visit family tombs and make food offerings to their ancestors. Traditional Korean costumes color every street in a festive and classical way.

1 October, Armed Forces Day – Colorful military parades, honor guard ceremonies, and other such martial activities honor Korea's defense forces. A major gathering of military personnel and citizens usually takes place at the reviewing plaza at Youido Island in the Han River region of southwest Seoul.

3 October, National Foundation Day – Also called Tan'gun Day, this national holiday recalls the day in mythical times when Tan'gun, the legendary son of a bear-woman, was born and became Korea's first human king. Tan'gun's reign is said to have begun in 2333 BC, continuing till 1122 BC.

9 October, Han'gul Day – Han'gul Day joyfully and respectfully recalls the anniversary of the promulgation by King Sejong of *han'gul*, Korea's indigenous alphabet. Sejong commissioned the creation of this unique phonetic writing form in mid-15th century.

25 December, Christmas Day – Because of a large Christian community, Christmas is observed as a national holiday in Korea in about the same way as it is observed in most Occidental countries.

RELIGIOUS SERVICES

Christian Science Society – Miju Apartment House (behind Daehan Theater), 62-16, Pil-dong 3, Chung-gu, Tel: 7904-3702

International Lutheran Church – Hannamdong on road to Pusan Expressway, Tel: 794-6274

Seoul International Baptist Church – Yoido, next to Dong office, Tel: 324-2896

The Memorial of the Catholic Joil du Sans Martyrs – 96-1 Hapchong-dong, Mapo-ku, Tel: 322-2973

Jewish Services Center – Yongsan Base, Building T-3601, gate passes at Gat 10, Tel: 7904-4113

Yoido Full Gospel Church (evangelical) – 1-20 Yoido-dong, Yongdungpo, Tel: 782-9673, 782-4851/5

COMMUNICATIONS

MEDIA

The Press: There are 10 national newspapers, seven morning and three evening. In addition there are four national economic dailies. Three English-language dailies – *The Korea Herald, The Korea Times* (morning) and *The Korea Daily* (evening) – use international wire services and are available at news-stands and bookstores. Papers do not publish on public holidays. The pacific edition of *Stars and Stripes*, a U.S. military newspaper, is sold at U.S. military institutions and nearby hotels and to subscribers in Seoul. *The International Herald Tribune, The Asian Wall Street Journal* and *The Financial Times* are circulated locally.

PERIODICALS

Weeklies, semi-weeklies, bi-weeklies, monthlies and bi-monthlies flood the bookstores. The top publications are the weekly *Sisa Journal* and the monthly *Wolgan Chosun, Shindongah, Wolgan Joongang* and *Observer*.

The most popular English language monthlies cater for foreign businessmen. They are *Business Korea*, *Korea Business World* and *Korea Economic Report*. Other periodicals are *Korea Journal*, published by UNESCO, and *The Korea Post*. There are several academic quarterlies published by institutes, among them *Korea* and *World Affairs*, *Korea Observer* and the *Journal of East and West Studies*. The Royal Asiatic Society stocks these publications and has also published its own annual *Transactions* since 1900.

RADIO

In the winter of 1980, Korean radio broadcasting was forcibly consolidated by the government into three broadcasting stations: Korea Broadcasting System (KBS), a government-owned station; Munhwa Broadcasting Company (MBC), owned by a semi-government foundation; and the Christian Broadcasting System (CBS), established by religious sponsors in 1945.

In recent years, however, new stations have been launched – SBS, which broadcasts in the Seoul area; PBS, a Catholic-owned station; and TBS, a traffic station. The U.S. Armed Forces Korea Network (AFKN) offers English programs with news every hour on the hour, 24 hours a day, to its military community.

TELEVISION

Television broadcasting in Korea began in 1956 with a privately-owned, commercial station which burned down three years later. On 31 December, 1961, the government established its own network, the Korea Broadcasting Service (KBS-TV). Presently, the channels are: KBS-1, KBS-2, KBS-3 (an educational channel), MBC and SBS in the Seoul area. Experimental cable TV also began in 1991 and is expected to develop through the decade. Korea does not permit satellite broadcasting, which means it is one of the few countries where CNN is not available in hotels. AFKN-TV (American Forces Korea Network) is watched by the foreign community and by many Koreans. It has news bulletins from CNN and news programs, dramas and sit-coms from other American networks. Public service announcements, such as warning to guard against terrorist, in the place of advertising, remind the non-military viewer that the network is catering for the American soldier. Broadcasting hours vary from station to station, but AFKN is the only network broadcasting 24 hours. Daily program schedules are listed in the English-language papers.

POSTAL SERVICES

The first modern post office was opened in 1884 in Seoul on An'guk Street to the right of the Chogyesa Buddhist temple. It was burned during a political riot soon after opening, but was reconstructed into a Communications Memorial Center in 1969. On display are old telegram sheets designed in 1904, a map showing the layout of telephone subscribers in Inch'on in 1900, official seals, records, documents and other relics. In addition, a collection of stamps – dating from the first issues – is also displayed. All these stamps – from the T'aekuk-design stamps in 1884 to the 1988 Olympics – present the commemoration of some key historical events in the country. Commemorative stamps are sold here, as well as at regular post offices and in *up'yo* (stamp) shops around town. The memorial is open business hours weekdays and until noon on Saturday.

The contemporary central post office, however, is located on Chungmu Street across from the Chinese Embassy, a block east of Shinsegye Department Store. Two other post office branches are located near the corner of T'aep'yong-no and Chong-no and on Yulkok Street between the U.S. Embassy Housing Compound and the An'guk Immigration Office. General post office hours are 9 a.m. to 6 p.m. Monday to Saturday (5 p.m. in the winter months).

Aerograms are W500. A 10-gram airmail letter to Europe, North America and Middle East is W440, and to Hong Kong or Japan, W370. Postcards are W300 to all destinations. Letters to the United States and Europe take seven to 10 days.

TELEPHONE & TELEGRAM

Intra-City Calls: Red and gray public pay phones take two W10 coins per intra-city call. The call automatically disconnects after three minutes.

Inter-City Calls: Large rectangular public telephones are used for inter-city calls. To place a direct dial inter-city call, use the following prefixes before the desired phone number:

Anyang	0343
Ch'olwon	0353
Ch'ongju	0431
Ch'unch'on	0361

Cheju City	064
Chonju	0652
Inch'on	032
Iri	0653
Kanghwa-Si	0349
Kangnung	0391
Kumi	0546
Kuri	0346
Kwangju	062
Kyongju	0561
Masan	0551
Mokp'o	0631
P'ohang	0562
Pusan	051
Seoul	02
Sogwip'o	064
Songnam	0342
Suwon	0331
Taegu	053
Taejon	042
Uijongbu	0351
Ulsan	0522

Overseas Calls: Overseas calls can be dialed direct from major hotels by dialing the international access code (001) plus a country code and the number. Calls can also be made from public phones labeled "Home Country Direct" To book an oversea call, dial 007 for the international operator.

Telegrams: The Korean Int'l Telecommunications Office at 21, 1-ga Chungmuro Chung-gu (Tel: 005), handles telegram messages over the telephone. To make sure the message is conveyed correctly, write it out at the office. There are three types of telegrams: Urgent, which takes about six hours to reach its destination; Ordinary (ORD), 12 hours; and Lettergram (LT), about 24 hours. There is also a special telegram service for the press. Office hours are 9 a.m. to 5 p.m. Monday to Friday, 9 a.m. to 1 p.m. Saturday.

EMERGENCIES

MEDICAL SERVICES

Many kinds of medicines and health care goods – from bottled sweetened vitamin tonics to contraceptives – are available at local pharmacies. Many drugs are imported. Except for the sales of narcotics and barbiturates, there is little government control over these business, and drugs are sometimes diluted or mixed, repackaged, and then sold. Placebos are not unheard of. Hospital pharmacies are more reliable drug outlets.

Dentists and optometrists are generally reliable and their work is reasonably priced.

Major hotels have house doctors. For medical attention in hospitals, below are some of their phone numbers.

LOSS

To recover lost possession, including those left in taxis, contact the nearest police box or ask the hotel front desk clerk to help you do so. Call the Seoul police Lost and Found Center at 755-4400 or 778-4400.

GETTING AROUND

FROM THE AIRPORT

The airport bus has two lines which run every 10 minutes from 5:20 a.m. to 9:30 p.m. daily. Follow the signs at the airport to the stop in front of the terminal. Line 1 runs from Kimp'o to the Seoul Garden Hotel, the Koreana Hotel, Sheraton Walker Hill Hotel and back. Line 2 runs from Kimp'o to the Palace Hotel, the Express Bus Terminal in Panpodong, the Riverside Hotel, Nam Seoul Hotel, the Korea Exhibition Center, the Olympic Sports Complex and back. Both bus trips cost W500 one-way and take about one hour to Walker Hill and 45 minutes to the Sports Complex.

City bus #41 runs every five minutes from the airport to Midop'a Department Store in downtown Seoul. It cost W180 and the pick-up point is at the bus terminal, located next to the airport parking lot. However, for the traveler with a lot of baggage, the city bus is not recommended.

DOMESTIC TRAVEL

By Air: Korea Air has daily flights from Seoul to Cheju (60 minutes), Pusan (50 mintues), Taegu (50 mintues), Yosu (60 minutes), Kwangju (50 minutes), Sokch'o (40 minutes), Chinju (60 minutes), Ulsan (50 minutes) and P'ohang (50 minutes).

Asiana Airlines flies to Cheju, Pusan, Kwangju, Taegu and Yechon (40 minutes).

Tickets are available at major hotels and tourist agencies or can be simple purchased at the airport. Security is tight and passports are required.

BY SEA

Numerous ferries and fishing boats make regular connections between the coasts and the outlying islands. The schedules change frequently and boats will cancel trips at any time if the weather gets bad. Travel arrangements should be made with travel agents and time should be allowed for last minute changes if you travel during the monsoon season.

Several routes on the south coast in the Hallyo Waterway may be traveled either by ferry or by hydrofoil. Although the hydrofoil is faster, it is small and cramped.

If time allows, the ferry is by far the more pleasant mode of transportation and it allows the passengers to take in some scenery. There's not much of a view from the hydrofoil and those prone to seasickness should definitely avoid it.

You may call any of the following ferry terminals for further details:

Pusan
international	(051) 463-3161
domestic	(051) 44-0117
Cheju	(0641) 2-4225
Kunsan	(0654) 3-2936
Inch'on	(032) 882-1714
Masan	(0551) 2-8301
Mokp'o	(0631) 2-4226
P'ohang	(0562) 2-0711
Yosu	(0662) 63-2441

BY RAIL

The introduction of the locomotive to Korea was not without political motives. Several foreign powers, including Russia, Japan, France, and the United States, bid hard for the contract, which was eventually awarded to an American, James R. Morse. Soon after initiating construction, Morse, beset with financial difficulties, was forced to pass the project to the Japanese. The Korean government directed Japan to complete the line in the standard gauge system Morse used rather than import arrow gauge rails in from Japan.

The first railroad, which linked Seoul to Inch'on, was opened in September 1899. Other major lines were laid by the Japanese, including lines originating in Mokp'o, Masan, and Pusan to Seoul and to Sinuiju in North Korea, which linked with the Trans-Siberian Railway.

At one time, a serious traveler could travel by train from Pusan to Paris. The railroad suffered considerable damage during various wars, but since 1953 the railway system in South Korea has been steadily modernized over the years to accommodate locals and tourists comfortably.

Today, five kinds of train services are available. Their classifications in order of increasing speed, comfort and punctuality are: *wanhaeng* (stops at each station along the way), *pot'ong kuphaeng* (ordinary express with berths, stops frequently and runs at night), *tukkup* (limited express, reserved sets available, occasionally with diner car), *udung* (air-conditioned), and *Saemaul Ho* (luxury, air-conditioned super express with diner car).

It is advisable to purchase tickets in advance, especially during the summer vacation months. If you require any details about trains, call (02) 392-0078.

BY ROAD

Inter-City Buses: Eight expressways cut across the farmlands and mountains of Korea: the Kyungjin (Seoul-Inch'on); Yongdong (Seoul-Kangnung); Tonghae (Kangnung-P'ohang); Kuma (Taegu-Masan); Kyongbu (Seoul-Pusan); Namhae (Masan-Kwangju); Honam (Kwangju-Taejon); and the '88 Olympic (Taegu-Kwangju) Expressways.

There are three kinds of inter-city buses: *kosok* (highway express bus – the speediest, and therefore the most dangerous), *chikhaeng* (first class local and direct route), and *wanheang* (round about with frequent stops). Because of the high rate of occupancy, it is advisable to buy bus tickets in advance for a reserved seat. Listed below are nine main bus stations in Seoul and their more popular destinations:

Ch'onho-dong Bus Terminal – Located southeast of Seoul city limits; service to Namhan-sansong Fortress in southern Seoul, Kwangju. (Tel: 478-2159)

Dong Seoul (East Seoul) Terminal – Service is almost same as the Kangnam Terminal. (Tel: 447-5131)

Kangnam Kosok Bus Terminal – Located across the Han River in Banpo-dong. (Tel: 591-3402; 598-4151)

Miari Bus Terminal – Service to Soyosan (north of Uijongbu, and Tongduch'on) for mountain climbing. (Tel: 994-0634)

Nambu Bus Terminal – In south Yongsan along the main road; service to Kanghwa-do, Kosam, Taech'on Beach, Puyo, Kongju, Chonju, Songni-san, Ch'ongju, Taejon. (Tel: 521-8549/50)

Sangbong Bus Terminal – In Majang-dong; several meters away from city bus #41 stop; service to Ch'unch'on, Sorak, Sokch'o, Yangyang, Yongmun-sa, Kangnung, Yoju, Chungju, Kwangju, Wonju, Andong. (Tel: 493-5471)

Seoul Sobu Bus Terminal – In Pulkwang-dong (northern Sodaemun-ku); service to Haengju-sansong, Uijongbu. (Tel: 356-3516)

Sinchon Bus Terminal – Service to Kanghwa-do: 6 a.m. to 8 p.m.; trip takes 1 hour 15 minutes. (Tel: 324-0611)

Yok Chon Terminal – Across the street from Seoul Train Station, to the left of the Daewoo building; service to Suwon, Inch'on, P'yongt'aek. (Tel: 755-0988)

PUBLIC TRANSPORT

The majority of people living in Seoul depend on public transportation. Previous government statistics show that 70 percent of the traffic was handled by approximately 5,000 city buses; 11 percent by subway; and 7 percent by the city's 50,000 taxis.

The subway costs only W250 and is the most convenient form of public transportation for visitors. It covers 116.5 km with four lines and hooks up with Korean National Railroad. Trains run from 5 a.m. to midnight at three minute intervals during rush hours, and six minute intervals at other times.

Three transportation alternatives to and from downtown Seoul are: taxi (about W4,000), the airport bus (W500), and regular city buses (W180). Passengers should be on their guard to avoid being heavily overcharged by taxis at the airport. Make sure the meter is on as soon as you step into the taxi.

There are two airport buses which run every 20 minutes from 6:30 a.m. to 10:30 p.m. daily. Follow the signs at the airport to the stop in front of the terminal. Line 1 runs from Kimp'o to the Seoul Garden Hotel, the Koreana Hotel, Sheraton Walker Hill and back. Line 2 runs from Kimp'o to the Palace Hotel, the Express Bus Terminal in Panpodong, the Riverside Hotel, Nam Seoul Hotel, the Kortea Exhibition Center, the Olympic Sports Complex and back. Both bus trips cost W550 and take about one hour to Walker Hill and 45 minutes to the Sports Complex.

CITY BUSES

During less hectic commuting hours, getting around on the local city bus can be interesting, quick and cheap. The driver usually turns up his radio so all may listen to the local baseball game, a melodrama, or to the latest rock'n roll or classical hits. Confucian ethics generally prevail on board the bus: students offer their seats to mothers toting babies and to grandfolks, and out of mutual consideration, those seated relieve those standing of their schoolbooks and shopping bags. Smoking is prohibited.

Buses run frequently from 5 a.m. to around 11:45 p.m. daily. Tokens available at most stops cost W170. Fares paid in cash cost an extra W10 payable upon entrance.

In addition to the regular city buses, there are express buses, which follow similar routes but with fewer stops and for a somewhat higher fare (W470). These are designed for commuter use and generally make few stops downtown.

A word of caution: beware of pickpockets on the bus and at crowded bus stops.

Destinations are written on the side of the bus in *han'gul* and on street signs at the bus stops. Route maps for the entire system are virtually non-existent and change so frequently that it is impossible to keep track. The routes are mapped out on a panel inside the bus, but destinations are again written only in *han'gul*. The best way to get around the matter is to take the subway, and with directions from a hotel concierge or a business partner, it is possible to brave the crowds. Two rules of thumb: when the bus comes, run to where it stops and leap on; at the other end, get to the exit before the bus stops and jump off just as fast.

TAXIS

Taxis are queued in front of the customs exit door ready to whisk passengers off to any destination.

By far the most expedient public transport, taxis are everywhere – weaving in and out of city traffic and darting along rural roads. Fare for regular taxis begins at W750 for the first 1¼ miles (two kilometers) and W50 for each additional 400 meters. The taxi meter also runs on time when movement is slower than 15 meters per hour. Medium-size "88" taxis start at W800. The beige radio call taxis are more expensive: W1,000 for the first two kilometers and W100 for each additional 400 meters. You may call for these taxi services in Seoul at (02) 414-0150/2. Another class of taxis in Korea is the "Hotel Taxi" found near major hotels, and the meter begins at W1,000. Visitors can hire at W7,000 per hour daytime. Call (02) 333-1238 for this service.

Cabs may be hailed to curbside and shared with other passengers bound in the same direction. Each passenger pays only for the distance he travels (two or more traveling as one party pay as one passenger). This taxi-sharing system is called *hapsong*.

After midnight, passengers are expected to pay a 20 percent surcharge on taxi fares.

The driver should have a chart available listing officially calculated surcharge totals.

Long-distance rides can be bargained for. Few drivers understand English, so try to have your destination written in *han'gul* before entering the cab.

U.S. military I.D. holders may also use Army-Air Force Exchange taxis, which charge slightly higher rates in dollars.

Kiamaster pick-up trucks transport bulky baggage and packages at metered and negotiated rates.

SUBWAY

The subway costing W200 anywhere in the city is also heavily used and it is the most convenient form of public transportation for visitors. Korea's subway system opened in August 1974, covers 116.5 km with four lines and hooks up with the Korean National Railroad. From Seoul Railway Station, it goes to six major destinations: Chongnyang-ni Train Station and Songbuk district to the north, and, to Inch'on (24 miles/39 kilometers west), Suwon (26 miles/41 kilometers south), Chamsil and Kuro. Three more lines are under construction and to be completed by 1995. Smoking is prohibited in the cars.

Following are points of interest within walking distance of each subway stop within the city walls:

City Hall (T'aepyong-no)
– City Hal, Toksu Place
– British Embassy
– Major hotels, banks, department stores
– Seoul Tourist Information Center

Chonggak (Chong-no)
– Posin-gak (city bell tower)
– Bookstores (with foreign language sections)
– Korean National Tourism Corporation
– Ch'ogye-sa (Buddhist Temple)
– Communications Memorial Center
– Seoul Immigration Office
– Kyongbok Palace, National Museum, Folk Museum
– Embassies of U.S.A., Japan, Canada
– Sejong Cultural Center
– Yi Sun-sin statue at Kwanghwa-mun Intersection

Chong-no 3-ka
– Pagoda Park and shopping arcade
– Chongmyo (Royal Confucian Shrine)

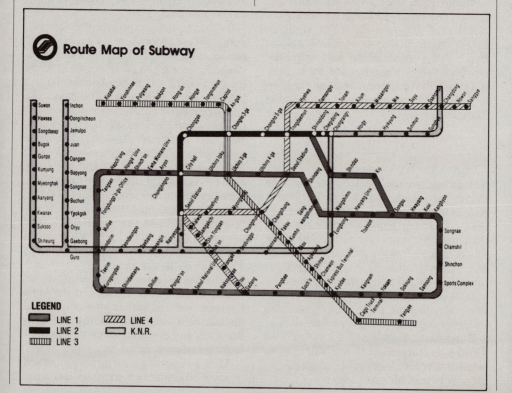

Route Map of Subway

LEGEND
LINE 1
LINE 2
LINE 3
LINE 4
K.N.R.

- Insa-dong (Mary's Alley antique shops, art galleries, etc.)

Chong-no 5-ka
- East Gate marketplace, herb shops

Tongdae-mun
- Big East Gate, Seoul Baseball Stadium

PRIVATE TRANSPORT

Car Rentals: Foreigners are advised to avoid driving in Korea if possible. The accident rate is high and in legal disputes over accidents, foreigners tend to come off worse.

However, for the brave there are several car rental firms: **Daehan** (tel: 585-0801); **Sambo Rent Car**, a joint venture with National, (tel: 797-5711); **VIP Rent Car**, a joint venture with **Avis** (tel: 557-8081); and **Kumho**, which has a joint venture with Hertz (tel: 798-1515). Charges are around W55,000 a day for a four-door Hyundai Stellar sedan to W150,000 for Hyundai Grandeur 2.4 with driver.

WHERE TO STAY

Several kinds of accommodation are open to the visiting foreigner:

HOTELS

For all the comforts, conveniences, and privacy of home, nothing beats western-style hotels which range in standard and price. (* denotes deluxe hotel)

SEOUL

(prefix 02 to telephone numbers)

DELUXE

* **Hyatt Regency Seoul**, Tel: 798-0061/9
* **Inter Continental**, Tel: 533-8181
* **Lotte**, Tel: 771-10
* **Lotte World**, Tel: 419-7000
* **Ramada Renaissance**, Tel: 555-0501
* **Seoul Hilton International**, Tel: 753-7788
* **Seoul Plaza**, Tel: 771-22
* **Sheraton Walker Hill**, Tel: 453-0121
* **Shilla**, Tel: 233-3131
* **Swiss Grand**, Tel: 356-5656
* **Westin Chosun**, Tel: 771-05

FIRST CLASS

Capital, Tel: 792-1122
King Sejong, Tel: 776-1811/9
Koreana, Tel: 730-8611/9
Nam Seoul Washington, Tel: 552-7111
New Seoul, Tel: 735-9071/9
New World, Tel: 557-0111
Pacific, Tel: 777-7811/9
President, Tel: 753-3131/9
Ramada Olympia, Tel: 353-5121
Riverside, Tel: 543-1001
Seoul Garden, Tel: 717-9441
Seoul Palace, Tel: 532-0101
Seoul Royal, Tel: 771-45
Seoulin, Tel: 732-0181/8
Sofitel Ambassador, Tel: 275-1101/9
Tower, Tel: 236-2121
Yoido Tourist, Tel: 782-0121/5

SECOND CLASS

Astoria, Tel: 267-7111/8
Bukak Park, Tel: 352-7101/8
Central, Tel: 265-4120/9
Daehwa Tourist, Tel: 265-9181/9
Empire, Tel: 777-5511/9
Hamilton, Tel: 794-0171
Metro, Tel: 752-1112
New Kukje, Tel: 732-0161/9
New Naija, Tel: 737-9011/5
New Oriental, Tel: 753-0701/6
Savoy, Tel: 776-2641/50
Seoul Prince, Tel: 752-7111/9
Seoul Rex, Tel: 752-3191/4
Seoul Tourist, Tel: 735-9001/5

THIRD CLASS

Boolim Tourist, Tel: 962-0021/5
Chonji Tourist, Tel: 265-6131/5
Eastern, Tel: 764-4101/9
Hangkang Tourist, Tel: 453-5131
YMCA Tourist, Tel: 732-8291/8

PUSAN

(* denotes deluxe hotel; prefix 051 to telephone numbers)

* **Hyatt Regency Pusan**, Tel: 743-1234
* **Paradise Beach**, Tel: 742-3131
* **Westin Chosun Beach**, Tel: 742-7411
Bando, Tel: 44-0561
Commodore, Tel: 44-9101
Crown, Tel: 69-1241
Dong Yang, Tel: 245-1205
Ferry, Tel: 463-0881
Haeundae, Tel: 741-5300
Kukdong Hotel, Tel: 72-0081
Kukje, Tel: 642-1330
Moon Hwa, Tel: 806-8001
Pusan, Tel: 241-4301
Pusan Plaza, Tel: 463-5011
Royal, Tel: 241-1051
Shin Shin, Tel: 88-0195
Sorabol, Tel: 463-3511
Tai Yang, Tel: 465-7311
Tong Nae, Tel: 555-1121
Tower, Tel: 241-5151
UN, Tel: 255-5181

TAEGU

(prefix 053 to telephone numbers)

Kumho, Tel: 252-6001
Dong In Tourist, Tel: 46-7211
Dongsan Tourist, Tel: 253-7711/6
New Yongnam Hotel, Tel: 752-1001
Royal Tourist, Tel: 253-5546
Taegu Soosung, Tel: 763-7311

INCH'ON

(prefix 032 to telephone numbers)

Bosung Tourist, Tel: 433-2221/7
Bupyong Tourist, Tel: 527-2331/6
Olympos Tourist, Tel: 762-5181
Songdo Beach, Tel: 865-1311/20

KWANGJU

(prefix 062 to telephone numbers)

City Hill Tourist, Tel: 524-0025
Kukje Tourist, Tel: 673-0700
Kwangju, Tel: 292-6231/5

Kwangju Grand, Tel: 224-6111
Kwangju Palace Tourist, Tel: 222-2525
Kwangju Tourist, Tel: 232-6231/9
Riverside Tourist, Tel: 223-9111
Shinyang Park, Tel: 27-0671/9

CHEJU-DO

(prefix 064 to telephone numbers)

*
Cheju Grand, Tel: 42-3321
Cheju KAL, Tel: 53-6151
Cheju Prince, Tel: 32-9911/32
*
Cheju Shilla, Tel: 33-4466
Cheju Washington, Tel: 42-4111
*
Hyatt Regency Cheju, Tel: 33-1234
Paradise Hotel Sogwip'o, Tel: 33-5161
Sogwip'o KAL, Tel: 32-9851/3
Sogwip'o Lions Tourist, Tel: 62-4141/4

CHOLLABUK-DO

Chonju, Tel: (0652) 83-2811/5
Kunsan, Tel: (0654) 3-4121/5
Naejangsan Tourist, Tel: (0681) 535-4131
Victory Tourist, Tel: (0654) 2-6161/3

CHOLLANAM-DO

Chirisan Plaza, Tel: (0664) 2-2171/80
Sejong Tourist, Tel: (0662) 62-6111
Shinan Beach, Tel: (0631) 43-3399
Sunchon Royal Tourist, Tel: (0661) 74-7000
Yosu Beach, Tel: (0662) 63-2011/5

CH'UNGCH'ONGBUK-DO

Chechon Tourist, Tel: (0443) 43-4111/4
Ch'ongju, Tel: (0431) 64-2181
Core, Tel: (0652) 85-1100
Suanbo, Tel: (0441) 42-2311
Songnisan Tourist, Tel: (0433) 42-5281/8
Waikiki Suanbo Tourist, Tel: (0441) 42-3333

CH'UNGCH'ONGNAM-DO

Jeil Tourist, Tel: (0418) 44-6111/25
Joongang Tourist, Tel: (042) 253-8801/5
Riviera Yusong, Tel: (042) 823-2111
Taejon Tourist, Tel: (042) 253-8131/9
Togo Spa Tourist, Tel: (0418) 42-6031
Yousung Tourist, Tel: (042) 822-0611/5

KANGWON-DO

Chunchon Sejong Tourist, Tel: (0361) 52-1191
Dragon Valley Tourist, Tel: (0374) 32-5757
Naksan Beach, Tel: (0396) 672-4000/13
New Sorak, Tel: (0392) 34-7131/49
Sorak Park, Tel: (0392) 34-7711/24
Soraksan Tourist, Tel: (0392) 34-7101/5
Wonju Tourist, Tel: (0371) 43-1241

KYONGGI-DO

Brown, Tel: (0331) 46-4141/50
New Korea Tourist, Tel: (0343) 48-6671/8
New Prince Tourist, Tel: (032) 654-3391/5
Pyongtaek Tourist, Tel: (0333) 54-3331
Songtan Tourist, Tel: (0333) 4-5101/5
Youlim Tourist, Tel: (0351) 5-2101/4

KYONGSANGBUK-DO

Bulkuksa, Tel: (0561) 746-1911/9
***Concorde Kyongju**, Tel: (0561) 745-7000
***Kyongju Chosun**, Tel: (0561) 745-7701
***Kyongju Kolon**, Tel: (0561) 746-9001
***Kyongju Hilton International**, Tel: (0561) 745-7788
Sang Dae Hot Spring Tourist, Tel: (053) 82-8001/2

KYONGSANGNAM-DO

Changwon Tourist, Tel: (0551) 83-5551/60
Daewoo Okpo Tourist, Tel: (0558) 687-3761/5
Diamond Tourist, Tel: (0552) 32-7171/7
Lotte Crystal Tourist, Tel: (0551) 45-1112
Masan Royal Tourist, Tel: (0551) 44-1150
4 Samch'onpo Beach Tourist, Tel: (0593) 32-9801/5
Ulsan Koreana Tourist, Tel: (0522) 44-9911/20

YOGWAN & YOINSUK (INNS)

Yogwan: Korean guests might request *pori ch'a* (barley tea), *yo* and *ibul* (mattress and blanket, respectively), *pyogae* (pillow), *ondol* (heated floor), and inexpensive home-cooked Korean meals. Some inns prepare a communal hot bath. Prices range from W5,000 upwards for single occupancy outside the city. In Seoul, prices can vary between W8,000 to W15,000.

Yoinsuk: The *yoinsuk*, another type of Korean inn, offers lodging in a private compound and isn't as consistently clean, convenient, nor as appealing as the *yogwan*. But the room rates are usually lower – W2,000 upwards. Accommodation is native all the way.

YOUTH HOSTELS

A chain of youth hostels has been established in many of the provinces, and such facilities are open to international members. Membership is open at any of their branches. Some of the hostels, such as the Seoul Bando Youth Hostel and the Puyo Youth Hostel, are a combination hostel-hotel, with communal rooms as well as plush, private rooms and suites.

Below is a list of youth hostels in Korea.

Seoul:
  Academy Youth Hostel, Tel: (02) 993-6181
  Bando Youth Hostel, Tel: (02) 567-3111

Pusan:
  Ae-Rin Youth Hostel, Tel: (051) 27-2222

Ch'ungch'ongbuk-do:
  Hanal Youth Hostel, Onchon-ri, Chungwon-gun, Tel: (0441) 846-3151

Ch'ungch'ongnam-do:
  Puyo Youth Hostel, Tel: (0463) 835-3101

Kangwon-do:
  Naksan Youth Hostel, Chunjin-ri, Yangyang-gun, Tel: (0396) 672-3416
  Sorak Youth Hostel, Sokch'o, Tel: (0392) 34-7540

Kyongsangbuk-do:
  Kyongju Youth Hostel, Kyongju, Tel: (0561) 746-0601

OTHERS

The *hasuk chip* (boarding house) has its place among students, working bachelors, and itinerants. Rooms are rented by the month, usually to long-term residents. Rent includes very simple home-cooked meals.

For the working foreigner, the *setbang* – a rented room in a local home – is yet another option. Except for the fact that he happens to share the same roof with others, the tenant is generally on his own.

FOOD DIGEST

WHAT TO EAT

Barbecue Meat Restaurant (*Pul Koki Jip***)** – Beef (*so-koki*) and pork (*toechi-koki*) and short rib (*kal bi*) are marinated in soy sauce, sesame oil, garlic, green onions, and toasted sesame seeds, then char-broiled.

Raw Fish Restaurant (*Saengson Hoe Jip***)** – Fresh raw fish is served sliced with a soy sauce (*kan-chang*) or red pepper sauce (*cho-chang*). Other kinds of fish dishes such as *maeun t'ang* (hot pepper soup of fish, soybean curd, egg, and vegetables) are served.

Ginseng Chicken Dish Restaurant (*Samgyae T'ang Jip***)** – Chicken stuffed with rice, white ginseng, and dried oriental dates are steamed and served hot. Deep-fried chicken and other chicken dishes are also served.

Dumplings Restaurant (*Mandoo Jip***)** – Meat, vegetables, and sometimes soybean curd are stuffed into a dumpling and steamed, fried or boiled in a broth. Chinese-style cookie pastries baked in the restaurant fill the display window.

Noodles Restaurant (*Poonsik Jip***)** – Noodle dishes are the specialty but so are easily prepared rice dishes. Some of the popular dishes are *Momil kooksoo* – buckwheat noodles served with a sweet radish sauce; *Naengmyon* – cold potato flour or buckwheat flour noodles topped with sliced meat, vegetables, a boiled egg, and a pepper relish sauce and ice; *K'ong kooksoo* – wheat noodles in fresh soymilk; *Odaeng kooksoo* – wheat noodles topped with oriental fishcake in a broth; *Ramyon* – instant noodles in instant broth; *Udong* – long, wide wheat noodles with onions, fried soybean curd, red pepper powder, and egg; *Pipim-pap* – rice topped with parboiled fern bracken, bluebell root, soysprouts, spinach, and a sunny-side-up egg, accompanied with a bowl of broth; and *Chap Chae* – rice vermicelli stir-fried with vegetables and meat slices.

Steamed Rice Restaurant (*Paekpan Jip***)** – A bowl of rice is served with a variety of *kimch'i, namul* (parboiled vegetables), fish, and soup (usually made of soybean paste) – the basic Korean meal. Other simple dishes, such as *naengmyon* and *pipim-pap* are often on the menu. In the evening, the *paekpan jip* switches into a *makkolli jip*.

Dog Meat Soup (*Posin T'ang Jip***)** – *Posin-hada* means to build up one's strength. Thus, to the people, dog meat soup, *Posin t'ang,* is considered to be a delicacy. Other popular Korean dishes include: *Sinsullo* – chopped vegetables, meat, quail egg, fish balls, and gingko nuts in a brazier; *Sollong t'ang* – rice in a beef and bone stew; and *Pindaettok* – the Korean bean flour and egg pancake filled with different combinations of vegetables and meat.

WHERE TO EAT

Chinese Shantung restaurants are as popular as Korean restaurants. They are designated by a red or green door plaque draped with a red strip of cloth. Homemade wheat noodles with various sauces make for a slurpy meal. *Tchajangmyon* is a popular order consisting of pork, seafood, and vegetable tidbits stir-fried in a sweet-sour black bean sauce, and topped with a boiled egg. Larger Chinese restaurants have a more varied menu that includes delicacies such as sweet-sour fried fish and meat.

Japanese restaurants complete with *sushi* (laver-covered rice rolls), *sashimi* (raw fish), and *tempura* (deep-fried batter-covered fish and vegetables) bars are scattered all over Seoul, and are even more common in the southern part of Pusan.

While in Seoul, the traveler may have noticed that Koreans always seem to be eating or drinking. They are always stopping at little food tents on the streets to eat hot potatoes and chestnuts and silkworms in winter and sausages on sticks and seafood in the summer. Unfortunately, one of the former charms of the city, the *pajangnaja* or mobile food stalls have been banished to the suburbs because they were regarded as eyesores by the government.

The **best places** are any of the many small **backstreet venues**, where you can buy a portion for W5,000 or less. In recent years several top quality "garden" restaurants have sprouted up south of the Han River. Among the best is the **Samwon Garden**. Located in the posh district of Apkujongdong, it features waterfalls, indoor and outdoor restaurants and ushers dressed in traditional costume. Tel: 544-5351. Prices for barbecued beef and ribs start at around W10,000 a head.

Another good barbecue beef restaurant is **Pine Hill** which has two outlets. One is in Namsan and the other and more famous one in Kwonchol-dong, just across the road from the fashionable Myong-dong district. The latter has some of the best beef to be found in Seoul. Normally in these restaurants there are three grades of beef. Two portions of beef come to W16,000 for A grade beef. Tel: 732-3162.

A point for gourmets to remember in sampling the local fare is that, unlike in Japan, in Korea you eat your *pap* or rice with your spoon not with your chopsticks.

For those wanting to combine culture with their food there is **Korea House** in Chungmuro, **Pil-dong**, a traditional style building housing a theater restaurant. There are three ondol rooms where you can eat traditional Korean food served in white china dishes. Tel: 266-9101. Booking is essential and the cost is around W20,000 per head.

The best **Korean restaurant** in the hotels is the newly renovated **Asadal** in the Plaza Hotel. Its eel and noodles are particularly good. The restaurant is pricey. Count on spending W40,000 for a meal for two. Tel: 771-22. Anyone with a taste for something spicier should try any of the numerous city restaurants specializing in dishes from the southwestern Cholla provinces.

Those not wishing to go ethnic will find the only really good western food in the hotels, with exceptions of course.

The best **French restaurants** are **Hugo's** in the Hyatt hotel, the **Four Seasons** in the Hilton and the Westin Chosun's **9th Gate**. Hugo's specializes in duck cooked with cognac, mullet cooked with champagne, liver with cognac and champagne and all kinds of fresh salads. Reservation is required. Tel: 798-0061. Four Seasons roast beef on the trolley is especially good for the 9th Gate the ambience and view of the garden makes up for the more mediocre fare. Four Seasons tel: 753-7788, 9th Gate: 771-05. Eating out in these plush French restaurants costs about W80,000 for two without wine.

The Hilton also has the best Italian restaurant in town, **II Ponte**, which is particularly good for its pasta and veal. Take W40,000 to cover a good meal for two. The Intercontinental also has a good Italian restaurant called **Firenze** which has a choose your own pasta feature. Prices are higher because of the plusher decor, ranging from W60,000 for a modest dinner for two. Tel: 555-5656.

Outside of the hotels is **La Cantina**, next to the American Cultural Center, a popular spot with foreign diplomats and journalists. Marble busts and shady corners make an intimate and slightly cheaper dinner for two. Price for two: around W35,000 with local house wine. Tel: 777-2579.

The best Chinese restaurants in town are in **Daesanghae** in the Korean (tel: 730-9911, W30,000 for two) and the Hilton's **Phoenix** (about W60,000 for two).

The best Japanese hotel restaurant is the Sunwon in the Seoulin hotel where high-ranking Korean officials and politicians bring their guests. The tempura is reputed to be the best in town. Count on about W40,000 for two. Tel: 732-0181. Japanese food, especially raw fish, can be expensive. But a tempera or noodle meal can be reasonable at under W5,000. Watch out for Japanese restaurants in the hotels which can be up to W150,000 for two.

Notable exceptions to the only good western food being in the hotels are the **Moghul** (Tel: 796 5501), Korea's only Pakistani restaurant, and the **Chalet Swiss** and **Old Germany** (Tel: 795-8780, 795-1723), both serving top quality European food. All three are located in It'aewon and provide excellent quality food at an average W15,000 – W20,000 a head. Old Germany is the cheaper of the three at around W10,000 a head for a good meal.

Also in It'aewon is Korea's only Indian restaurant Ashoka, in the Hamilton hotel. Tandoori chicken plus a curry dish will come to around W25,000 for two. Tel: 792-0117.

DRINKING NOTES

Potable water is available in hotels. In establishments for locals, *bori ch'a* (roasted barley boiled in water), distinguished by its light brown color, is served instead. Another popular water substitute is *sungnyung,* tea boiled from browned rice gathered from the bottom of a rice pot. It is also quite safe to drink water which spring from certain mountain sites at temples in the countryside. Unboiled tap water is never advised for drinking. Bottled water can be purchased for use in private residences from Diamond Water. The company will deliver the water, which costs about W500 per liter, to your doorstep on a regular basis (Tel: 324-3907/8).

TABANG (TEA-ROOMS)

Tabang (or *tasil*) is one of the most common signs in any Korean town. Koreans go to the *tabang* for everything but tea (in fact, the tea is free) or coffee. It is where businessmen strike deals, where students practice English with "native speakers", where friends gather to gossip, joke, and listen to music, and where lovers tryst. It is also where the honk, grind and smoke of the city is rivaled – but nobody complains. A cup of thin coffee is but a token to hours of socializing. The *tabang* has become a vital institution in contemporary Korean culture; a meeting hall outside the home and office for young and old, male and female. And with 10 million souls in the capital alone, there is always room for one more tearoom to open above, below, or next to all the others.

Unlike teahouses or coffeeshops elsewhere, the Korean *tabang* provides a personal delivery service: a girl dressed in a uniform will deliver a hot cup of coffee in a scarf-wrapped thermos bottle to customers who call in orders and clearly indicate their whereabouts.

Things to Do

Businessmen visiting Korea, like readers of economic journals around the world, know that Koreans are reputed to be among the most diligent workers on earth, logging endless hours to keep production at a peak, and to ensure the perpetual prosperity of the country's export-oriented economy.

Foreign residents too, both old-time and new, generally concur with characterization, but also know that the "Land of the Morning Calm" harbors some of the world's most hearty and enthusiastic drinkers, who are often loath to abandon their watering holes before dawn.

These two stereotypes do seem to complement each other, since a people who work hard might naturally be expected to play hard as well, but there is yet a third side to the modern-day Korean – a passive but pleasing contrast to the other two, which is somewhat less well known to the outside world.

During the Yi Dynasty, a proper Confucian gentleman might have found calm and contentment in an after-dinner ritual with his pipe, filling its small brass bowl with Korean tobacco, and drawing slowly through the long bamboo stem to cool the soothing smoke. His descendants today can seek diversion in a variety of establishments offering all manner of indulgences and female companionship. These range from beer halls where the waitress might share a drink and squeeze one's hand, to secret salons where the whiskey flows freely and the customer's every wish is his hostess-cum-partner's command.

Somewhere between those ancient and modern extremes on the spectrum of hedonistic delights, there lie a number of common pleasures available, in startlingly similar forms, to contemporary Koreans ranging from day laborers to tycoons.

When a Korean has been working or playing (or both) with perhaps more zeal than wisdom, he is likely to seek refuge and relief through one of the few such simple pleasures which remain amid the excesses and inconstancies of urban industrialization. Depending on his whim, he might well choose a bathhouse or a barber shop, both of which abound in every urban setting, as well as in most sizable rural communities.

MOGYOKT'ANG (BATHHOUSE)

Just as a visit to the barber shop involves more than a simple haircut, so a call at the bathhouse offers much more than a mere turn in the tub. For the seeker of a slightly more active treatment for weary bones, the bathhouse (*mogyokt'ang*) presents a moderate alternative to the passive pleasures of the barber's chair.

At the baths, one is free to set one's own schedule, regimen, timing and style. That last choice offers perhaps the widest variety of options, and the images conjured up by the behavior of an ordinary bathhouse's clientele might run the gamut – from scolded puppies to walruses in rut.

There is quite a range of bathhouse types as well, but all offer the same basic accoutrements, focusing around the same essential enjoyment of a steamy, soothing soak. As visitors to Japan learn from their guidebooks – or perhaps from an embarrassed or offended Japanese – the proper form is to bathe before entering the communal tub, and in Korea too, soap and dirt should be kept out of the bathwater.

One begins by soaping up, shampooing and rinsing down, either by dipping a basin at the edge of the main tub, or under a shower, if there is one. Next should come a leisurely soak in the central tub, where muscles can relax and pores dilate. Then, back on the curb-like lip ringing the tub, it's time to commence some serious scrubbing, again using a basin.

Westerners seem to cling to the illogical conviction that towels should be kept dry, although they only perform their rightful function by getting wet. In the *mogyokt'ang*, a handtowel is just the right size, doubling both as an ample washcloth and as a fig leaf substitute – for modesty's sake – as one moves around. Small red washcloths are available, too – very abrasive, but very popular for doing away with dead and dying skin and stubborn city grit. And for the patron who doesn't savor the strain of a vigorous scrub, attendants are usually on hand to rub, rub, rub with cloths until the customer's skin approaches the hue of that raspy red fabric.

A scrubbing session is by far the most apropos opportunity for a shave. Steam, suds and sweat combine to create the fleeting impression that there is no blade in the razor – an innocent illusion swiftly given the lie if one later slaps on a little aftershave.

All that accounts for the literal *"mogyok"* (bathing) in *mogyokt'ang,* but one is no more restricted to a mere bath in a bathhouse than to only a haircut in a barber shop. Time and the facilities at hand are the only limits, and none but the improvident take towel in hand with less than an hour or two to kill.

Nearly every ordinary bathhouse (*taejungt'ang,* or "masses' bath") offers, in addition to the central tub and showers, an extra-hot tub, a cold tank and a sauna dock as well. These offer many alternatives to the basic cycle of bathe, soak, bathe.

The properly heated hot tank greets the bather with a sharp tingling sensation that is easily mistaken for pain, but which gradually mellows into simply stimulating heat. (If the tank is overheated, on the other hand, it turns out to be real pain.) The sauna is often so hot that it hurts to inhale quickly, and persons with abnormal blood pressure or heat sensitivity are advised to exercise appropriate caution.

Alternate visits to the sauna and hot tub, interspersed with breathtaking plunges into the cold tank, can give the pores a healthy workout. A few such rounds, however, can leave one a bit light-headed, not a little enervated, and frankly ready for a short nap. A well-planned bathhouse will have a corner, or perhaps even a mezzanine, where those with the time can stretch out and doze off.

The last step in the bathing area is usually a final rinse under the shower – hot or cold, or both. But that is hardly the end. There is more to enjoy out in the dressing room. After all that time in the baths, most patrons seem to feel it a bit abrupt simply to dress and leave. Smokers smoke; thinkers sit and think; trimmers trim (a nail clipper is usually available); and browsers read ads on the walls for products such as soap, ginseng nectar, and "Happiness" – a mysterious compound touted as an aid to a happy married life. Some people, of course, simply dry themselves at considerable leisure, perhaps in front of a fan, but better yet, while grabbing one last catnap. (That soggy handtowel, once wrung out, turns out to be quite up to the task.)

Gentlemen can get the same finishing touch they would in a barber shop, while on the ladies' side, bathers can relax one last time under a hair dryer. Eventually though, everyone has to leave. Korean bathhouses, incidentally, close around 8 p.m., hours earlier than the counterpart *ofuro* in Japan, but they open earlier as well, about 5 or 6 a.m.

HAIRCUT & MASSAGE

A haircut is ever so much more than cutting hair in a Korean barber shop (*ibalso*). One can easily spend an hour, and perhaps two, in laid-back languor as a crew of young ladies and gentlemen attend to nails, whiskers, face, ears, muscles, aches and – not to be forgotten – hair.

The actual clipping is mere prologue, a ritual of 10 minutes or so more aptly termed a "trim", lest the customer be tempted to wait too long before his next visit. A manicure is usually begun just about the time one's stockinged feet get comfortably settled on a cushion placed over the sink, and it inevitably lasts much longer than the haircut.

As soon as the barber has dispensed with his proforma exercise, he disappears, and the chair is tilted into a full reclining position for more leisurely informalities. The sequence is not strictly prescribed, but those interested in a shave generally get one quite soon after the haircut. Young ladies traditionally perform this service, which is not always limited to the conventional heavier growths of whiskers; upper cheeks, noses, foreheads and even selected parts of the ear are all fair game for a well-trained and unrestrained Korean razor maid.

The next step is often a face massage (*massaji* in Korean, after the Japanese rendering of the English). This can, with luck, encompass the scalp as well, along with those chronically understimulated muscles and vessels around the base of the skull. Between soothing applications of a hot towel, the young lady in charge might apply a plastic-like facial pack, peeled off later like congealed glue, or perhaps just a simple layer of cold cream. In either case, as the face is absorbing allied benefits, the lady will produce an ear spoon, preferably made of bamboo, and carefully begin to excavate hidden reserves of wax – unless the client recalls the old doctor's dictum that only one's elbows are to enter one's ears. When the delicate digging is done, each ear is given an unnerving twirl with a tool resembling a doll house duster – a tympana-tickling sensation comparable to hearing kittens' claws on a blackboard.

By this point, someone has no doubt already begun a body massage (*anma* in Korean, from two Chinese characters roughly meaning "press" and "rub"). This can coincide with other services, and can involve a number of people who come, go, and reappear, according to the needs of other customers. It is not uncommon to have three or four girls and fellows at work in a single curtained cubicle, each kneading a separate extremity. One of them is usually a young man equally well versed in Oriental finger pressure therapy and the orthopedic limitations of the human anatomy – although he occasionally loses his feel for the fine line between stimulation and pain.

Even as a joint effort, a body massage can last half an hour or longer. Ordinarily, it concludes with an extraordinary ritual. First one's wrists, then palms, and then fingers are firmly massaged. Next the young lady gives each finger a sharp, snapping tug, perhaps to realign the knuckles. Finally, she interlocks her fingers with the client's, bends his hand backward, and, while gently running her thumbnails across the taut palm, blows on it ever so softly, telegraphing tingling signals up well past the elbow.

After all this, it's time for a nap, presuming the customer has time. (If he doesn't, he should have postponed his visit until another day.) A towel placed over his eyes softens any harsh visual stimuli, and he is left to dreams and fantasies.

Later on, someone eventually has to mention the code word "shampoo", and the customer knows his respite is nearly over. Not only is the barber chair about to be raised abruptly to the upright position, but that foot-supporting cushion will also be removed from the sink. Within seconds, said groggy gent is roused from his delightful daydreams – not just sitting up, but bent over a basin, head soaked and soapy.

The end comes quickly. A brief towel fluffing is followed by the barber's final touch – the *turai* (dry) with a comb and hand-held blower – as the client receives a ritual offering: a cigarette and a shot of sweet yogurt drink. Then it's time to button up, straighten up, settle the tab (W15,000–W20,000) and bid a fond, but hardly final, farewell to tonsorial therapy.

SAUNA

The man with a little extra cash, and a yearning for a little extra luxury, is likely to patronize a so-called "*saunat'ang*", essentially a plusher version of the *taejungt'ang*. For perhaps five times the ordinary bathing fee, the customer can spend all day – if he likes – soaking, sweating, napping, snacking or even negotiating business deals over coffee, clad only in a towel or short gown.

One of the oldest and most popular of such establishments in Seoul is in the Shin Shin

Hotel, a modest brick complex in the alley beside the Bank of Korea's head office (across a broad intersection from the Shinsegye Department Store). The *saunat'ang* in the Shin Shin's main building provides each guest with his own private section of warm pillow and sheets, dressing gown, adjacent mini-closet and a menu listing every type of refreshment. There is also a spacious lounge with well-padded easy chairs, a television set and a lunch counter.

Those who make it to the Shin Shin's bathing area check their gowns with the young attendants on the way in, and grab fresh towels from a handy pile. Numbered signs mark a seven-step circuit for the uninitiated, beginning with a dip in the main tub or pool (the *ont'ang*). A small statue of an elephant helps establish the tropical mood.

Next are the two sauna docks – hot and hotter. One can perspire surrounded by the warm tones of golden-grained wood, gazing at quotations on the wall such as "Patience is the skill of having hope".

From the sauna, of course, one could proceed only to the cold tank (*naengt'ang*), which is appropriately adorned with a statue of a polar bear. A helpful sign notes that there is no further benefit to be gained from remaining in the 18°C water after one has rinsed off all that sweat.

The fourth stop is the hot tub (*yolt'ang*), kept at 48°C, which should loosen up the pores again. The *yolt'ang* leaves one well prepared for the next stop, the vigorous rubbing away of grit and grime and (hopefully) dead skin by one of a squad of young men.

By this point, one might well feel a bit groggy, in which case Stop No. 6 comes just in the nick of time. It's called *rireksyon* in Korean, a slight muddling of "relaxation", and that's exactly what it entails. At a row of massage tables, more young fellows administer 20 or 30 minute rubdowns, using either cold cream or mentholatum.

The last stop, once again, is the shower, for a final soap and rinse. Stepping out of the bathing area, one promptly receives another fresh (and *dry*) towel and, moments later, the same, carefully cared for dressing gown. The remainder of one's time can be spent eating, drinking, reading or watching TV. One can also request the services of a blind masseur, should a few kinks or wrinkles have survived the bathing process. And, of course, one can simply sleep, for a good session in any sort of *mogyokt'ang* can turn even the most tense or torpid physique into a tingling and squeaky-clean bundle of bait for the sandman.

Nearly every Korean *saunat'ang* offers comforts and accommodations like those at the Shin Shin, with the little extras (rubdown, scrubbing, etc.) costing, naturally, a little extra. Another establishment in downtown Seoul boasts a cold tank reputedly filled with mineral water piped directly from nearby Namsan (South Mountain); and one might also find such conveniences as a five-minute hourglass in the sauna dock, or a urinal right in the bathing area (to spare customers the indignity of having to relieve themselves over the drains).

Actually, the clientele in the plusher *saunat'ang* facilities seem more interested in loafing and laying about than in bathing per se, since they probably can afford to bathe in hot running water at home. Thus they embody the core spirit of Korea's modern pleasure principle, as pursued by those fortunate enough to have the means.

To observe the spirit of Korean humanity at large, however, foreign visitors ought to bathe at least once in an ordinary *taejungt'ang* where everyone can be seen doing his own thing. Europeans sometimes attract a few stares, but they should most certainly feel free to return the compliment.

There are many styles to observe: while one unassuming soul sits modestly facing a wall, another may appear to be drilling for the national splash-and-thrash platoon, exalting in generating frothy waves accompanied by ecstatic grunts and harrumphs to the assembled. Many bathers concentrate on modified calisthenics, such as "push-up" against the edge of the main tub, or deep knee bends in the cold tank. Some simply fashion a pillow from an overturned basin and a towel, and sack out on the tiled floor.

All in all, the public bathhouse is perhaps the most egalitarian of the institutions to be found amid the considerable Confucian influence in contemporary Korea, stripping customers of all trappings of wealth or power (except perhaps a prodigious stomach), and offering each an identical opportunity to play any role he or she pleases. And that equality does extend generally to the sexes, for while they are strictly segregated in the public facilities, the two remain equal in terms of opportunities for indulgent enjoyment. The sauna remains an exception with only a handful catering for women. Two of the best women's saunas to be found at the Capitol Hotel, which includes a ginseng bath, and the Riverside Hotel.

There are a host of other comforts related to the *mogyokt'ang*, or at least appealing to the same more or less wholesome hedonism that keeps bathhouses and barber shops in business. At a large *mogyokt'ang*, for example, one might find a private bathing room upstairs (called a *tokt'ang*) suitable for a couple or a family. Visitors are advised that many establishments which offer massage provide sexual services to male clients. In particular, Turkish baths (*tokit'ang*), saunas and barber shops in 4-star hotels and many ordinary barber shops (except those in buildings owned by major companies or organizations). However, there is little pressure to accept these services and a simple "No" will suffice.

Another facility, the *anma sisulso*, specializes in the services of blind masseurs and masseuses. Those services can often be obtained more conveniently – and more cheaply – by phoning to summon the masseur/masseuse to one's lodging or home. Downtown hotels and *yogwans* should be able to offer such arrangements, and some apartment complexes in Seoul have round the clock, on-call massage.

TOURS

Guided Bus Tours: Seoul city tours and excursions outside the capital are conducted by numerous commercial tour guide agencies. Some agencies with English and Japanese speaking guides are:

Aju Tourist Service	755-5845 (Seoul)
	22-2222/4 (Pusan)
East-West Travel Service	734-1612
Global Tours Ltd	323-0131
Hana Tours	725-0071
Hanjin Tours	777-0041/7
Hannam Sightseeing Co.	753-0601
International Air Travel Service	777-6545/9
Korea Express Co.	753-1631
Korea Tourist Bureau	585-1191
Korea Travel International	777-31
Korea Travel Service	778-1941

Lotte Travel Service	273-4161
ODCO Travel Service	762-8770
Orient Express Corporation	735-0641
Oriental Air Travel Service	753-9233
Samyong Travel Service	719-4814
Sana Travel Service	778-3101
Seoul Tourist Corporation	566-0211
Universal Travel Service	733-5341
Walker-Hill World Travel Ltd	776-9801
World Tours Ltd	313-3401
Y.S. Travel Agency Ltd	23-0311/4

Two organizations which plan tours particularly for resident foreigners and welcome outsiders are:

The Royal Asiatic Society (RAS), Christian Building, 6th Floor, Room 611, Chong-no 5-ka, Tel: 763-9483

The United States Service Organization (USO), 104 Kalwol-dong, Yongsan-ku, Tel: 795-3028/3063

KTB Tours: The Korea Tourist Bureau (Tel: 722-1191/6) offers tours to Panmunjom, the Folk Village, Kyongju and Pusan, Kyongju, and around Seoul by day and night. The main office number in Kangnamgu is 5855-1191; and the Head Office KTB is (02) 757-2345.

Tours to Panmunjom must be reserved 48 hours in advance with full name, nationality and passport number. The trip, including lunch and a "briefing," takes 7 hours, and kids under 10 years of age are not admitted. Travelers must wear good clothes and pointing at the DMZ or speaking with north Korean officers at the DMZ is strictly forbidden. Buses leave Monday through Friday from the Lotte Hotel, but guests registered at the Chosun can be picked up from there as well.

CULTURE PLUS

Korea's cultural history is vividly displayed in numerous museums (municipal and national) and cultural centers. Drama theaters and libraries present more contemporary perspectives.

MUSEUMS

Listed below are the larger public and private museums and cultural centers.

National Museum and National Folklore Museum – Located on the grounds of Kyongbok Palace, the National Museum houses excavated and national treasures. The National Folklore Museum just west of the National Museum renders articles and settings of traditional treasures: Palsang-jon (the five-story pagoda at Popju-sa), Hwaom-sa and Kumsan-sa.

National Museum of Contemporary Art – A permanent collection of Korean modern art and special shows during the year are held in this museum at Seoul Grand Park.

Onyang Folk Museum – The largest and finest collection of Korean folk art is exhibited in Onyang, a pleasant country town southwest of Seoul. It is especially rich in crafts, but is limited in folk painting.

Puyo and Kongju National Museums – Museum collections include archaeological finds made in the vicinities of these two ancient Paekche (18 BC-AD 660) capitals. At the Kongju National Museum, treasures on display are from King Muryong's tomb, excavated in 1971. The tomb itself is a few miles away and is open to the public.

Kwangju National Museum – This two-storey museum in Chollapuk-do was recently built specially to house Yuan Dynasty bounty salvaged from a sunken 600-year-old Chinese ship discovered in west coast waters in 1976. Cholla-do treasures are displayed on the second floor.

Kyongju National Museum – Opened in 1975 on the site of an ancient Silla building, the Kyongju National Museum is located on the outskirts of Kyongju town. Silla dynasty articles, including the famous Emille Bell, the largest Buddhist temple bell in Korea (cast in AD 771), are on display. There is also a folk museum in the center of the town.

Ancient Tombs (*Tumuli*) Park, Kyongju – This cluster of 21 tombs built before the unification of Silla lies on the eastern fringe of the city. Excavation from 1973 to 1975 led to the discovery of King Mich'u's tomb (AD 262-285) and the tomb with the mysterious "Flying Horse" painted on a saddle. Some of the original relics and some replicas (many originals are in the National Museum) are exhibited.

The Korean Folk Village – In Suwon, a complete traditional Korean village has been recreated for visitors to wander through and observe the folk customs and lifestyle. Food and drink are prepared and sold here.

Emille Museum – The world's largest collection of Korean folk painting is newly housed in Songni-san, near Popju Temple. The Emille Museum is privately owned by Zo Zayong, author of several art and cultural books about Korea.

Sejong University Museum – Located in eastern Seoul near Children's Park, this museum is one of six folk museums in Korea. Over 3,000 articles, especially of traditional dress, ornaments, furniture, and art paintings are on display.

Lotte World Folk Village – A history and folk exhibition hall with intricately-made exhibits such as a miniature village and traditional market. Located in the Lotte World Complex in southeast Seoul.

CONCERT HALLS & THEATERS

Open Music Hall – Periodic Korean and western concerts are given here on the western slopes of Namsan near the Central National Library.

Sejong Cultural Center – Opened in 1978 near Kwanghwamun, the Sejong Cultural Center (81-3, Sejongno, chongno-gu, Tel: 02-736-2721), holds foreign and Korean classical and contemporary concerts and dramatic plays.

Drama Center – The Drama Center (tel: 02-778-0261) is off Namsan Street, at 8-19,

Yejang-dong, Chung-gu. Everything from P'ansori to Shakespeare is performed. Check the newspapers for current performances.

Korea House (Tel: 266-9101) – Situated on the slopes of Namsan off Toegyero. Korea House stages free folk dance performances at 3 p.m. on Saturday and Sunday. Art displays decorate the rooms and Korea-related books are sold in their bookshop. A Korean restaurant overlooks an oriental garden.

National Classical Music Institute (Tel: 02-274-1151) – Just past Tower Hotel on the slopes of Namsan is the school where many of the nation's finest classical musicians of different genres, including Royal Court musicians, practice and teach their art. Performances are given in the concert hall.

Space Center – Housed in an architectural artpiece near the Secret Garden of Ch'angdok Palace (219, Wonso-dong, Chongno-gu), the Space Center (Tel: 02-763-0771) stages a variety of shows from classical *kayakum* (Korean zither) solos to Dixieland jazz to drama. The Center also publishes a cultural magazine called *Space*.

Seoul Arts Center – The new Seoul Arts Center (Tel: 580-1114) hosts concerts and exhibitions. It has an Art Information center, a Film Preservation room and an Art Training room. A drama theater and opera house are under construction and are expected to be completed in 1993.

MODERN DRAMA THEATERS (SEOUL)

Madang Cecil Theater, 3-2, Chung-dong Chung-gu, Tel: (02) 737-5773

Elcanto Art Theater, 50-1-ka, Myong-dong, Chung-gu, Tel: (02) 776-8035

Min Ye Studio, 56-1, Daehyun-dong, Sodaemun-ku, Tel: (02) 744-0686

Munyae Theater, 1-130, Tongsung-dong, Chongno-ku, Tel: (02) 762-5231

National Theater, San 14-67, Changch'ung-dong 2-ga, Chung-gu, Tel: (02) 274-1151

Silhom Theater, 114, Unni-dong, Chongno-ku, Tel: (02) 765-4981

MOVIES

Giant painted billboards of *kungfu* duels, infernal disasters, love, and despair draw thousands of people to Korea's commercial theaters. Foreign films, including an occa-sional American film, are also screened, usually with Korean subtitles.

The **Center Culturél Français** (tel: 734-9768), located on the right side of Kyongbok Palace, just past the Hyundai Modern Art Gallery and Andre Kim's boutique, is a multi-media oasis where one can browse through a modern art gallery, sit and view French cultural videotapes or, for a token W100, watch a classic French film subtitled in English in a small theater downstairs. The CCF is open from 12 p.m. to 6 p.m. daily. A variety of films are films are shown from noon to 6 p.m. except Sundays.

Films undergo government censorship and sometimes are edited if too long to allow impressarios to squeeze in a maximum number of showings. During cold months, hot water pipes heated on the floor provide some warmth in the theater. Check the entertainment section of *The Korea Times* or *The Korea Herald* for current engagements.

LIBRARIES

Royal Asiatic Society (RAS) is the Korean chapter of an international British association. Its office is in the Christian Center Building (136-46 Yunjidong, Chongno-gu, Tel: 763-9483) near Chongno 5-ka. There you'll find most books written locally in English about Korea and a complete collection of their magazine, *Transactions*, which contains Korea-related articles that have been written by lecturing members since 1900. Visitors are welcome to sign up for tours conducted by the RAS and by an affiliate, the Korea Art Club.

Korean Research Center is located at Pyong-dong, Chongno-ku, near Sodae-mun Rotary (Tel: 723-4533). The Center publishes cultural research articles in Korea with some translations in English but also provides a quiet library of old and recent Korea-related books written by foreign explorers, diplomats, and expatriates. Some current periodicals written in other languages are available. The Center is open weekdays from 9 a.m. to 5 p.m.

United States Information Service (USIS) (Tel: 732-2601) offers an art gallery and library for public viewing and study. It is located across the street from the Lotte Hotel on Ulchi-ro. Passport identification is needed. Art gallery hours are 8:30 a.m. to 5 p.m.

weekdays and library hours are 9:30 a.m. to 6 p.m. weekdays.

UNESCO Library – Back issues of the *Korea Journal* and *The Courier*, as well as Korean cultural magazines are available, the latter in English, French, and Spanish. The Library is also stocked with other reference publications.

British Council Library (Tel: 738-7452) is located just beside the Anglican Church on the cul-de-sac leading to the British embassy, the library is open weekdays and offers good British reading, including newspaper and magazines, and educational videotapes.

Lotus Lantern International Buddhist Center (Tel: 735-5347) – Founded in 1987, the center is run by a Korean monk, Won-myong Sunim, and offers a wide variety of classes and workshops open to people of all nationalities and religious backgrounds. In addition, there is a weekly meditation session on Thursdays at 7:00 pm and a weekly bowing/chanting services on Sundays at 6:30 pm.

Ewha, **Sogang**, **Yonsei** and other universities also invite foreigners to use their library.

NIGHTLIFE

Seoul lacks sophisticated Western nightlife and is a desultory place for the lover of live music, entertainment and dance. There are many fine local dance and drama troupes, but a real absence of Western-style culture, except for the odd fleeting appearance by a visiting ballet company or orchestra.

Western movies are very popular with Koreans, but the packed cinemas and the long queues make foreigners shy away and return home to watch the local American Forces Korea Network TV, which serves up *Dynasty* and the like. The main movie belts are Chong-no and Toegye-ro streets in the city center.

There is live Korean pop music featuring top stars in the **Holiday in Seoul**, next to the Pacific Hotel, and in other city center venues and folk music in the Taehak-no student zone. Many of the hotels feature foreign crooners and Filipino bands, particularly the pseudo-English pub called the **Bobby London** at the Lotte Hotel, and the posher **9th Gate** bar at the Westin Chosun Hotel.

For jazz lovers there is **J.J. Mahoneys**, which is the "jewel in the crown" of the nightlife scene for foreigners. Located in the basement of the Hyatt Hotel beside the swimming pool "J.J.s" is the only place in town offering food, darts, pool, jazz, and disco.

Another haunt for music lovers is **All That Jazz** in It'aewon. Many It'aewon bars play country and western music, but the new midnight closing time has reduced these haunts to shadows of their former selves.

Risking disappointment nightclub lovers can choose from the **Rain Forest** at the Hilton, the **Bistro** and **Annabels** (featuring topless foreign dancers) in the Lotte and the **Point** at the Shilla Hotel. At the **Sheraton Walker Hill**, slightly out of town beside the Han River and boasting the best view in the city, there are two nightly performances of the Paris Express, a topless revue featuring foreign and Korean dancers. The hotel also has the city's only casino.

For wealthier Koreans and Japanese visitors, prepared to pay several hundred dollars for a night out, **Kangnam**, south of the Han River, boasts high class hostess clubs.

There are myraid bars ranging from Japanese-style *karaoke* joints to stand bars, where there is a strip show and live singing. Some "cabarets" and bars can be a rip-off with customers obliged to pay W30,000 for an obligatory plate of peanuts. Outside of It'aewon, visitors may try bars such as **Tiger House** and **Man's Bar**, which have English-speaking hostesses, behind the Plaza Hotel. In regular bars and beer halls, there is local OB and Crown beer (*maekchu* in Korean), and rice wine (*makkolli*) served with hors d'oevres (*anju*).

Seoul has some of the most notorious red-light areas in Asia. Deliberately buried out of sight of most of the tourist areas, the fleshpots of Chongryang-ri, Yongsan and Mia-ri will have the eyes popping.

SHOPPING

WHAT TO BUY

Korea's unique arts and crafts and the towns which traditionally produce the best of particular products are :
1. **Bamboo craft** – Tamyang
2. **Brassware** – Ansong, Taegu
3. **Hemp cloth** – Hansan, Andong
4. **Lacquerware** – Wonju
5. **Oriental paper** – Chonju
6. **Pottery** – Ich'on
7. **Porcelain** – Ansong
8. **Ruchecraft** – Kanghwa City
9. **Silk** – Ch'unch'on, Kanghwa City

SEOUL SHOPPING

Popular merchandise and where to shop for them in Seoul include:
1. **Antiques** – Ahyon-dong, Insa-dong, Chun-gang Sijang (Central market), It'aewon
2. **Brassware** – It'aewon
3. **Boutique goods** – Myong-dong, Idae-ap
4. **Calligraphy paint brushes** – Insa-dong, Kyonji-dong
5. **Korean costumes** – Tongdae-mun Sijang, and most other marketplaces
6. **Korean cushions and blankets** – Insa-dong, marketplaces
7. **Korean herbal medicine** – Chong-no 5-ka, Chong-no 6-ka
8. **Name seals** (custom-made name seals in stylistic characters carved of hard wood, stone, etc.) – along the busy streets
9. **Oriental paper** – Insa-dong, Kyonji-dong
10. **Silk Brocade** – Tongdae-mun Sijang (2nd floor), Chong-no 2-ka, Myong-dong (K'o Silk Shop)
11. **Sweatsuits and athletic shoes and gear** – It'aewon, Namdae-mun Sijang (across the Tokyu Hotel)
12. **Topaz, "smokey topaz", amethyst, jade** – underground arcades

The most popular shopping venue is still It'aewon, once the fabled "fakes paradise" where you could obtain counterfeit Rolex watches, Chanel and Polo sweatshirts and Gucci bags and a host of other times. Some of the fakes are still there, but the trend is waning.

Top buys in It'aewon are athletic shoes for men women with names like Reebok (the real thing as well as fakes) and L.A. Gear, costing between W7,000 and W20,000. Another favorite is high quality leather and lambskin jackets selling at W65,000 to W195,000. Leather gloves can be picked up for W7,000 and eelskin wallets, gloves and bags are well stitched and prove popular with tourists.

Casual sweaters, jeans and windsheeters, emblazoned with Gucci and other big brand and angora cardigans sell from about W35,000 to W85,000. Imitation Benetton and Lacoste sweatshirts sell at about W7,000, while the real thing costs around W21,000.

For those looking for high fashion the choices are the central district of Myong-dong, where most of the designer clothes are, and the expensive department stores such as Lotte, Shinsegae, Midopa and Printemps. In the city center, there are many labyrinth-like shopping malls near the subway stations, while over the river in the posh Kangnam district you can shop in stores, such as Hyundai and the Lotte World and fashionable boutiques.

Usually, high on the businessman's shopping list is the obligatory suit made from the ubiquitous Mr. Lee or Mr. Kim the tailor. However, with high labor costs, the prices have doubled to a starting price of about W220,000 with no guarantee of quick delivery as in the old days. Men's suits in Seoul are nevertheless much better made than before with many local tailors teaming up with foreign designers such as Yves St. Laurent.

Shoppers looking for a more exotic touch of the east would do well to visit Insa-dong, the area of oriental paintings and colorful silks. Genuine antiques are also available in Insa-dong and other areas.

DEPARTMENT STORES

One needn't even go outside of Seoul to find the above products. Huge marketplaces and alleys unfold bounteous displays that exhaust most shoppers. Department stores help narrow down the choices somewhat.

Major Seoul shopping areas outside central city hotels are:

Lotte Shopping Center, 1, Sogong-dong, Chung-gu, Tel: (02) 771-25

Midopa Dept. Store, Store 123, Namdaemun 2-ga, Chung-gu, Tel: (02) 754-2222

New Core Shopping Center, 257-3, Panp'o 3-dong, Soch'o-gu, Tel: (02) 533-1001

Saerona Dept. Store, 1-2, Namch'ang-dong, Chung-gu, Tel: (02) 778-8171

Shinsegye, 52-2, Ch'ungmuro 1-ga, Chung-gu, Tel: (02) 754-1234

Yong Dong Dept. Store, 119, Nonhyon-dong, Kangnam-gu, Tel: (02) 544-3000

UNDERGROUND ARCADES

Specialty shops can be found in underground shopping malls. Don't let the price tags intimidate you from bargaining. The larger more centrally located arcades are:

1. Namdaemun Arcade
2. Myong-dong Arcade
3. Sogong Arcade
4. Hangram Arcade
5. Ulchi-ro Arcade
6. Lotte Center 1st Avenue Arcade
7. Arcade Bando-Chosun
8. Dongbang Plaza

MARKETPLACES

Seoul marketplaces run on for blocks. Anyone who has anything to sell is out there – from the button merchant to the antique dealer to the rice cake *ajumoni*, including *chige* (A-frame) bicycle and Kiamaster delivery men and haggling shoppers. The distinguishing feature of Korean markets, however, is that shops with the same goods tend to group together, and even set up the shops the same way. Merchants say they are not hurt by competition caused by the close proximity; instead, the area becomes known for specializing in, say, second-hand books, sinks or antiques. Almost anything can be found at the markets.

BOOKSTORES

Reading materials in English or European languages are difficult to locate in Seoul but there are several places where these can be regularly found. The major hotels have bookstores which carry periodicals although they are usually late in coming and are extremely expensive. For the latest issues (also at high prices), the most reliable bookstore is in the basement of the Kyobo Building which is near the American Embassy on Taepyong-ro 2-ga.

Used books and magazines can be found in Myong-dong just across from the Chinese Embassy. There are several small shops here overflowing with books and old magazines which are sold for much less than their original cost. You can also trade in your own used paperbacks or bargain for lower prices, particularly if you purchase several books at a time.

On the outskirts of It'aewon, about halfway toward the third tunnel through Namsan, there is another foreign bookstore which both buys and sells. The titles here are, however, limited to especially adventure stories and war novels. The owner also drives a hard bargain.

SPORTS

Volleyball, soccer, basketball, tennis, table tennis, baseball, swimming, shooting, wrestling, gymnastics, and track and field are some of the western sports that have been integrated with Korean sports and are enthusiastically supported. Korea first participated in the Olympic Games under her own national flag in 1948 in London. These days, athletes train at an indoor 18-acre camp at T'aenung on the eastern outskirts of Seoul. Sports facilities at T'aenung include an indoor swimming pool, shooting range, and gymnasiums for wrestling, boxing and weightlifting. All kinds of sports events were held at the Olympic Sports Complex in Chamsil which was built for the 1988 Seoul Olympics. The stadium here has a seating capacity of 100,000 and there are facilities for a wide range of games.

Other sports which draw wide attention and participation by visitors are:

MARTIAL ARTS

T'aekwon-do, literally the way of combat kicking and punching, is a martial art exercise that has been developing in Korea for more than 2,000 years. It focuses the combined strengths of body, mind, and spirit in devastating fist and foot blows. This empty hand-fighting technique was originally learned from China during the T'ang dynasty and has been developed since the Three Kingdoms Period (post AD 650) into the form in which it is practiced today.

The National T'aekwon-do Association has a membership of 80 nations. In Korea, students train at some 1,100 centers. The World T'aekwon-do Federation (Tel: 566-2505) has its headquarters at Kukki-won, the main t'aekwon-do practice gymnasium in the southern outskirts of Seoul. Regular exhibitions are staged there for tourists.

Yusul ("soft art"), another martial art, was introduced from China to the Korea Royal court in 1150, but declined in popularity by the 17th century. It was a characteristically passive defense which consisted of throwing, choking or blocking an aggressor, *Yusul* was taught to the Japanese, who called it *judo* and was later reintroduced to Korea during the Japanese Occupation when it was restyled and called *yudo*. It is now a compulsory martial art for Korean policemen.

Ssirum, Korean wrestling was introduced by the Mongol invaders during the Koryo Period. Once a form of self-defense, *ssirum* today is a simple folk sport for students and villagers. Contestants hold each other around the back and wrap a cloth strip around their opponent's thigh, they then try to throw each other down using leg, hand, and body maneuvers. *Ssirum* matches are held during Tano and Ch'usok (spring and autumn festivals, respectively). Western wrestling is taking a firm hold on Koreans, since their enthusiasm was fueled by a major victory in the 1976 Montreal Olympics (in the featherweight freestyle event) and successes at the 1988 Seoul Olympics.

KOREAN ARCHERY

Once a means of hunting, a weapon of war, and a prerequisite for Yi dynasty military leaders, Korean archery is perpetuated these days as a recreation. Contests are held at various traditional sites annually by the Korean Archery Association. One of these ancient sites, the Pavilion of the Yellow Cranes, is located above Sajik Park in Seoul.

HIKING & MOUNTAINEERING

A visitor flying into Korea for the first time finds himself surprised by the mountainous panorama of the country.

The approach to Kimpo airport reveals serried ranks of distant, and some not-so-distant hills. Indeed, the typical bird's-eye image of Korea, both north and south, is of layers of peaks separated by boiling mist.

Once on the ground, one is soon caught up in another Korea: the day-to-day thrust-and-parry of life in some of the most overcrowded, dynamic cities in the world.

The frantic pace of urban Korea can itself be attributed, partly at least, to mountains. The cities are so chock-a-block with people because over 75 percent of the land is taken up by mountains and is deemed uninhabitable. It is not long before the mountains start to beckon the city-weary, especially in autumn, when the blazing colors of the *tanpung* (color-changing) season rival the splendid greens, russets and golden yellows of any Canadian fall.

But, newcomers be warned, mountaineering and hill-walking in Korea seldom means "getting away from it all." When you go to the most popular mountain trails you will find that half the population seems to have had the same idea on the same weekend.

But, if you like people as well as mountains, the best areas to visit are the officially-designated national parks. Here are some of the best:

SORAK-SAN

This "Snow Peak Mountain" is actually a series of peaks in the central part of Taebaek Mountain range, which forms the spine of the Korean peninsula. Just to the north lies the fabled Kumgang-san ("Diamond Mountains"), an equally stunning series of jagged peaks and tumbling waterfalls which is visible on a clear day.

Travelers are advised to book hotels well in advance, especially around the tanpung time as Sorak-san is perhaps the most-visited of all Korean tourist venues.

The quickest way to get there from Seoul is to fly from Sokoho. The 40-minute flight then requires a 20-minute bus or taxi ride to Sorak-dong, where the hotels are.

For those coming by coach or private car, the journey by expressway from Seoul takes around 5 hours. Once passed the town of Inje, you can take either the southern route through the Haugye-ryong Pass (3,281 feet/1,000 meters) or the northern route through the Chinpu-ryong and Mishi-ryong Pass (2,033 feet/620 meters).

Among the numerous courses are a 7km walk in the Outer Sorak area from Sorak-dong which takes in two main peaks, Hwachae-bong (4,329 feet/1,320 meters) and Taecheng-bong (5,602 feet/1,708 meters). Two other peaks, in South Sorak, are Kari-bong (4,982 feet/1,519 meters) and Chombong-san (4,671 feet/1,424 meters). In Inner Sorak there are several courses from Paekdam-sa, a Sorak temple made famous once as the much-publicized place where disgraced ex-president Chun Doo-hwan served out his self imprisonment.

SOUTH CHUNGCHONG PROVINCE

The best way to get to this region (between Taejon and Kongjuis) is by bus: Seoul to Taejon takes 1 hour and 50 minutes, and Seoul to Kongju, 2 hours 50 minutes.

For those who prefer the luxuries of an overnight stay, Sorak-san and Halla-san are better bets. Kyeryong-san, however, does have decent *yogwan*, or inns, although an overnight stay can frequently be spoiled by rowdy groups of neighbors. For history buffs, a stop of the Kap-sa temple is a must.

NAEJANG-SAN

This national park includes several peaks in the 2,296-foot (700-meter) range and features several attractive waterfalls. However, Naejang-san's most noted feature is its dramatic display of its tree-covered slopes changing color in autumn. But, even for the people-person, Naejang-san is too crowded during this brief two-week period in September. Visitors compare it to a Seoul subway during rush-hour.

Set in the Cholla provinces, the area is in easy reach of Chongju, a 3½-hour car, coach or train journey from Seoul.

PUKAN-SAN

Situated aside the sprawling northeast suburbs of Seoul, this area is accessible from the city center in 30 minutes, give or take a few traffic jams. Half of Seoul goes out to climb Tobong-san (2,352 feet/717 meters) regularly. You can join the exodus on bus Nos. 2 or 9, or by subway line No. 1. Also located in the park are the North Han Fortress (Pukhan Sansong) (bus No. 156) and several temples and other sites. For rock climbers, Insu-bong (2,634 feet/803 meters) is the most popular.

HALLA-SAN

This extinct volcano dominates Cheju Island, off the southern Korean coast, geographically and culturally midway between Korea and Japan, which is being developed as the "Hawaii of the East." If you feel sorry for the locals and the destruction of their peaceful life and wince at the inappropriate sound of one-arm bandits in the international hotels, take refuge here.

As befits its legendary associations – most recently the hideaway in the late 1940s of anti-government guerrillas – Halla-san is frequently wreathed in mist. Its peak contains a small lake, called the Paekrok-dam ("dam" means "pond"), reminiscent of the mystical Chunji pond at the top of Paektu-san (9,000 feet/2,744 meters), which is in North Korea and is the peninsula's highest peak. At 6,396 feet (1,950 meters), Halla-san, is the highest in South Korea.

You can fly to Cheju from Seoul in 55 minutes, or from Pusan in 50 minutes, and do the 30-minutes drive in a taxi or hired car to the foot of the mountain, effectively beginning your hike half-way.

HUNTING & FISHING

Hunting on Cheju Island and other particular areas is allowed in the fall to those with a proper license. Hunting equipment, rifles, and dogs are rented. Game animals include the male ring-necked pheasant, quail, turtledove, wild boar, hare, and rive and roe deer.

Fishing is a leisure activity enjoyed along rivers, lakes, reservoirs and along the sea coasts. Fishing gear is sold at sporting goods shops everywhere.

SKIING

Regarded as a preserve of the rich in the country, skiing was virtually unpromoted in Korea as a tourist attraction in the past. The country's many slopes, regards as some of the most exciting for skiing in Asia, with plentiful snow and crisp winter days, have been frequented mainly by a select band of Korean ski enthusiasts who were introduced to the sport through visits to Europe or the U.S. Occasionally, U.S. servicemen would venture out to the slopes on their days off.

As skiing become increasingly more popular among Asians, and some of the better known resorts in the region, such as in Japan, become increasingly crowded, the KNTC (Korea National Tourism Corporation) hopes to lure more skiers to Korea. Already, the nation's reputation is catching on fast as a budding ski resort with many expatriates in Hong Kong, Singapore, Manila and Bangkok heading here in the winter.

Condominiums are especially popular with Korea's new generation of skiers. At present ski resorts range from the highly developed to the primitive. At the top end of the scale is the **Dragon Valley complex** at Palwangsan Mountain in Kangwon Province. Its 13 slopes include a 2,800-foot (850-meter) "golden slope" and it has lighting facilities for night skiing. The fastest way to get there is to take a 50-minute flight from Seoul to Kangnung (W29,000 return fare) and then a 30-minute bus and taxi ride. Accommodation ranges from W11,000 to W102,000. A night at the Yongpyong condo is W80,000.

The **Bears Town Ski Resort** represents the less developed end of the scale. The resort is 20 miles (32 kilometers) from Seoul at Chukumsan Mountain. In between ski resorts are at Yongin and Chonmasan, both under an hour's drive from Seoul and the Alps Ski Resort at Masanbong, in Kangwon Province.

SWIMMING (BEACHES)

Every year when summer strikes, Korean newspapers carry photographs of the gracious curve of sand of Pusan's **Haeundae Beach** awash with parasols and people. If the captions are to be believed the mile-long strip holds half a million people on a good day.

Nearer Seoul, weekenders or daytrippers may prefer **Taechon Beach**. A favorite of resident foreigners in Korea ever since the first missionaries in the 19th century established it as their holiday spot, Taechon is in South Chungch'ong province and has the largest beach on the west coast. The sandy two-mile stretch is set off beautifully by several cliffs and woods visible from the shore.

A popular east coast resort is **Naksan Beach**, located in Kangwon-do, near Sorak Mountain. Pine trees back onto the two-mile (3.2-kilometer) sandy beach and fishing is permitted in a nearby lake. The area offers accommodation from a quality hotel to a campsite. Early risers can treat themselves to the spendid sunrise over Uisangdae Peak. From Seoul travelers can take the twice daily flights to Kangnung (W14,200) or Sokch'o (W17,500). Buses leave from Seoul every 10 minutes and cost around W4,000 for the four-hour journey.

Dubbled as Korea's "holiday paradise", **Cheju Island** has a host of **beaches**. From the **Chungmun Beach** at the south coast Chungmun Resort Complex near Sogwip'o, romantics may gaze out to sea and imagine an almost-straight line taking them across open seas to Darwin on the northern coast of Australia.

Travelers who hire a car for the round-island drive can find many **small beaches** on **Cheju**, where they can swim.

Other beaches to try are:

Yonpo Beach, southwest of Taean, South Chungch'ong province; beautiful white sand beach set off with pines and flowering bushes.

Mallipo Beach, also near Taean; great sunsets.

Kyongpodae Beach, east of Kangnung, Kangwon province; long beach within easy access of the Yongdong Expressway; tends to be crowded.

Yongok Beach, north of Kangnung; thick pine forest backdrop.

Sanju Beach, south of Namhae, South Kyongsang province; good access from Namhae Expressway.

GOLF

There are 16 golf courses operated on a membership basis but guests are welcome. Most of the courses are just outside of Seoul. All of them are 18-holed. Korea is on the ninth leg of the annual Asian Circuit with a W21 million prize.

HORSE-RACING

Korea's only horse-racing tracks is in Kwachon, southeast of Seoul. It is run by the Korean Equestrian Association, which is affiliated to the Ministry of Agriculture and Fisheries. Races are held three days a week on Friday, Saturday and Sunday. The horses are imported mainly from Japan and the United States and none are privately owned.

TRADITIONAL GAMES

Nearly 70 per cent of the folk games in Korea are said to have been created and played during the winter. Traditional games and recreation which are still the delight of Koreans include:

Chess (*Ch'anggi*): *Ch'anggi* is the Korean version of chess which was introduced from Mesopotamia through China. Men can be seen crouched over engrossing games on sidewalks, in shops, and in parks. Sixteen pieces are given per player: one general, two chariots, two cannon, two horses, two elephants, two palace guards, and five soldiers, which are represented by Chinese characters written on checkers. The object of the game is to checkmate the general.

Game of Wits (*Paduk*): *Paduk* (called *go* in Japan) is a contest of wits between two players to occupy more territory (houses) on a board divided by 19 vertical and horizontal lines. Black and white button-like stones are used as markers. Once the game of only high officials during the Koguryo and Paekche days, *paduk* increased in public popularity after 1945. In fact, paduk halls have been established in almost every town, and national tournaments in the spring and autumn are held by the Professional Paduk Association in Seoul.

Cards (*Hwat'u*): Korean playing cards are called *hwat'u*. A pack consists of 48 matchbook-sized cards, representing the 12 months of the year. January is symbolized by a pine tree; February, a plum tree; March, cherry; April, bush clover; May, orchids; June, peony; July, iris; August, the moon; September, chrysanthemum; October, maple; November, paulownia; and December, rainfall. A bit of gambling spices the game.

These flower cards are also used for fortune-telling, and in Japan are called *hanafuda* cards.

Backgammon (*Yut*): *Yut* is a form of backgammon that is sometimes seen played on the ground by young men. Four 10-inch sticks used as dice are tossed in the air, and the player moves his pawns according to the number of backs or faces that turn up on the sticks. The first player who gets all four of his pawns to a goal wins.

Kite-Flying: Perhaps kite-flying was originally used in 1380 by a Koryo general in his conquest of Cheju Island, but it has seen a series of uses since then. Not too long ago, it was a pastime of children during the winter months. Children traditionally flew their kites on the 15th of January (by the lunar calendar) and strung names of evil spirits and diseases onto the kites in hopes of ridding themselves of all evil. Kite-flying contests are held annually. One is held in Seoul by *The Korea Times* newspaper – usually in January or February according to the lunar calendar. The participants aren't all children either. Kite strings are reinforced with ceramic filings to sharpen them for combat against other kites. Most are constructed of bamboo and paper and are judged in various divisions.

Swinging and **Jumping-Seesaw**: The simple pleasures of swinging and jumping-seesaw are traditionally celebrated by women these days on Tano. Young girls stand on swings which are suspended by 20-foot (6-meter) lengths of rope, and gleefully pump their way skyward. The jumping-seesaw also draw giggles as girls on either end of a solid length of wood set on large bag stuffed with rice straw, spring each other into the air. Some say these recreations were designed to allow the aristocratic Korean women of old to see up and over their compound walls, as they were not permitted to step outside their premises during the day.

295

Photography

Opportunities for photography in Korea abound but it is important that the visitor respects the privacy of his hosts. Koreans do not always like ceremonies to be photographed and older Koreans especially do not like to be photographed. Ask before you shoot.

Black and white film is hard to come by and be processed. But color film is available everywhere and there are numerous 40-minute processing shops in city centers.

Language

Korean *han'gul* is romanized in two ways: by the Ministry of Education system and by the McCune-Reischauer system, an internationally recognized romanization scheme. Both romanizations are used in literature, maps, and signs, which can confuse those unacquainted with the language. Thus, learning the Korean alphabet, which is simple, would prove most beneficial, especially for the lone traveler.

Provided below are commonly used questions and statements romanized according to the McCune-Reischauer system. No matter what village, town or city in Korea you visit, you should be able to survive with the following common questions and statements. At least this simple lesson will lead you to a taxi, bus or train station, and then to food, shelter and a hot bath.

NUMERAL SYSTEM

The following is a list of basic numbers and their Korean pronunciation:

1	*Il*	60	*Yuk-sip*
2	*Ee*	70	*Ch'il-sip*
3	*Sam*	80	*P'al-sip*
4	*Sa*	90	*Ku-sip*
5	*0*	100	*Paek*
6	*Yuk*	200	*Ee-paek*
7	*Ch'il*	300	*Sam-paek*
8	*P'al*	567	*O-paek yuk-sip*
9	*Ku*		*ch'il*
10	*Sip*	1,000	*Ch'on*
11	*Sip-il*	2,000	*Ee-ch'on*
20	*Ee-sip*	4,075	*Sa-ch'on ch'il-*
30	*Sam-sip*		*sip o*
40	*Sa-sip baek*	13,900	*Man Sam-*
50	*O-sip*		*ch'on ku-baek*

USEFUL PHRASES

the airport	*konghang*
the subway	*chihach'ol*
the taxi	*taeksi*
Seoul train station	*Seoul yok*
express bus terminal	*Kosok t'ominal*
the ticket office	*p'yo p'a-nun kos-i*
entrance	*ipku*
exit	*ch'ulku*
public bathhouse or private bathroom	*mogyokt'ang*
the restroom	*hwajang-sil*
the restaurant	*sik-tang, umsik-chom*
the tea or coffee house	*tabang*
the bank	*unhaeng*
the hotel	*hotel*
a good Korean inn	*cho-un yogwan*
the post office	*uch'e-guk*
the post box	*kyongch'al-so*
the embassy	*dsea-kwan*
Telecommunication Office	*chonhwakuk*
the dry cleaners	*saet'ak-so*
the public telephone	*kongchung- chonhwa*
the department store	*paekhwa-jom*
the duty free shop	*myonse-p'um-jom*
the marketplace	*sijang*
the souvenir shop	*t'osang-p'um-jom*

USEFUL QUESTIONS & SENTENCES

How many kilometers is it from here?
Yogi-so myot kilo im-nikka?
How long does it take to go there?
Olmana kollimnikka?

It takes 30 minutes / one hour.
Samsip-pun/han si-gan kollimnida.
Please call a taxi for me.
Taeksi jom pullo ju-seyo.
Just a moment, please.
Cham-kkan man kitari-seyo.
Please go straight.
Ttok paro ka-seyo.
Please stop here.
Sewo ju-seyo.
What is this place called?
Yogi-nun odi imnikka?
Hello (to get the attention of a waiter, sales clerk, etc.)
Yobo-seyo.
Please give me some coffee.
K'op'i-rul chu-seyo.
May I have more beer?
Maekchu to ju-seyo.
May I have the bill?
Kaesanso-rul chu-seyo.
Do you have amethyst?
Chasujong iss-umnikka?
Please show me another one.
Tarun kos-ul poyo ju-seyo.
How much does it cost; what is the price?
Olma imnikka?
Can you give me a discount?
Tisukauntu rul hal-su iss-umnikka?
It's too expensive.
Nomu pissamnida.
Thank you.
Kamsa-hamnida.
I will buy this.
Ee kos-ul sa kess-umnida.
Good-bye (to someone not departing).
Annyong-hi ke-seyo.
Good-bye (to someone who is also departing).
Annyong-hi ka-seyo.
Can you speak English?
Yong-o halsu-issum-nikka?
Do you understand me?   Yes / No.
Ee hae ha-seyo?   *Ne / Anio.*
Please bring me some…
…chom katta ju-seyo.
  …beer   *maekchu…*
  …cold drinking water   *naeng su…*
  …hot water (for bath)   *ttugo-un mul…*
  …barley tea   *pori ch'a…*
  …Korean food   *Han chong sik…*
Good morning / Good afternoon / Good evening.
Annyong ha-simnikka.
Excuse me.
Sille-hamnida.

I am sorry.
Mian-hamnida.
You are welcome.
Ch'onman-eyo.
(Something, someone is) good.
Cho ssumnida.
(Something, someone is) bad.
Nappumnida.

KOREAN LANGUAGE CENTERS

Korean language courses are offered at a few institutes in two- or three-month terms. Student visas can be arranged. Among the prominent schools are:

Language Teaching Research Center – 16-17, T'aep'yong-no, 1-ka, Chong-dong, Chong-no ku, Tel: 737-4641

Yonsei University – Korean Language Institute, Taek 134, Sinch'on-dong, Sodaemun-ku, Tel: 392-6405

Ewha Womans University – Tel: 362-6151

FURTHER READING

Adams, Edward B. *Korea Guide*. Seoul International Tourist Publishing Co., 1977.

Kyongju Guide: Cultural Spirit of Silla in Korea. Samhwa Printing Co., 1979.

Palaces of Seoul: Yi Dynasty Palaces in Korea's Capital City. Taewon Publishing Co., 1972.

Through Gates of Seoul: Trails and Tales of Yi Dynasty. Vol. I and II. Saham-bo Publishing Corporation, 1971, 1972.

Bartz, Patricia M. *South Korea*. Clarendon Press, 1972.

Berger, Carl. *The Korea Knot: A Military-Political History*. Philadelphia: University of Pennsylvania Press, 1957.

Bishop, Isbella B. *Korea and Her Neighbors*. Yonsei University Press, 1970.

Brandt, Vincent S. *A Korean Village Between Farm and Sea*. Cambridge: Harvard, 1971.

Buck, Pearl S. *The Living Reed.* New York: John Day Co., 1963.

Bureau of Cultural Properties, ed. *The Arts of Ancient Korea.* Kwang Myong Publishing Co., 1974.

Carpenter, Frances. *Tales of a Korean Grandmother.* Seoul: Royal Asiatic Society, 1973.

Choe, Sang-su. *Annual Customs of Korea.* Korea Book Publishing Co., 1960.

Clark, Allen D. *An History of the Church in Korea.* The Christian Literature Society of Korea, 1971.

Clark, Allen D.; Clark, Donald N. *Seoul: Past and Present, A Guide to Yi Taejo's Capital.* Seoul: Royal Asiatic Society, 1969.

Clark, Charles Allen. *Religions of Old Korea.* The Christian Literature Society of Korea, 1961.

Crane, Paul S. *Korean Patterns.* Seoul: Royal Asiatic Society, 1967.

Daniels, Michael J. *Through a Rain Spattered Window. Essays on Korea.* Taewon Publishing Co., 1973.

Deuchier, Martina. *Confucian Gentlemen and Barbarian Envoys.* Seoul: Royal Asiatic Society, 1977.

The Traditional Culture and Society of Korea: Art and Literature. Honolulu: University of Hawaii Center for Korean Studies, 1975.

Lee, Sun-ju. *Korean Folk Medicine.* Publishing Center of Seoul National University, 1966.

MacMahon, Hugh. The Scrutable Oriental. Sejong Co., 1975.

Mattielli, Sandra. *Virtues in Conflict.* Tradition and the Korean Woman Today. Royal Asiatic Society, 1977.

Mattielli, Sandra; Rutt, Joan Lee. *Wade's Korean Cookbook.* Pomso Publishers, 1974.

McCann, David R. *An Anthology of Korean Literature.* Ithaca, New York: China-Japan Program, Cornell University, 1977.

McCann, David R.; Middleton, John; Shultz, Edward J., editors. *Studies on Korea in Transition.* University of Hawaii Center for Korean Studies, 1979.

McCune, E. *The Arts of Korea.* An Illustrated History. Charles E. Tuttle Co., Inc., 1962.

McCune, Shannon. *Korea: Land of Broken Calm.* Princeton: D. Van Nostrand Co., Inc., 1966.

Korea's Heritage: A Religious and Social Geography. Charles E. Tuttle Co., Inc., 1956.

Michener, James A. *The Bridges at Tokori.* New York: Fawcett Crest, 1953.

Middleton, Dorothy H.; Middleton, William D. *Some Korean Journeys Seoul.* Royal Asiatic Society, 1975.

Moffett, Samuel H. *The Christians of Korea.* Friendship Press, 1962.

National Academy of Arts. *Survey of Korean Arts: Folk Arts.* Information Service Center, 1974.

Osgood, Cornelius. *The Koreans and their Culture.* Charles E. Tuttle, Co., Inc., 1954.

Phil, Marshall R. *Listening to Korea: A Korean Anthology.* New York: Praeger, 1973.

Rees, David. *Korea: The Limited War.* New York: St. Martin's Press, 1964.

Ridgeway, Matthem B. *The Korean War.* New York: Doubleday & Co., 1967.

Rutt, Richard, editor and translator. *The Bamboo Grove: An Introduction to sijo.* Berkeley: University of California Press, 1971.

Korean Works and Days: Notes from the diary of a Country Priest. Taewon Publishing Co., 1973.

Sohn, Ho-min. *The Korean Language: Its Structure and Social Projection.* 1975.

Stewart, Ruth. *Under the Snow the Bamboo Shines.* 1973.

Wade, James. *Early Voyagers.* Hollym Corporation Publishers, 1969.

One Man's Korea. Hollym Corporation Publishers, 1967.

Wickman, Michael. *Living in Korea.* Seoul: The American Chamber of Commerce in Korea, 1978.

Won, Pyong-o; Gore, M.E.J. *The Birds of Korea.* Charles E. Tuttle Co., Inc., 1971.

Rare and Endangered Species of Birds and Mammals in Korea. Korea Association of Conservation of Nature, 1975.

Yi, Sun-sin; translated by Ha, Tae Hung. *Najung Ilgi: War Diary of Admiral Yi Sun Sin.* Yonsei University Press, 1977.

Zong, In-sob. *Folk Tales from Korea.* Hollym Corporation Publishers, 1970.

USEFUL ADDRESSES

TOURIST INFORMATION

Enquiries and information for tourists can be sourced from the head office of KNTC (Korean National Tourism Corporation) at: 10 Da-dong, Chung-ku, C.P.O Box 903, Seoul, Korea. Tel: 757-6030, and also at the following:

Seoul Tourist Information Centers

City Hall	735-8688
Kimp'o Airport	665-0988
Korea Tourist Association	757-2345
Korea National Tourism Corp	757-0086
Korea Tourist Bureau	722-1191/6
Seoul Railroad Station	392-7811
Kangnam Express Bus Terminal	537-9198
Chonggak	732-0088
Myong-dong	757-0088
Namdae-mun	779-3644
Tongdae-mun	274-8588

USEFUL TELEPHONE NUMBERS

Emergency

Police	112
Fire	119
Ambulance	119
Time	116
Weather	737-0365
Information	114
International Calls	007
International Calls Information	004
Telegrams	115

Hospitals

Cheil Hospital	274-1231
Ewha Women's Univ Hospital	762-5061
Hanyang Univ Hospital	293-3111
Korea Univ Hospital	762-5111
Kyunghee Univ Hospital	962-2411
National Medical Center	265-9131
Seoul Adventist Hospital	244-0191
Seoul Red Cross Hospital	737-4581
Seoul National Univ Hospital	761-0114
Severance Hospital (with international clinic)	392-0161
Chungang Hospital	
Asan Foundation	480-3114
(with international clinic)	480-3026
Alarm Center (24-hours)	356-0981

Seoul Post Offices

Central	777-0004
Kwanghwa-mun	732-0004
International	645-0004

Immigration Offices / Airport

Seoul Immigration Office	653-3041
Airport Customs Office	636-7070
Airport Information	660-2114
Lost and Found Center	755-4400

Call-a-Cab Service — 414-0150/2

Train Information — 392-7788

Ferry Information

Cheju	(064) 57-0117
Chungmu	(0557) 43-0364
Donghae	(0394) 31-5891
Inchon	(032) 882-1714
Kunsan	(0654) 3-2936
Masan	(0551) 45-0116
Mokpo	(0631) 43-0116
P'ohang	(0562) 42-0111
Pusan (international terminal)	(051) 4633161
(domestic terminal)	(051) 44-0117
Yosu	(0662) 63-0116
Wando	(0633) 52-0116

AIRLINES

Aeroflot	569-3271/5
Air France	773-5171
Air India	778-0064
Alitalia Airlines	779-1676/8
All Nippon Airways	752-5500
American Airlines	778-3351/3
British Airways	774-5511
Canadian Pacific Airways	753-8271/5
Cathay Pacific Airways	773-0321
China Airlines	755-1523
Continental Airlines	778-0394
Delta Airlines	754-1924
Garuda Indonesian Airways	779-1694
Gulf Air	779-1675

Iberian Airlines	782-7445
Japan Air System	752-9090
Japan Airlines	757-1711
KLM	753-1093
Korea Airlines	756-2000
Kuwait Airways	753-0041
Lauda Air	232-8515
Lufthansa German Airlines	777-9655
Malaysian Airline System	777-7761
Northwest Airlines	734-7800
Philippine Airlines	725-1401
Qantas	777-6875
Sabena Airlines	778-0394
Saudi Arabian System	755-5621
Scandinavian Airlines System	752-5123/4
Singapore Airlines	755-1226
Swiss Air	757-8801/3
Thai Airways International	779-2621
Trans World Airlines	777-4864
United Airlines	757-1691
Varig Brazilian Airlines	779-3877

BANKS

Domestic

Bank of Korea	759-4114
Bank of Pusan	051-67-3151
Bank of Seoul	771-60
Citizens National Bank	771-40
Cho Heung Bank	733-2000
Commercial Bank of Korea	771-30
Donghwa Bank	733-7171
Export-Import Bank of Korea	784-1021
Hanil Bank	771-20
Industrail Bank of Korea	729-6114
Korea Bank	731-8114
Korea Development Bank	733-2121
Korea Exchange Bank	771-46
Korea First Bank	733-0070
Korea Housing Bank	784-6611
Kwangju Bank	062-27-0161
Shinhan Bank	756-0505

Foreign

American Express Bank	753-2435
Australia and New Zealand Banking Group	753-8411
Bank of America	733-2455
Bank of California	736-5431
Bank of Montreal	732-9206
Bank of Tokyo	752-0111
Banque Indosuez	732-7611
Banque Nationale de Paris	753-2594
Barclays Bank	754-3680
Chase Manhattan Bank	758-5354

Citibank	731-1114
Credit Lyonnaise	778-3811
Dai-Ichi Kangyo Bank	756-8181
Daiwa Bank	752-0831
Deutsche Bank Aktiengese Ilschaft	754-3071
Development Bank of Singapore	732-9311
First National Bank of Boston	733-6981
First National Bank of Chicago	753-8980
Fuji Bank	755-1281
Hong Kong and Shanghai Bank	739-4211
Kyowa Bank	755-9048
Lloyds Bank	754-2711
Mitsubishi Bank	734-9561
Mitsui Bank	757-4631
National Bank of Canada	733-5012
Royal Bank of Canada	730-7791
Saitama Bank	738-5183
Sanwa Bank	757-6850
Societe Generale	753-9400
Standard Chartered Bank	757-5131
Sumitumo Bank	732-1801
Taiyo Kobe Bank	777-7092
Toki Bank	739-9810
United Overseas Bank	739-3916

NOTED ORGANIZATIONS

Chambers of Commerce

American	753-6471
British (contact UK embassy)	735-7341
German	776-1546/9
Japanese	755-6672
Korean	757-0757
Korea Trade Promotion Corp	551-4181
Korea Exhibition Center	551-0114
Korea Red Cross	755-9301
Korean UNESCO	774-3956
Lions International	734-5111
Seoul JAYCEES	244-9521
Seoul Rotary Club	266-1860
YMCA	730-9391
YWCA	777-5725
FOCUS (foreigners' community service)	797-8212

RELIGIOUS ORGANIZATIONS

Anglican Church	738-6597
Assemblies of God	737-1915
Seoul Int'l Baptist Church	782-3395

Catholic Church	771-76
Catholic Martyrs	
Memorial Church (Choltusan)	335-0212
Chogye Order (Buddhist)	732-2115
Ch'ondokyo	732-3956
Confucian Society	734-1637
Hanolkyo	737-3551
Jingak Order (Buddhist)	913-0751
Lutheran Church International	794-6274
Methodist Church	399-2029
Mormon Church	232-1441
Muslim Federation	794-7307
National Council of Churches	763-8427
Presbyterian Church in Korea	763-7934
Presbyterian Church of Korea	741-4350
Salvation Army	739-5141
Taego Order (Buddhist)	745-2030
Taejongkyo	289-8617
Unification Church	716-9001
Wonbulkyo (Won Buddhism)	814-4312
Yoido Full Gospel Church	780-5111

FOREIGN EMBASSIES

Argentina: 135-53 It'aewon-dong, Yongsan-gu, Tel: 793-4062

Australia: 11th Floor, Kyobo Building, Chongno-ku, Tel: 730-6491/5

Austria: Room 1913, Kyobo Building, Chongno-ku, Tel: 732-9071/2

Bangladesh: 33-5, Hannam-dong, Yongsan-ku, Tel: 796-4056

Belgium: 1-65, Dongbinggo-dong, Yongsan-ku, Tel: 797-7517

Bolivia: Room 1501, Garden Tower Building, 98-78, Unni-dong, Chongno-ku, Tel: 742-7170

Brazil: 301/6, New Korea Building, 192-11, Ulji-ro, Chung-ku, Tel: 776-4717

Brunei: 1-94 Dongbinggo-dong, Yongsan-ku, Tel: 797-7679

Bulgaria: A-906, Namsan Foreign Apt, 21-139 It'aewon-dong, Yongsan-ku, Tel: 796-3426

Canada: 10th Floor, Kolon Building, 45, Mugyo-dong, Chung-ku, Tel: 753-3605/8

Chile: 9th Floor, Youngpung Building, 142, Nonhyun-dong, Kangnam-ku, Tel: 549-1654

Republic of China: 83, Myong-dong 2-ka, Chung-ku, Tel: 776-2721/5

Colombia: 125, Namsan Foreign House, It'aewon-dong, Yongsan-ku, Tel: 793-1369

Costa Rica: 133, Namsan Village, It'aewon-dong, Yongsan-ku, Tel: 793-0652

Denmark: Room 701, Namsong Building, 260-199, Itaewon-dong, Yongsan-ku, Tel: 795-4187/9

Dominican Republic: A-212, Namsan Village, It'aewon-dong, Yongsan-ku, Tel: 744-1803

Ecuador: 133-20, It'aewon-dong, Yongsan-ku, Tel: 795-1287/1195

EC: 109 Changchoong-dong 1-ka, Chung-ku, Tel: 271-0781

El Salvador: 1002, Garden Tower Building, Chongno-ku, Tel: 741-7527

Finland: Room 604, Kyobo Building, Chongno-ku, Tel: 732-6223/6737

France: 30, Hap-dong, Sodaemun-ku, Tel: 392-3272

Gabon: Room 202, Kunchang Building, 23-5, Nonhyun-dong, Kangnam-ku, Tel: 548-9912

Germany: 51-1 Namchang-dong, Chung-ku, Tel: 779-3271/5

Guatemala: A-206, Namsan Village, It'aewon-dong, Yongsan-ku, Tel: 790-3265

Haiti: House 165, Namsan Village, It'aewon-dong, Yongsan-ku, Tel: 796-0570

Holy See: 2, Kungchong-dong, Chongno-ku, Tel: 736-5725

Honduras: 3rd Floor, Daisuh Bldg, 1428-3 Soch'o-dong, Soch'o-ku, Tel: 582-4725

Hungary: 1-104 Dongbinggo-dong, Yongsano-ku, Tel: 792-2103

India: 37-3, Hannam-dong, Yongsan-ku, Tel: 798-4257

Indonesia: 55, Yoido-dong, Yongdeungpo-ku, Tel: 783-5675

Iran: 726-126, Hannam-dong, Yongsan-ku, Tel: 793-7751/3

Iraq: 33-6 Hannam-dong, Yongsan-ku, Tel: 792-6671

Italy: 1-398, Hannam-dong, Yongsan-ku, Tel: 796-0491

Ireland: Daehan Fire and Marine Insurance Building, 55-1 Namchang-dong, Chung-ku, Tel: 774-6455

Japan: 18-11, Chunghak-dong, Chongno-ku, Tel: 733-5626

Liberia: 657-42 Hannam-dong, Yongsan-ku, Tel: 793-6704

Libya: 4-5, Hannam-dong, Yongsan-ku, Tel: 797-6001

Malaysia: 4-1, Hannam-dong, Yongsan-ku, Tel: 795-9203

Mexico: Room 901, Garden Tower Building, 98-78, Unni-dong, Chongno-ku, Tel: 741-0380

Morocco: S-15, UN Village, 270-3 Hannam-dong, Yongsan-ku, Tel: 793-6249

Myanmar (Burma): 4-28 Hannam-dong, Yongsan-ku, Tel: 792-3341

Netherlands: 14th floor, Kyobo Building, Chongno-ku, Chongno-gu, Tel: 739-9514

New Zealand: 18th Floor, Kyobo Building, Chongno-ku, Tel: 730-7794

Nigeria: 158 Hannam-dong, Yongsan-ku, Tel: 797-2370

Norway: 124-12, It'aewon-dong, Yongsan-ku, Tel: 795-6850/1

Oman: 1-35 Shinmun-ro 2-ka, Chongno-ku, Tel: 736-2432

Pakistan: 58-1, Sinmun-ro 1-ka, Chongno-ku, Tel: 739-4422

Panama: Room 1101, Garden Tower Building, 98-78, Unni-dong, Chongno-ku, Tel: 765-0363

Paraguay: 1-68 Dongbinggo-dong, Yongsan-ku, Tel: 794-5553

Peru: 129, Namsan Village, It'aewon-dong, Yongsan-ku, Tel: 797-3736

Philippines: 559-510, Yeoksam-dong, Kangnam-ku, Tel: 568-9131

Poland: 135-17 It'aewon-dong, Yongsan-ku, Tel: 796-5753

Portugal: 8th floor, Citicorp Building, 89-29 Shinmun-ro 2-ka, Chongno-ku, Tel: 738-2078

Rumania: Chunghwa Apts Building 8 Apt 305, 22-2 It'aewon, Yongsan-ku, Tel: 797-4924

Saudi Arabia: 1-112, Sinmun-ro 2-ka, Chongno-ku, Tel: 739-0631/5

Singapore: 7th floor, Citicorp Bldg, 89-29 Shinmun-ro 2-ka, Chongno-ku, Tel: 722-0442

Spain: 726-52, Hannam-dong, Yongsan-ku, Tel: 793-5703

Sri Lanka: Room 2004, Kyobo Building, Chongno-ku, Tel: 735-2966

Swaziland: Room 1706, Garden Tower Building, 98-75 Unni-dong, Chongno-ku, Tel: 744-0263

Sweden: 108-2, Pyong-dong, Chongno-ku, Tel: 720-4767

Switzerland: 32-10, Songweol-dong, Chongno-ku, Tel: 739-9511/4

Thailand: 653-7, Hannam-dong, Yongsan-ku, Tel: 795-3098

Tunisia: 7-13 Dongbinggo-dong, Yongsan-ku, Tel: 790-4334

Turkey: 726-116, Hannam-dong, Yongsan-ku, Tel: 794-0255

United Arab Emirates: 5-5 Hannam-dong, Yongsan-ku, Tel: 790-3235

United Kingdom: 4, Chong-dong, Chung-ku, Tel: 735-7341/3

United Soviet Socialist Republics: 261-1 Hannam-dong, Yongsan-ku, Tel: 790-3581

United States of America: 82, Sejong-ro, Chongno-ku, Tel: 732-2601/9

Uruguay: Room 1802, Daewoo Center Bldg, Namdaemun, Chongno-ku, Tel: 753-7893

Venezuela: Room 1801, Garden Tower Building, Chongno-ku, Tel: 741-0036

Yugoslavia: 1-88 Dongbinggo-dong, Yongsan-ku, Tel: 793-7727

Zaire: 15-4 Nonhyun-dong, Kangnam-ku, Tel: 544-7411

ART/PHOTO CREDITS

INDEX